The Concept of Academic Freedom

The Concept of
Academic Freedom

EDITED BY EDMUND L. PINCOFFS

UNIVERSITY OF TEXAS PRESS, AUSTIN AND LONDON

Library of Congress Cataloging in Publication Data

Conference on the Concept of Academic Freedom,
    University of Texas at Austin, 1972.
    The concept of academic freedom.

    Sponsored by the American Council of Learned
Societies and the University of Texas Graduate School.
    Bibliography: p.
    Includes index.
    1. Teaching, Freedom of. I. Pincoffs, Edmund L.,
ed. II. American Council of Learned Societies Devoted
to Humanistic Studies. III. Texas. University at
Austin. Graduate School. IV. Title.
LB2332.C67 1972   378.1'21   74-20852
ISBN 0-292-71016-X

CONTENTS

PART FOUR

PART FIVE

INTRODUCTION

BY EDMUND L. PINCOFFS

Whoever has been caught up in the tight tangles of academic-freedom cases must be aware that his practical problems often result from theoretical problems. Not only is it sometimes hard to distinguish the heroes from the villains on the academic stage, but also it often is not easy to be sure how to go about making the distinction: to know what should count for or against the claim that someone is violating the academic freedom of someone else. There is, one soon discovers, no clear and widely accepted definition or justification of academic freedom and no settled account of the way in which claims of violation may be assessed.

The papers in this book were originally drafted for presentation at a conference called to discuss these fundamental conceptual and justificational matters.[1] Some revisions have been made in the papers there delivered, and writers of the principal papers have been given an opportunity to reply to their respondents. The discussion at the conference was a searching one and tended to return repeatedly to the four topics around which I will organize this introduction: (1) the nature of the social and political reality presupposed by claims to academic freedom; (2) consequentialist vs. nonconsequentialist grounds for the justification of academic-freedom claims; (3) special theories deriving academic freedom from a

[1] The Conference on the Concept of Academic Freedom, at The University of Texas at Austin, April 13–16, 1972, held under the gratefully acknowledged auspices of the American Council of Learned Societies and The University of Texas Graduate School. I should like to thank Hardy Jones and Milton Fisk for helpful criticisms of an earlier draft of this Introduction.

conception of the function of the university vs. general theories in which academic freedom is a branch of civil liberty; and (4) competing conceptions of the academic community.

Descartes maintained that it is useful from time to time to turn out all our beliefs, like apples from a basket, so that we can pick out and reject the unsound ones, retaining only those that bear close examination. The papers in this volume constitute an exercise in apple sorting. They are concerned not only with whether the apple in question is a sound one, but also with just what kind of apple it is: not only, that is, with the justifiability of claims to academic freedom, but also with the nature and the presuppositions of such claims.

Social Reality and Academic Freedom

When a professor or a student claims that he is entitled to academic freedom he is generally understood to be claiming the right to *pursue the truth unhindered.* This understanding is nearly as vague and full of difficulties as the general understanding that the *summum bonum* is happiness. Radical critics of academic pretensions are especially alert to the ways in which rhetoric and special pleading can pass for impartial analysis and reasoned defense.

It is the general position of the radical skeptic that academic-freedom claims must be understood in the context of a power struggle between classes with conflicting interests and that the various definitions offered of "pursuit," "truth," and "hindrance" will be persuasive ones that simply reflect the interests of the defining parties. Professors themselves are an interest group, but more importantly they are the "functionaries" of interest groups. In a capitalist society they are hired and supported by a class whose interest is in the exploitation of labor. While professors claim to be politically neutral, in the pursuit of their academic interests, they are, it is held, not really so. Assessment by professors of their peers, for retention or promotion, masks political judgments under the cover of professional ones. They are simply maintaining the public orthodoxy. The sponsoring of research by funding agencies, especially the government, is said to be inherently political, yet since research requires funds, the decision not to grant funds is a hindrance that counts as a limitation on academic freedom. Again, professors are professionals who must develop and sell their competences with an eye to the market for them. Feeling the insecurity of all who are subject to the swings of the market, they demand the right to be judged only on professional grounds by their peers, as opposed to being judged as plentiful or scarce commodities on the labor market. Academic-freedom claims become too easily just ways of defending job security.

As the radical theory works out, the professor is and should be loyal to his own class interests, which are in turn identified with the interests of the class which supports him economically. The aim of reform or revolution should not be to change this fact of life, but to alter or abolish the class relationships that presently obtain; to make the professor the functionary of a governing laboring class, or of a classless social order, rather than of a class of capitalists; to remove him from the role of entrepreneur in his own interest; and to persuade him to identify his interests with those of laboring men. It is felt that this change of identification will be necessary since, among other things, the professor cannot at once pursue the truth and serve as a functionary of capitalism. He cannot do so, because capitalism is inherently exploitative, and the pursuit of the truth will inevitably reveal its exploitative nature.

When academics appeal to their right to be free of hindrance in the pursuit of truth, what we are to understand, on the radical analysis, is that "right" is a partisan term, as opposed to a universal one. The notion of rights that apply to all academics is itself simply a product of class history. To claim rights is ideally to exhibit class awareness, awareness of class interests that are in conflict with the class interests of others.

The radical analysis implies that professors can be functionaries of a class even though they do not know that they are. They can be hired and fired by the capitalist class, which simply makes use of "professional peer" procedures. The analysis also implies that the tasks academic functionaries perform need not be directly related to the interests of the class by which they are hired. They may also engage in "diversionary" tasks that indirectly promote those interests. For example, they may engage the young in philosophical speculation that will serve to keep them diverted from the pursuit of their own true interests, which may be in conflict with the interests of the capitalistic classes.

These latter implications of the radical analysis are seized upon by critics. The suspicion is mooted that the radical argument is a "built-in" one, in that it is so stated that nothing can count as evidence against it, that it cannot be falsified. For if it is shown that many academics are in fact not in sympathy with the interests of the capitalistic classes, then the reply can be that they are functionaries even if they do not know that that is what they are. If it can be shown that many academics do pursue the truth wherever it may lead, it can be argued from the radical position that the pursuit is covertly guided so that it does not endanger the interest of the capitalist classes. If it be argued that there are a great many pursuits in research and teaching that do not even remotely advance the interest of the capitalist class, of which the academic is supposedly the functionary, it can be answered by the radical that in fact these pursuits do advance the capitalist-class interest by diverting the potentially active and revolutionary young from the roles that, had they not been diverted, they might otherwise play in bringing about social change. They are reading Roman law instead of picketing the courts, conjugating Swahili rather than burning ghettos.

Let us return to the common conception of academic freedom as the right to pursue the truth unhindered. When, to begin with, may the scholar be said to be *pursuing* the truth? "To pursue" is generally taken to mean to do research, to engage in scholarship, to teach, or to learn. When, then, is the academic properly said to be engaged in research or scholarship? When, on the other hand, is the academic engaging, even though unconsciously, in the rationalization of conclusions already accepted, or in apologetics for ideologies taken as given? Consider the economist who spends his life investigating questions that can only be taken seriously by a capitalist (or by a Marxist), never questioning the ideological presuppositions of his undertakings. Can this economist rightly be said to be engaged in the pursuit of truth? It is easy to answer too hastily. Perhaps the vast majority of academics, including many of those who win international prizes for their contributions, seldom question the fundamental assumptions of the ideology that informs their work.

The matter is relative. It makes no sense to suppose that a person could simultaneously investigate the truth of a proposition and of all the indefinitely many propositions that are presupposed by it.

Yet it does make sense to require some degree of critical awareness if his activity is to be accepted as "pursuing truth." There are unavoidable questions of intention, practice, and good faith. If orthodoxy throws a fence around the mind, the fence is not always easy to detect. Appeals to the requirements of sound methodology, for example, can mask ideological motives, conscious or unconscious.

There are infinitely many true propositions and another infinity of false ones. What, then, does it mean to pursue *the truth*? Some selection between truths that are and are not worth pursuing is inevitable. But what is the basis of this selection to be? How are we to distinguish between acceptable and unacceptable criteria? Is such a distinction possible on impartial, universal grounds? Or must it be merely a reflection of the interests, especially the economic interests, of the class to which the academic belongs or with which he identifies his interests?

The nearly inevitable move is to appeal to procedural "criteria": the professional judgment of one's peers. One's academic peers will consider it worth one's while to investigate the autobiographical allusions in Shakespeare's sonnets but not to count the number of apostrophes in *King Lear*, worthy of a scientist to probe the secrets of the behavior of matter at high temperatures but unworthy to determine whether this behavior was predicted by the prophets. Yet there remain the questions of how one determines who one's academic peers are and whether *this* judgment can be independent of ideology and class interests. Purely formal "criteria" will not do. Membership in professional associations and possession of certain degrees provide no guarantee of nonbiased judgment.

Truth is a notoriously difficult term. What *kinds* of truth may properly be pursued with an academic community? Does the inner "revelation" that results from the use of LSD count as truth? Those who, in the context of art criticism or religious teaching, speak of truth as experience would find it difficult to explain why drug-induced experience cannot be truth as well. Is there a truth perceived only by the Loyal American, to which the participant in Un-American Activities is blind? Can a political scientist who is an anarchist teach "the truth" about political life? Or suppose that a sociologist holds that students can only grasp the truth about American communal life by involvement in protest movements and assigns participation in organizing, in picketing, and in sit-down strikes.

At this point we approach one of the central contemporary difficulties in understanding the justification and limits of academic freedom. Practical problems arise for academics not as much over the abstract question of the nature and varieties of truth as over the permissible activities in which they may engage, or require or encourage their pupils to engage, in the pursuit of truth. A professor of history may, for example, because of his pedagogical beliefs about the necessity for an atmosphere conducive to communal learning, require his students to engage in "sensitivity sessions" as a preliminary to the semester's work. "Sensitivity session" is a broad concept and can include exercises in warm swimming pools that may well raise questions about the limits of academic freedom. A professor of sociology may insist that his discipline requires the experimental inducement of social change, for example of patterns of land ownership. While such an experiment may raise no questions if confined to a hacienda in Peru, it will surely do so if conducted in a neighboring region of large landholdings. Our sociologist may hold not merely that there should be experiments in land ownership but also that the experiments should be conducted in such a way, with respect to participation and publicity, as to encourage beneficial change in society and that the measure of his success as a sociologist is precisely the degree to which his efforts result in such change. Truth easily becomes indistinguishable from ideology, and the pursuit of truth from political activism. It is worth bearing in mind that, although academic freedom has been oppressed in our time, it has also been pressed—toward limits about which we are not so clear as we should like to be.

What kind of *hindrance* should we regard as a violation of academic freedom? Bad weather or faulty equipment can hinder a research project; a broken-down elevator in the stacks can hinder scholarship. The sort of hindrance relevant for our purposes must be attributable to the activities of persons, as opposed to the occurrence of natural events. The Bermuda high that is slowing the progress of this introduction is not, for our purposes, a relevant hindrance. But to say that the hindrance must be attributable to the activities of persons does not carry us very far. There are innocent and not-so-innocent person-attributable hindrances. The problem is how to distinguish between the two.

Consider the funding of research. When is failure to provide continuing funds for research in progress a violation of academic freedom? It will be useful to bear in mind here that there are two different ways in which we may apply the principle that academic freedom should not be violated. We can say of a given case: (*a*) that the withdrawal of funds is a violation of academic freedom and is therefore unjustified, or (*b*) that it is a violation of academic freedom and is nevertheless justified. If we think of the preservation of academic freedom as a necessary condition of correct administrative action as in (*a*), we are likely to be more cautious about identifying a case as a violation of academic freedom.

The withdrawal of funds for a research project may be a violation of academic freedom if the purpose of the withdrawal is to hinder the (professionally desirable) project. In circumstances in which funds must be cut somewhere to ensure the survival of the institution, the purpose of withdrawing funds from a project is not to hinder it but to save money. When academic freedom is violated, the funds are withdrawn *so that* the project will not continue, it being understood that the project is desirable as judged by "professional peers."

Consequentialist vs. Nonconsequentialist Grounds for Academic Freedom

Academic freedom is a practice within an institution, the institution of the university. In discussing the justification for protecting the academic freedom of the faculty, one must begin with the aims of the university. If there is little agreement at less general levels, nevertheless there is general agreement that universities aim at the discovery, publication, and teaching of the truth. It is usually argued that this is necessary for well-being, or at the least for the avoidance of misery. It is commonly then assumed that this general justification of universities somehow also justifies academic freedom for the academic. The steps of the argument are like this: (1) the aim of the university is to advance well-being, or at least to minimize misery; (2) a necessary condition of the advancement of either of these ends is the discovery, publication, and teaching of the truth; (3) the discovery, publication, and teaching of the truth can only take place in the presence of academic freedom; and (4) therefore academic freedom should be allowed to each academic.

This argument has a number of defects, the most glaring of which is the hiatus between steps 3 and 4. It does not follow that because in general academic freedom should be allowed, it should therefore be allowed to everyone. The right a given academic had to academic freedom might on these premises be a differentially qualified one, depending on the extent to which he was in a position to discover or promulgate truth that was for the happiness of everyone. If he should discover or promulgate truths that caused misery, then he would presumably be under an obligation to hide them. If, because of his ineptitude, laziness, bad luck, or assignment within the academy, he was unlikely to find any truths at all that would affect well-being very much, then his entitlement to academic freedom would be tenuous at best.

One "nonconsequentialist" suggestion that is offered in this volume is that the academic has a moral right to academic freedom, which is based not on the instrumental value of the activities in which he engages, but on the consideration that it is simply unfair to set him the socially useful task of discovering the truth and then not to allow him to accomplish, or to hinder him in the accomplishment of, what he has been set to do. It is further argued that this "setting" is what in fact occurs in universities. Faculties are in fact recruited on the understanding that they will actively seek, publish, and teach the truth, and that advancement and honor will turn on their success in these endeavors. So far, this argument is only partially nonconsequential. It justifies the general practice of seeking the truth on consequential grounds and ensuring academic freedom for the individual on nonconsequential ones. A further nonconsequentialist move is to argue that the very practice of seeking the truth can be justified on moral grounds: that the discovery of the conditions of life and of the consequences of different policies is itself a necessary condition of, and hence required by, the attempt successfully to do that which is right for everyone.

The central issue in these maneuvers is whether academic freedom can truly be said to be a moral right, or whether it is a "right" that can at best be justified prudentially. The dispute presupposes that prudentially justifiable rights are distinguishable from, and are not, moral ones. The issue may seem moot to the uninitiated, since it may seem that at the most general level prudential concerns cannot be distinguished from moral ones: that if a policy is likely to result in general misery it is a policy that ought not to be pursued, and that the question whether the "ought" is a prudential or a moral one insists upon a nonexistent distinction. The reluctance to identify moral and prudential concerns often stems from the feeling that there is a quality of moral judgments that cannot be reconciled with what is held to be the irremediably instrumental quality of prudential ones. The objection to instrumental judgments, from the moral point of view, is that they are never firm, never categorical. They can always be overridden by the judgment that the prudential desideratum, the antecedent of the hypothetical imperative, is dispensable or not essential, as once it was thought to be. But whether the avoidance of general misery or the attainment of general well-being are, as overall ends, dispensable in this way is, to say the least, questionable. If these ends are indispensable, the distinction between moral and prudential judgments, at the highest level of policy, may break down.

The consequentialist vs. nonconsequentialist argument can take a different turn. Another nonconsequentialist tack is to hold that to set academics to pursue the truth and then to hinder them in its pursuit is simply inconsistent and as such, regardless of morality, indefensible. Thus, supposing that he is truly committed to the pursuit and discovery of the truth, the president who threatens an assistant professor with nonrenewal if he continues to probe the locally touchy question of the legal validity of claims to offshore minerals is acting inconsistently and hence irrationally. We move closer to the rationale for the staunch defense of academic freedom when we consider the moves open in such a situation. Suppose the president answers that the university is committed only to the pursuit of those truths that, in the pursuit, do not weaken the support of the university. It requires no imaginative feat to see that this policy may well result in the tailoring of the activities of academics to the likes and dislikes of the legislators and contributors who provide their salaries. Since these likes and dislikes will probably turn on questions of special interest and advantage, the guidance they offer will have little relation to the uncovering and publication of truth.

Of course, there may be institutions that are not committed to the pursuit of truth and that are consequently involved in no inconsistency in throwing roadblocks against employees who pursue it. But it would be difficult to maintain that an institution is at once entitled to the honorific name of "University" and not concerned with finding and publishing the truth.

There is, even in the moral and logical versions of nonconsequentialism mentioned above, more than a small residue of consequentialism. For the pursuit of truth is on neither side claimed to be an activity that may have value in itself. Yet if we are to take our cue from Aristotle[2] or to learn from our own experience or that of others who engage in scholarly or scientific work, there is much to be said for the pleasures of pursuit. We might well ponder the question whether life would be richer or poorer if it were possible to find the answers to all our scientific and scholarly problems by pressing buttons on a Universal Encycloputer. One line of justification for academic freedom might be that there is a burden of proof upon him who would interfere with activities that are intrinsically valuable and, in consequence, on him who would interfere with the development of and instruction in intrinsically valuable activities.

A consequence of this conception of academic freedom, as freedom to engage in one of many kinds of intrinsically valuable activity without interference, is that academic freedom so conceived is simply a part of civil liberty. Freedom of speech and assembly and freedom to engage in activities that harm no one include the freedom of academics to engage in research and publication and to teach the truth as they discover it. But academic freedom can also be conceived as a special right and not as part of a general one, a right that belongs exclusively to members of an academic community in virtue of that membership.

Special vs. Nonspecial Theories of Academic Freedom

Is the academic entitled to freedom in virtue of his membership in the academic community, or in virtue of his rights as a citizen? The "or" need not be an exclusive one, but if he is entitled to freedom both as an academic and as a citizen, how are these two roles related in the justification of his claims to freedom?

[2] Aristotle, *Nicomachean Ethics*, Book X.

The "special theory" of academic freedom holds that the rights to teach, do research, or publish without lay interference "are not general human rights like the right to free speech. They are special rights that derive from particular institutional structures, which are created by quite specific sets of constitutive rules."[3] It is a theory that, given that knowledge is highly valued and that the freedoms mentioned are necessary means to it, would and does obtain even in polities in which there is no general freedom of speech and publication. It apparently obtains to a considerable degree in the Soviet Union and did obtain in Imperial Germany. The theory is adequate to cover many of the cases in which we would all be concerned that academic freedom is being violated. But, so it is held, the theory is not by itself enough to cover all the cases that most of us would want to call violations of academic freedom. For example, it does not cover cases of reprisals against professors for engaging in political activity, or interference with "private clubs" on campus by political fanatics, or cases in which professors are prevented from speaking on campus on political matters that are outside their professional competence.

The "general theory" is the theory that "professors and students have the same rights of freedom and inquiry, freedom of association, and freedom of publication in their roles as professors and students that they have as citizens in a free society, except insofar as the mode of exercise of these freedoms needs to be restricted to preserve the academic and subsidiary functions of the university."[4] This theory does not, of course, find support in an unfree society, not in Imperial Germany, not in the Soviet Union. The same theory would justify claims to freedom of speech, research, and publication in nonacademic institutions within a free society, for example, oil companies, social clubs, neighborhood organizations, and fraternities. But in each case, as with universities, the special function of the institution in question will impose limits on academic freedom. Thus, the employee of an oil company is not allowed the freedom to publish the secret formulae, the log data, or the future exploration plans of his company; and the member of a swimming club is not allowed to hold political assemblies in the pool. Anal-

[3] John Searle, *The Campus War* (New York: World Publishing Co., 1971), pp. 184–191.

[4] Ibid., pp. 191–197.

ogously, so it is argued, students do not have "equal time" with professors in the classroom; and professors may not use the classroom as a political forum. The function determines the limitation. This "general theory" can, as by itself the "special theory" cannot, account for the claim that the professor who engages in politics outside his competence and is punished for it has had his academic freedom violated. What has been violated is his freedom as a citizen to engage in politics, supposing that there is no special reason related to the function of a university that would place restrictions on his political activity. Similarly, interference with private clubs on campus is a violation of academic freedom, just because it is a violation of civil liberties that cannot be warranted by appeal to the function of a university, and professors, whatever their field of competence, cannot be prohibited from speaking to members of the campus community, because, like other citizens, they have a right to that freedom, and there is no adequate ground for overriding that right.

The chief objection to an analysis that emphasizes the "general theory" is that one risks confusing academic freedom with general civil liberties. The "general theory" is not a theory of *academic freedom* but of freedom of speech and assembly, of civil liberties available to all. When a university exercises its power to restrict a professor's right to take part in political activity, it infringes his civil liberties. To identify such infringement as of academic freedom is to invite the response that, if academic freedom is to be given a special prominence and role in civil life, then academics should be required to restrict their public utterances and performances according to academic standards and should be punished if they do not do so. The *1940 Statement of Principles on Academic Freedom and Tenure* falls into just this difficulty. By failing to recognize that academics are citizens entitled to the freedom they claim, the authors of the Statement think they must stipulate that "he should remember that the public may judge his profession and his institution by his utterances. Hence he should at all times be accurate, should exercise appropriate restraint." The "should" may originally have been intended as cautionary and friendly; but it has become a hard quasi-legal restriction on the freedom of academics in their extramural lives.

The response to this objection is that, unless one grants that there is a general theory according to which academic-freedom claims can be justified, unwanted consequences follow. For example, the nonrenewal of a professor because of his political utterances will *not* be a violation of academic freedom. Academic freedom, understood so narrowly as not to include the violation of civil liberties of academics, will, so it is argued, not be much under threat. The chief threats to academic freedom, properly understood, come as threats to the civil liberties of professors, as threats of reprisals for their taking an active part in political affairs, in particular.

Should we say that Angela Davis, nonrenewed by the Board of Regents of the University of California because she was a Communist, had suffered at their hands a violation of her academic freedom? On one view it was a violation. On another, it was wrong, and a violation of Miss Davis's civil liberties, but nevertheless it is not good policy to claim that the sin against Miss Davis consists in a violation of her academic freedom. She did not, on the latter view, need to claim any special status as an academic to show that she had been treated in an indefensible way; and for her to claim special status as the grounds of her complaint is to risk being held to the standards in her public utterances that that status supposedly requires.

It may be useful to put the problem of the relation between the special and general theories in a different way. Let us contrast the freedom of the academy, the freedom that is found within the academy, with the freedom of academics, the freedom that members of the academy have in their individual lives whether outside or inside the academy. Let us say that the freedom of the academy is violated when, and only when, within the academy, a professor or student is hindered in that he is threatened by or subject to reprisal, coercion, or restriction on nonacademic grounds. Thus, the freedom of the academy will have been violated if an academic is dismissed, not because his teaching or research is unsatisfactory as judged by his peers, but because he has assigned a text of which the Board disapproves or because he is investigating a question (of the intellectual ranking of races, for instance) of which students and faculty disapprove. The freedom of an academic, on the other hand, is the freedom he has, without fear of reprisal, to engage in politics, give speeches, write letters to the newspaper, take part in demonstrations, and in general live his private life as he pleases under the protection of the Bill of Rights. The freedom of the academy is a guarantee that within the university an academic's performance will be judged and rewarded only by his peers on the canons appropriate to his profession. The freedom of academics is the freedom that academics have in their lives as citizens in a given polity. It is clear that the freedom of academics can in some polities be severely limited at the same time as freedom within the academy flourishes. This will be so when it seems evident to all that knowledge and the development of its applications are of great value, that universities are places where knowledge is found and passed on, and that these functions cannot be performed in the absence of freedom of the academy, at the same time as, for reasons of their own, the government or the majority makes no bones about restricting speech, assembly, and publications.

Given this distinction, the question can now be phrased: Is the freedom of academics best described and defended as "academic freedom"? The arguments for doing so appear to turn around the point that academics can be singled out as a class for discriminatory treatment under the Bill of Rights and that the term, *academic freedom*, serves to call attention to this discrimination. For to discriminate against members of the academic profession may well be to chill their active pursuit of the truth within the academy, to soften and quiet the debates that are held within the walls. Because of the open way in which the intramural debates are conducted, academics are likely to be contentious and open in public and extramural debates. In a repressive political atmosphere, then, academics are likely to be especially troublesome to the regime. It is well to recognize that selective or discriminatory application of the laws to academics is just that and to mark this discrimination by the accusation that it is not merely freedom that is being violated, but the freedom of academics.

On the other hand, it is insisted that if the reprisals taken against an academic who exercises his political freedom are marked off as violations of academic freedom, rather than of freedoms that should be the possession of all, then dangerous inferences will be made. It will be, and is, reasoned that if the academic claims special status for himself, in that the violation of his political freedom is somehow a special case, then others will have the right to insist that academics live up to a special, academic standard of performance within the political arena, a standard to which other members of the public are not held. It may also be contended, wrongly, that it is only in virtue of adherence to this higher standard that the academic is entitled to the protections to which every citizen is entitled. Conversely, the insistence that there is something especially harmful about violations of the political freedom of academics is likely to be taken to imply that the violation of the political freedom of nonacademics is somehow less important because not marked off by a special term.

The distinction between the freedom of the academy and the freedom of academics is not parallel with that between intramural and extramural freedom. The freedom of the academic obtains both inside and outside the academy. Yet to protect the freedom he enjoys as a member of the academy it is often necessary to make the difficult distinction between the academic's intramural and extramural performances. It will often be unclear whether a speech that triggered a dismissal was addressed to the academic community or to the general public. The legitimate question at issue is whether the utterances in question are or are not to serve as evidence of the professional competence of the academic. A speech by a political scientist addressed to political scientists or other members of the academic community is generally evidence of competence, or the lack of it; a speech by the same political scientist on the steps of the Capitol to a demonstrating crowd should, arguably, never, and in any case seldom, be used as evidence of competence. But it is unfortunately often unclear whether the speech or publication that triggered a dismissal was addressed to the academic community. The academic community is not easy to delineate. It cannot be so tightly circumscribed as to include only the faculty of a given university. Professors are members of the faculties not just of universities but of university systems. They are practitioners of internationally practiced disciplines. They carry on their debates, in all sorts of journals and magazines, with persons who share their intellectual interests.

The distinction between the freedom of academics and of the academy is useful in clearing up a recurrent problem in the discussion of academic freedom: the question whether academic freedom is a collective or a distributive right. Is it a right that pertains to each academic in virtue of his active pursuit of the truth? Is it a right that he possesses merely in virtue of his membership in the academic community? How can a law professor, who has not published for twenty years and does not keep up with the development of law in his area of specialization, claim the right to academic freedom, if that right exists to protect the pursuit of truth? Why should a part-time instructor of optometry hired to teach students how to fit glasses, or an associate professor of education whose chief duty is to supervise the physical conditioning of the football team, be accorded academic freedom?

The answer to such questions should not be quick and doctrinaire. The notion that a man may demand the protection of a right that is contingent on a function that *he* does not perform may seem repugnant. Yet if universities do exist for the pursuit and dissemination of the truth, and if freedom of the academy *is* a necessary condition of successful pursuit, then it is so far worthy of protection. If the test of contribution to knowledge as a precondition of academic freedom is imposed, abuse by freedom's enemies is invited. The burden would then be upon the individual academic to show that he is immune to hindrance because of the accomplishment or promise of his research. But it is not usually easy to prove that one is contributing, or is likely to contribute, to the advancement of knowledge. The freedom of the academy indeed presupposes not only that such determinations be made, difficult as they may be, but also that the burden of proof will be imposed by academics on academic grounds. It presupposes as well that the questions at issue are retention and advancement, not entitlement to academic freedom.

Competing Conceptions of the Academic Community

It is nearly certain that discussions of the nature and justification of academic freedom will end in discussion of the nature and justification of those academic communities we call universities. The present papers, and the discussion of them in conference, provide no exception. The question what *kind* of academic community we are talking about becomes particularly pressing in discussing tenure and disruption on campus.

It is suggested in one of the following papers, and denied in others, that tenure as traditionally understood in the United States could be considerably modified in the interest of greater academic accomplishment without impairing academic freedom.

Suggestions of this kind immediately raise the question what, ideally, university communities should be like, and how they should be required to justify themselves before the community at large. On one view, the academic community is best thought of as analogous to a religious community to which members commit themselves for a lifetime of scholarships and research. If premises be added that assert the value of these occupations and the likelihood of attempts to hinder them by removing the academic from his post, some form of tenure is suggested.

It may be useful in this connection to compare the "tenure" enjoyed by a priest with that of the typical academic. There are two main points of comparison to be mentioned. One is that priests are ordained, that is to say, officially designated *as* priests. This designation—priest—now follows them into whatever monastery, church, school, or other organization they enter. Thus, there is, so far as this "tenure" is concerned, no question of a right to continue in one's position in a given ecclesiastical institution. The second point is that it is, by and large, up to the individual whether he leaves the priesthood. The weight of motivation is in our time nearly all against expulsion counter to his will. But ordination, or something analogous to it, would not likely serve the purpose of tenure. It would provide little protection against the person who would remove the academic from his institutional position for nonacademic reasons.

More to the point is the tenure of a judge. Here the purpose of tenure is relatively plain. The judge is not as subject to the inevitable pressure to decide cases the "right" way if no one can take his position away from him; and it is in the common interest that he should not be subject to such pressure.

If the university were a community of men who had dedicated themselves to the priesthood of truth seekers, tenure might still be necessary. But unlike the monastery, there are strong and recurrent motivations for depriving the academic of his position within the university community. Judges are quite clearly in need of the protection tenure affords; unlike academics, or most of them, the judge is entirely dependent on his office for the exercise of his function. Judges cannot be judges outside their offices.

Other suggestions have been made in these pages and elsewhere concerning the nature of a community of persons who are dedicated to the pursuit and publication of the truth. These suggestions turn partly on the foremost conception of the nature of the academic's truth-seeking activity. Is it a sort of meditation, a kind of building project, a joint venture for exploration, a critical dialogue? Given different conceptions of the activity, different conceptions follow of what it is tenure is supposed to protect.

These contrasting models of the pursuit of truth will also determine the attitude adopted toward the disruption of the activities that take place within a university, and of the relation between disruption and academic freedom. Depending on the model one has in view of academic activity, disruption can seem an unwarranted annoyance, an impediment to labor, a false scent, or an interference in the exchange of ideas. Yet there are those academics who hold, on principle, that there are some activities taking place within a university that should not merely be discouraged by budgetary and other administrative means but should also be disrupted, even by force. There are, they believe, speakers who should not be allowed to speak, researchers who should not be allowed to research. The pursuit of truth must be qualified by humane principles. Not just any methods or objectives will do, but only those that pass moral muster.

If the papers in this volume do not provide answers to all the questions they raise, that is to be expected. If they reveal a certain disarray in the ranks of those who would defend academic freedom, that is to be expected too. As times change, conceptions change—of the economic and cultural position of the professor, of the nature of the ideal political community within which the academic community finds its place, and of the academic community itself, of its structure and functions. Academic freedom is an ideal of very wide application, but only at the price of a certain flexibility.

The Concept of Academic Freedom

Part One

Most academic-freedom cases turn, these days, around the rights of professors who express radical views or engage in radical political activity, yet radicals have participated too little in the contemporary discussion of the nature of academic freedom. In the leading article in this part, Milton Fisk presents a radical analysis of the sociological and economic context within which, he argues, claims to academic freedom and attacks on academic freedom must be understood; and he offers an interpretation of academic-freedom claims that begins by focusing on professors as a class in a class society. If Fisk's interpretation is accepted, adequate analysis of the concept of academic freedom is impossible without prior understanding of the class structure and of conflicting class interests. Discussion of this radical claim is therefore given first place in this volume. For additional analyses from, or of, the radical point of view, see the articles by Richard Schmitt and Hugo Bedau.

Milton Fisk is professor of philosophy at Indiana University; Bertram Davis is past general secretary of the American Association of University Professors; and Hardy Jones is assistant professor of philosophy at the University of Texas at Austin.

1. Academic Freedom in Class Society

BY MILTON FISK

I shall try to indicate an important respect in which the right of academic freedom in the United States needs to be broadened. Its inadequacy is a result of the limited nature of the social institutions where it applies. Those institutions are limited in that they serve the preservation of capitalism in its currently destructive form.

Many rights have a dialectic that results in their approach to greater adequacy. The right to democratic government is no longer simply a device for unchaining the bourgeoisie from the restrictions of feudal privilege. Similarly, the right of academic freedom is not one to reject simply because of its current inadequacy. It can become more adequate by changing the role of institutions of higher education. Hysterical defenders of the status quo will surely say that I am out to destroy the university and academic freedom too. But their charge is groundless if capitalist social relations are but a stage in the history of society. Beyond them there are various stages in which both the university and the right of academic freedom express the needs of larger and larger segments of humanity and not, before all else, the needs of preserving a system of profit taking.

WHERE DOES ACADEMIC FREEDOM COME FROM?

Those who say that rights are discoverable by the mind by an inspection of our moral concepts, or by an inspection of independently existing moral forms or exemplars, or by an inspection of the nature of human beings as embodied in physical persons I shall lump together as moral idealists. It follows from the position of the moral idealist that human practice is only incidentally involved in the justification of rights. Rather the mind sees through human practice to a universal principle above or behind it, to which practice is then subjected. From the point of view of morality, human practice is simply an appearance that reflects to a greater or lesser extent the norms the mind beholds only by turning away from practice. Because it treats practice in the way metaphysical idealism treats nature, there is justice in calling this view moral idealism.

There are various forms of moral realism, one of which I should like to adopt as a working hypothesis for this discussion. According to what might be called descriptive moral realism, whatever is customary in practice is at least allowable, and one has a right to whatever one can expect to muster significant support for. But I wish to adopt a normative moral realism. On this view what is generally done need not be allowable, and what one can expect significant support for, one need not have a right to do. Rather, the very fact that an issue is a moral issue puts certain limitations on acceptable resolutions to that issue. In particular, I take it to be the case that, where the issue is over a right, acceptable resolutions are such that one never has a right to do what conflicts with the tendencies of the groups on which one must rely. It is understood that this reliance or dependence has a thoroughly group nature. It is a reliance or dependence on groups for the realization of interests arising from conditions that define the group or groups to which the individual with the right belongs. Hence it is clear that rights imply an avoidance of conflicts with the tendencies of the groups to which one belongs. This is not to say that inspection of the mind tells me what is right. I have not reverted to moral idealism. Rather, avoiding conflicts with the tendencies of groups on which one depends is a motive that one has in order to raise a question as to what is right to do. If one were not so motivated, then there would simply be no question of what one has a right to do.

This normative moral realism can be made more specific in one important respect. The groups on which one needs to rely to realize one's interests as a group member may manifest conflicting tendencies. What has been said so far provides no means of resolving these conflicts when I am deciding what I ought to do, what would be good to do, or what I have a right to do. Before concluding that an inspection of the mind is what is needed to save the day, it should be asked whether there is any ordering among the groups whereby one is dependent on another for the realization of its tendencies. I suggest that groups depend for the realization of their tendencies upon the adoption of these tendencies by a class. Thus, ultimately, by desiring not to conflict with the tendencies of any groups on which one depends in the above sense, one desires, knowingly or not, not to conflict with the tendencies of one's class or of an alien class with which one identifies. The kind of ordering among groups leading to the pre-eminence of classes advocated here is opposed to the pluralistic view of unordered groups. Moreover, in a classless society this specification of moral realism to class tendencies is inapplicable in that then the tendencies of society as a whole become controlling.[1]

We claim academic freedom as a right. How does the above conception of rights apply to it? I do not find the right of academic freedom to be self-evident—a clear result of a mental inspection of teaching and scholarship. I nonetheless recognize it as a right. And it may well have been a right that academics had before it was recognized that they had it. But it is a right now since academics, as integrated into institutions that work for the perpetuation of society in its present capitalist form, have, on the whole, defined their disciplines in such a way that what will be regarded as professionally responsible teaching and scholarship in those disciplines will not, on the whole, challenge the goals those institutions work for. This means that the tendency of academics, as members of a larger class, to perpetuate the capitalist order ensures that there is no conflict with the tendencies of the capitalist class arising from academic behavior that is professionally responsible. Of course, this means no conflict in the large, since more conflict is generated by attempts to stifle ineffectual dissent than by letting it ride. Thus, the base of the right to academic freedom in our society is the tendency of the class to which academics belong to serve the capitalist class by providing ideological props for the order in which that class is a ruling class.

[1] This class theory of morals is developed in a forthcoming paper of mine, "On the Inevitable Relativity of Morals in a Society with Classes."

My view here differs from that of those who say the right of academic freedom rests on the needs of society only in the respect that I
find the word *society* here implies a harmonization of classes that is
simply unrealized. Thus, in respect to the United States, I would
substitute *capitalist order* for *society*.

As I shall indicate more fully later, academics—both on the
campus and in the school—are members of a class of functionaries.
But this class has a status derivative from the class that is the ruling
class in the economic order. For the class of functionaries operates
to preserve an order in which the tendencies of the ruling class are
advanced. Since the ruling class here is a capitalist class, the rights
of functionaries are determined by the tendency of the functionary
class to preserve the capitalist order and therewith to preserve the
role of the capitalist class as a ruling class. In view of this tendency,
there is a coincidence of interest between functionaries and capitalists.

There is another facet to rights that provides an obvious complement to what has already been said. So far we have only seen why
academic freedom is allowable; it is allowable since it does not
conflict with the tendency of the functionary class to preserve the
capitalist order. But sufficient grounds have not been presented for
its being a right. For this we need to observe that the class on which
one depends must be prepared to intervene to assure the exercise
of the right. In fact, it ought to do this, and an "ought" has two requirements. If the class *ought* to intervene, then doing so will not
conflict with its own tendencies but will, in fact and not just in its
judgment, advance its tendencies. By and large these requirements
are satisfied in the case of intervention to support the right of academic freedom. Of course, at different times there will be variations
in the degree to which the capitalist class through its top functionaries will support academic freedom. Still, it would be superficial to
accept the alarmist view that academic freedom is now dead in view
of the fiscal crisis of the system of corporate democracy, in which
formal democratic procedures are combined with control by concentrated industrial and financial power. Fiscal crisis or not, the
benefits to corporate democracy from at least the universities are too
great to close professional forums to dissent. The words of Chief
Justice Warren in reversing a New Hampshire decision against one
of the great Marxists of the mid-twentieth century, Paul Sweezy, for

contempt of court, in 1957, still hold generally true: "To impose any strait jacket upon the intellectual leaders in our colleges and universities would imperil the future of our Nation."[2] Here "Nation," like "society," has a rhetorical, harmonistic impact, but descriptively it is to be read in the sense of the class theory of the state. To close professional forums—journals, symposia, and the lecture room—to dissent would be a gross failure to recognize just how deep the socialization into capitalist relations is in this country. Expressions of dissent from such forums are but a ripple, but once stopped their significance would become a deluge against that socialization. The resulting disruption would then interfere with the effectiveness of that group in the university that takes as their professional responsibility making repairs in the ship of capitalism and preparing beachheads for its imperialist expansion. In short, one has the right to academic freedom in the present context, since professional academic behavior does not, on the whole, conflict with tendencies of the functionary class to perpetuate the capitalist order and since the protection of such behavior from threat will, in view of the function of educational institutions, advance the tendency of functionaries to perpetuate capitalism.

I wish in what follows to prepare the ground for, though not to substantiate fully, two points already mentioned. The first is that the right to academic freedom in present American society is a right whose exercise has very limited social usefulness. It is a right whose exercise is limited due to its origin in a coincidence of interest with the capitalist class. This limitation implies a negative effect for teachers, for those who are students or potential students, and for the masses of working people. Teachers, who have the right to academic freedom, are not protected from the application to them of professional standards that conform to the advancement of capitalist tendencies. Students, who by academic freedom have the right to learn, can often exercise that right only in the lower tracks of educational systems that are stratified in response to industrial manpower needs. Working people see part of the profits they create go to protected academics—the Herrensteins, Huntingtons, Rostows—who tighten the noose of exploitation around their necks. The second point is that academic freedom will be a right the exercise of which

[2] Sweezy v. New Hampshire, 354 U.S. 250 (1956).

has greater potential for human advancement when it has its origin in a coincidence of interest between academics and a ruling working class. This coincidence will exist when the tendency of the functionary class is to perpetuate an economic order in which the working class is the ruling class. We have no precedents for precisely the situation I am envisaging here. The universities after the Great Proletarian Cultural Revolution in China may offer helpful information when more is learned about exact conditions within them.

FUNCTIONARIES AND OTHER CLASSES

Much thinking about academic freedom sees the basic polarity of human life as that between the individual and something called society. Each individual is to think of himself or herself as a center of autonomy that the mass of individuals is ready to grind to sand. This model has served the goal of fragmenting lower classes and destroying class solidarity in the face of the capitalist class and its agents in the class of functionaries. It not only serves this goal but also falsifies the facts in several ways. Since social mobility is not a reality for anything like a majority of those in the lower classes, there is a very real need for mutual reliance among members of those classes. Moreover, not only are individuals not fully autonomous due to this reliance, but also the many opposed to them do not compose a single entity—a society—but a multitude of antagonistic classes. The basic reality is, then, not a one opposed to a many but a one in a many opposed to a many. The model for thinking about academic freedom is, however, frequently the Millian one-vs.-many model.[3] The model I have suggested is somewhat closer to the one-in-many-vs.-many model.

I say *somewhat* closer only because the many the academic is in is the functionary class, and this class is opposed to the working class not just by being another class but more importantly because it represents the capitalist class in the work of exploiting the working class. Academic freedom exists now as a right for the academic not because he or she is an individual working as a teacher-scholar. It is a right for him or her because this work does not conflict with and, on the whole, does advance the tendencies of the capitalist class.

[3] John Stuart Mill, *On Liberty*, chap. 4.

Pluralist models of society as a multiplicity of complementary and basically harmonious groups give a reasonable description of the appearances during some epochs but fail to get at the forces at play. Pluralistic institutions are a response to the reality of class antagonism and are never more than a veneer laid over that antagonism. Though, until recently, there were those who supposed that pluralism could supplant a class theory, it is not pluralism so much as the old one-vs.-many theory that is operative in the literature on academic freedom. For example, in the AAUP's 1956 statement on academic freedom and national security it is suggested that the Communist is engaged in activities subversive of education itself and is thus unfit to teach.[4] The argument would seem to run as follows: The Communist is an enemy of society—that is, of corporate democratic society—but it is by serving the needs of society that the academic has the right to teach and study without threat of discontinuation. Thus, as an individual, he or she has forfeited the right of protection against the encroachments of society. There is no hint of pluralism in regard to the make-up of that society that individuals work either for or against.

Having made these observations about alternatives to a class theory, let us now try to see where academics fit into the class picture. Classes are groups in societies where the materials for satisfying human wants are in the hands of some one or several groups to the exclusion of others. The basis for the antagonism between classes is the fact that control over the means of production is limited. The power that this control gives is evident in the fact of exploitation. The condition of satisfying wants for a member of certain groups becomes the production of profit for owners. A portion of the worker's time is used in the production of profit that, as invested, may have little to do with his or her own further development.[5] Exploitation does not necessarily mean increased material misery; rather the degree of exploitation, in a context of high productivity per working hour, may be higher for the well-fed, housed, and transported worker than it is, in a context of low productivity,

---

[4] Louis Joughin, ed., *Academic Freedom and Tenure. A Handbook of the American Association of University Professors* (Madison: University of Wisconsin Press, 1969), p. 50.

[5] Karl Marx, *Capital* (New York: International Publishers Co., 1967), vol. 1, chap. 9, sec. 1.

for the poorly fed, ill-housed, and walking or cycling worker.[6] That part of the product of work that represents profit gains greater and greater control over the worker through its addition, year in and year out, to wealth concentrated in the hands of owners. Thus the increment of work done for profit—surplus work—not only is largely irrelevant to satisfying the wants of the worker's family but also is a device for making the worker powerless in the face of ever growing private wealth.

The specific form of class society we live in has generated a need for a large intermediate class between the working class and the ruling capitalist class.[7] The ever more complex work of the organization of actual production remains to be done. There is also the well-known need for knowledge and techniques related to the expansion of markets and production. In addition, as in all class society, there is a need for instruments of socialization that generate a noncritical acceptance of the fundamental principles of the economic order and the political order built around it. People employed for these tasks I have called "functionaries." Their task is not to produce, to transport, or to sell. Nor is their task to provide capital for the accumulation of greater wealth. It is the task of the functionary in a capitalist society to perpetuate the system that produces commodities for the accumulation of wealth. I use the term *functionary* in its old sense to refer to those who function to realize a goal set independently of them and not in the more limited sense it has had in recent centuries when it referred only to those who, by seeing to the day-to-day business of organizations, free others for either productive labor or broad policy matters.

In a capitalist order, the functionary is, however he or she may conceal the fact by explicit adoption of liberal stances, working to perpetuate, streamline, and expand the system of exploitation. With this role, functionaries, despite their ever increasing numbers, are not a primary class, but they merely mediate between financial and industrial capitalists, on the one side, and producers and service workers, on the other side. To say that functionaries should become the ruling class—by a managerial revolution—can only be true genetically, for as a ruling class they would no longer be inter-

[6] Ibid., chap. 17.

[7] Cf. Donald C. Hodges, "Old and New Working Classes," *Radical America* 5, no. 1 (January–February 1971): 11–32.

mediaries but controllers of the means of production and exchange.

It is thoroughly possible that a functionary could be both an exploiter, in the sense of one who oils the general machinery of the extraction of surplus, and at the same time exploited, in the sense of one from whom surplus is extracted for capitalist reinvestment. Top functionaries—members of the power elite in Domhoff's sense of those with key positions in institutions controlled by the big owners[8] —are definitely not exploited in that they are rewarded not only with the fruits of their own surplus labor but also with the fruits of that of innumerable others. They are profit takers—even though not necessarily accumulators of capital—of their own and others' profits. Middle functionaries, even when account is taken of the greater expense of the reproduction of their labor and hence of the greater value of their necessities of life as compared with those of less skilled labor, still generate an increment of value by their work that goes beyond the value of their necessities of life. But their salaries, like those of the top functionaries, are high enough to make it reasonable to say that in a significant number of cases they consume their own profit and are thus not genuinely exploited. However, there are two things to note about this. First, there is a qualitative difference between receiving part or all of the surplus one creates when one makes $15,000 a year and receiving the surplus of ten to twenty individuals when one makes $75,000 a year. Second, with the increasing size of the class of functionaries relative to the working class, middle functionaries will experience an increase in their degree of exploitation. Thus the prospect of unity between workers and middle functionaries around the issue of exploitation cannot be discounted. Bottom functionaries, including beginning university teachers, junior college teachers, teaching assistants, many schoolteachers, and social workers, are without a doubt exploited. Their aspirations to join the middle functionaries will serve to keep lines distinct between them and the lower classes—the working class and its lumpen —as long as middle functionaries do not feel the effects of exploitation.

The question of academic freedom for teachers applies predominantly to middle and bottom functionaries. Thus it is not universally characteristic of this group that it is exploited, though in a

[8] Cf. G. William Domhoff, *Who Rules America?* (Englewood Cliffs, N.J.: Prentice-Hall, 1967), p. 10.

period of fiscal crisis exploitation is an important factor as a basis for agitation in the group. It is universally characteristic of this group, as of all functionaries, that it acts to perpetuate the system of exploitation. This goal is built into the institutions of higher education through restrictive admissions, standards satisfied by attitudes and abilities appropriate to the profit system, and grants and lead money from foundations and the government that give direction to professional norms and to university expansion. Often the end of perpetuating exploitation is built into whole systems, as in the case of the Master Plan of 1960 for California higher education, which was designed not to satisfy educational needs but to produce a stratified work force required by the corporations.[9] A ruling-class foundation, the Carnegie Foundation, through a commission of top functionaries, will attempt to force a more elaborate system of educational stratification on the entire nation.[10] Since an overeducated work force is a political threat to the capitalist class, Clark Kerr and his colleagues on the Carnegie Commission on Higher Education are devising a way of meeting the growing demand for higher education by severely limiting admission to the third and fourth years of college in a way that will meet economic needs and discourage "experimentation in life styles."

Functionaries perpetuate an economic order, but it need not be one of limited ownership. It need not be one of profit taking for private investment. It may be one in which the working class controls the means of production and exchange. In such a case, all efforts directly related to perpetuating and streamlining exploitation cease, for the workers and functionaries share the surplus they have worked together to create. They do not alienate their surplus but invest it in their own way in projects for the improvement of their lives. One source of antagonism between functionaries and workers disappears, in that functionaries are no longer working to preserve and make more efficient a system of extracting profit. "In a cooperative factory the antagonistic nature of the labor of supervision disappears, because the manager is paid by the laborers instead of

9 William Barlow and Peter Shapiro, *An End to Silence* (New York: Pegasus, 1971), pp. 27–32, 178–186.

10 The Carnegie Commission on Higher Education, *Less Time, More Options* (Hightstown, N.J.: McGraw-Hill Book Co., 1971).

representing capital counterposed to them."[11] The antagonism does not fully disappear, but at least it is now that between one class and another derivative of it, not that stemming from a conflict between two primary classes.

The antagonism obvious between doing the work of exploitation and being exploited will be reflected in the relation between criteria for academic freedom and the interests of the working class. Angela Davis's statement in her letter from prison in September, 1971, to her brothers and sisters in the United Action Caucus of the American Federation of Teachers describes the situation accurately: "The myth of academic freedom has masked repression within the university but it has also blinded many educators to the more pervasive and brutal repression in the world outside the university." Those criteria reflect professional standards that have grown up in response to the reality that there would be no right to academic freedom in the capitalist order unless these standards did not conflict with the interests of the capitalist class and at least indirectly furthered those interests. Those standards have made education exclusive and have either geared the problems to those of corporate democracy or have fobbed off potential critical acumen with irrelevancies. On the other hand, functionaries of a ruling working class would derive their right to academic freedom from their definition of professional standards in a way that would further the interests of the working class. Functionaries would still have a derivative status, and that would be a source of antagonisms. But the choice of the major class on which the functionaries will be dependent is not one they, and in particular their academic colleagues, are free to make. The choice will be made for them in the struggle between the major classes themselves.

THE SOCIAL CONTEXT OF ACADEMIC STANDARDS

The frequent response to the class bias of actual standards is that incursions on neutrality are to be granted but that academic freedom cannot be faulted because of these incursions, since academic freedom is explicitly in support of treating a colleague's work in a purely professional way. This response must be deemed an elementary act of bad faith and is a way of protecting oneself from the responsi-

[11] Marx, *Capital*, vol. 3, chap. 23, p. 387.

bility involved in having accepted professional standards that serve the work of exploitation. It is so much more comfortable to be able to think of these standards as coming from the sky rather than from the practice of academic functionaries in the context of a capitalist society where they will be serving the capitalist class. The fact is, then, that the incursions are inherent in the standards of professional judgment. Academic freedom is a way of internally policing professional activity by these standards. There is less incidence of external policing with its potential for social disturbances. Academic freedom accomplishes greater consistency, less notoriety, and an appearance of universality in the selection of qualified academics.[12] Doubtless there is a gain in making the policing internal. But the thing to be kept in mind is that, up to a point, corporate society realizes the same goals by internal policing as it would by external policing, and it realizes them more efficiently by the former. Marx notes that the rise of Bonapartism in the aftermath of 1848 showed that the bourgeoisie had only intensified its own problems when it interfered on an ongoing basis with its functionaries in the state apparatus.[13] Bureaus of whatever kind need intellectual space to work their own problems out in, provided of course that those problems fit someway into the picture of advancing the interests of the ruling class.

According to one author in the AAUP Handbook, academic freedom protects teachers and students in higher education from threats that may inhibit them "from freely studying and investigating whatever they are interested in, and from freely discussing, teaching, or publishing whatever opinions they have reached."[14] As a description of a possible right, one can hardly object to this definition, but it is certainly not the case that anyone can now truly claim to have such a right. The disapprobation of one's colleagues when it comes time for reappointment is a threat that inhibits, or at least engenders anxiety about, one's freely teaching opinions one has reached. One's peers are honorable people and their judgment will be purely on

[12] Cf. Christopher Jencks and David Riesman, *The Academic Revolution* (New York: Doubleday and Co., 1968), pp. 199–206.

[13] Karl Marx, *The Eighteenth Brumaire of Louis Bonaparte* (New York: International Publishers Co., 1963), p. 67.

[14] Fritz Machlup, "On Some Misconceptions Concerning Academic Freedom," in *Academic Freedom and Tenure*, ed. Joughin, p. 178.

professional grounds. Yet it happens that the philosophical profession in mid-twentieth–century America is not what it was for Plato, Aquinas, Bentham, and Marx. Philosophy is now of a diversionary nature. It socializes students not by catechetical teaching of the sort that John Locke gave for the justification of property rights and of the role of the state in protecting them.[15] It can be assumed now that the philosophy of capitalism is well enough entrenched in the young mind in the United States by the time it reaches the campus. The threat is rather that critical tools should be mobilized for the examination of that philosophy and the philosophy of atomism and individualism that developed since the sixteenth century to provide it with a metaphysical base. To meet this threat one needs diversionary paths where sufficient technical difficulties are encountered to entice the potentially critical mind. The philosophical profession as defined by this diversionary effort has developed a thoroughgoing separation of thought and action, a commitment to ahistorical analyses, and the theoretical impossibility for the philosopher to see his or her practice as a philosopher in terms of the society conditioning it. The philosopher gives theoretical legitimacy to the given social situation around us, yet no more perceives the ideological bias of this legitimation than we smell air or taste water. If you reject the diversionary conception of philosophy and see philosophy as one tool for the acceleration of social change, professional judgment is quick to respond that you have sold your birth right for unprofessional activity and shall no longer inherit preferment in any of its various forms. Moreover, if you are not reappointed, your chances of becoming a member of the lumpen functionaries are great indeed. In practice, advocates of academic freedom admit that the judgment of your peers is, since it is a professionally respectable one, not an infringement of a right you have to teach and publish. Yet there is still the irresistible tendency to define academic freedom in a manner that ignores social context in order to be able to say that you have had a right violated, though it is one no power will support.

The academic disciplines have not set their standards of appointment and preferment in isolation. The hand of the foundation and of the governmental agency is evident in regard to many standards.

[15] John Locke, *The Second Treatise of Government*, nos. 27, 50, 123, 180 (Indianapolis: Bobbs-Merrill, 1952).

Ever since the requirement of the Ph.D. for departmental heads was laid down for a college to be eligible for participation in the Carnegie Foundation's pension fund—ultimately TIAA-CREF—the requirement of the Ph.D. became unchallenged. The behavioral approach in social sciences, with its inability to probe behind the social appearances and with its inherent acceptance of the given economic order, was a natural for the foundations to back. Had the foundations been hostile to the behavioral approach, its development would have been slower. In 1957, Ford and Carnegie funded the Harvard Center for International Affairs, whose objective was, according to a liberated document, to provide "training for civilians who might later be involved in the formation of defense policy."[16] Among the imperialist notables at or near its helm were McGeorge Bundy, W. W. Rostow, and Henry A. Kissinger. The demise of Ronald Hilton's *Hispanic American Report*, which was an embarrassment to foundation and defense-industry related officials at Stanford but a gold mine for independent Latin America watchers, was followed by a half-million-dollar grant from Ford for a Latin American Studies program of more pliable Latin Americanists. Standards set by the gentle pull of these monies at elite schools are quickly followed by those at other institutions. But at some nonelite schools the pull is also direct. The respectability of imperialist scholarship at Indiana University is not lessened when it reports one-half million from Ford to set up a business school in Dacca to teach the market economy to the Bengalis and thereby stem the trend to the left in that war-ravaged land.[17] In addition, Indiana University reported in 1971 that it was a corecipient with other MUCIA schools of one million from AID to study problems of setting up institutions, that is, of building the frontier of corporate democracy, in the underdeveloped world. David Horowitz, to whose writing I owe much of these data, concludes that "the saddest part is that the academics have become such eager victims. They have internalized the limits placed upon them. They fiercely uphold a strict academic professionalism. But it is no more than expert servitude to oppressive power."[18]

[16] David Horowitz, "Sinews of Empire," *Ramparts* 8 (October 1969): 38.

[17] *Research Reports*, Indiana University Foundation, no. 17 (1970–1971), p. 20.

[18] Horowitz, "Sinews of Empire," p. 42.

In short, the right to academic freedom is a right to publish and teach with impunity as long as there is general conformity to professional standards. But these standards of professional activity are fashioned by the tendency of the functionary class to perpetuate the order in which the interests of the ruling class are realized. The right does not extend beyond these social limits. Since, in the judgment of many, what is in the interests of the ruling class in mid-twentieth–century United States is destructive of the advancement of the human potential of a large segment of the human race, there is the suspicion—in the wake of Watts, Vietnam, East Pakistan, May Day 1971, and Attica—that many facets of standards of professional competence—though not all—are means of preserving a destructive system and hence that the right of academic freedom is not just powerless to initiate, but indeed an obstacle in the path of, social amelioration for the working masses of mankind. Academic freedom, like other rights, is no higher than the economic stage. A higher right of academic freedom—one that, by internalizing the tendencies of the broad masses of humanity, is not accomplice to the destruction of those tendencies—is only possible when functionaries identify with the working class in a common struggle. It is futile to try to extend a right beyond the limits of its social context without changing that social context. One cannot try to extend the right in this way by examining one's conscience on the content of professional standards. To try to purge those standards of all that is related to social context is futile for two reasons. In the first place, a profession in a given context cannot survive without adjustment to that context. In the second place, supposedly universal standards would be so general as to make drawing distinctions according to standards impossible.

BEYOND CAPITALIST SCHOLARSHIP TO THE WORKING-CLASS INTELLECTUAL

It is often helpful to distinguish between being a member of and identifying with a class. One's economic role determines membership; as someone employed to teach in a large United States university, I am objectively a member of the class of functionaries of capitalism. But this does not mean that, by contrast, it is sufficient to applaud the success and mourn the setbacks of another class to identify with it. Though identification is not membership, it does imply struggle for the realization of the tendencies of another class. Many functionaries identify with capitalism through endeavoring to make their work and that of those they can influence more effective in the realization of the tendencies of the capitalist class. But there are those that identify with the working class and the class derivative of it, the *Lumpenproletariat*. They struggle in, around, and in spite of their bureaus to make the operations of these bureaus less oppressive to these lower classes. Moreover, they recognize that in the end they can significantly advance the tendencies of these classes only by a reorientation of their bureaus from instruments of perpetuating exploitation to instruments of building workers' democracy.

But if moral idealism is to be rejected, how are we to justify identification with an alien class? Middle and bottom functionaries are, in general, if not exploited, at least not being compensated with much more than their own surplus. There is the threat that this situation will not be improved as demands are put into effect to increase the "productivity" of functionaries. Increasing productivity, in order to maintain an overall constant rate of return for the capitalist, increases the degree of exploitation of the functionary. The obvious fact that the salaries of top functionaries are largely profit and only in small part the value of their work, and that every effort will be made to maintain the high level of profit coming both to this power elite and to the owners, makes the fact of exploitation a galling reality not just for workers but also for the majority of functionaries. Clearly it is to the advantage of the majority of the functionaries to form a united front with working people to destroy the system that exploits them all, or at least threatens to do so.

There is a further fact of equal importance. The internal policing allowed some professions was seen, at the beginning of the section on the social context of academic standards, to be a condition of bureaucratic efficiency. But the sense of autonomy that is correlative with this internal policing is not merely a protective rationalization for having internalized the standards of the ruling class. It is a rationalization that has important social consequences. The academic, for example, begins to think that projects generated out of his or her discipline should be funded and that ideas taken from the institution of internal professional policing should be applied to the running of the entire university. Even if the academic does not go as far as Plato did, in the *Republic*, in proposing that the class of intellectual functionaries should supplant all contending major classes for the title of ruling class, at least the academic thinks he or she should have a voice in the control of monies to be spent in developing the university in new ways. When up against the reality that it is the government, the foundations, and the trustees—73 percent of whom are businessmen over fifty years old—that "dominate the margins of growth in the university system," the academic recognizes that he or she is united with the workers in their voicelessness as regards the ways in which capital development goes on.

The growth of identification within academic ranks with tendencies of the working class, based on the shared facts of exploitation and voicelessness, develops the possibility of a new category of academics. Antonio Gramsci wrote from one of Mussolini's prisons that as a class emerges into power it "creates with itself, organically, one or more groups of intellectuals who give it homogeneity and consciousness of its function not only in the economic field but in the social and political field as well."[19] Of course, the organic intellectuals of the working class must lead lives full of contradictions in present circumstances. Institutions alternative to the capitalist ones are not in existence except for a few editorial staffs barely eking out an existence. Thus a way needs to be devised in which an employee of a ruling-class institution can be an organic intellectual of the working class.

There are two things to be separated out here. First, there is the matter of developing the consciousness needed for a working-class intellectual while at the same time doing the work needed to keep a ruling-class institution going. Second, there is the matter of attempting to survive by extending the limits of existing academic freedom through a broadening of professional criteria that will make the activity of the working-class intellectual professionally acceptable while at the same time—before any broadening can take place— submitting oneself to the narrower criteria. Contradictions are always resolved in practice, and it is in the practice of the labor movement that both of these contradictions are resolved.

Exploitation and voicelessness are leading functionaries to organize in the way they have led many in the working class to organize.

[19] Antonio Gramsci, *The Modern Prince and Other Writings* (New York: International Publishers Co., 1957), p. 118.

As is clear from the study of Detroit workers by sociologist John C. Leggett, class consciousness is highest among union workers of all categories.[20] Union rank and file are most apt to recognize owners as their oppressors, to be willing to participate in demonstrative action, and to favor an equitable distribution of wealth. Correspondingly, in organizing around exploitation and voicelessness, academic functionaries will raise their consciousness through direct political experience of the structural limitations on their freedom in the corporate state.

Of equal importance, this consciousness will attempt to make itself felt in a shift of professional standards of acceptable research and of acceptable practico-theoretical endeavors. On current standards, it is inadmissible to set up a black-studies program that, like the one proposed by Nathan Hare at San Francisco State, attempts to avoid the cooptation of black leadership through liberal socialization. But there is acceptance, at places like Yale, of Ford Foundation–sponsored programs whose aim is not the improvement of conditions within the black community but the siphoning off of potential black leaders—only two in a hundred go back—to maintain peace in the immense reserve labor army. Acceptable scholarship, in the view of top functionary John Bunzel, cannot emphasize "motivation and commitment" to return to the black community. One is to infer that the academic traits of "independence, skepticism, and critical inquiry" exist only where one emphasizes a motivation and commitment to an identification with the ruling class, such as Ford sponsors.[21] Unionization will stop the liberal doublethink that separates exploitation at Ford Dearborn or Ford Rouge from the litany of progressive purposes that surrounds Ford Foundation President McGeorge Bundy.[22] And the double standard that sanctions ruling-class but forbids working-class practico-theoretical endeavors will be recognized for what it is. The shift of standards of professional acceptability that is thus implied would mean a broadening of academic freedom. For, given the principle of internal policing, academic freedom means more or less, according

[20] John C. Leggett, *Class, Race and Labor* (New York: Oxford University Press, 1968).

[21] Barlow and Shapiro, *An End to Silence*, pp. 139–145.

[22] Robert L. Allen, *Black Awakening in Capitalist America* (New York: Doubleday and Co., 1970), pp. 70–77.

to how few or many capitalist goals are reflected in the standards by which that policing is done. Internal policing clearly does not mean full autonomy for functionaries. The standards by which the policing is done have a class content. Functionaries of the working class who police themselves largely internally apply to their work standards that, when satisfied, advance the tendencies of the working class. In all, organization around issues that will develop an identification with the working class and a sense of the need to rely on working-class power will not just develop organic intellectuals of the working class but also provide protection that academic freedom does not now provide. This will come about both through political support from the working class and through a broadened concept of academic freedom.

However, identification with the labor movement can only be a bare beginning. Union practice can tear the veil from the capitalist standards of the disciplines and can afford some breathing space for this demythologizing. But unions generally accept the supremacy of the capitalist class and content themselves with maintaining enough power to reduce exploitation. Rank and file are less likely to entertain rosy, harmonistic myths than unorganized functionaries are, since organizing makes conflict visible and institutionalizes it. It is necessary for middle and bottom functionaries to organize, even though this is only a beginning, if the formulation of professional standards is not to be left to those functionaries who either identify with or unquestioningly serve the capitalist class.

The question is not one of whether professional standards should be broadened to include demonstrative actions as well as thought.[23] There is generally no basis for saying that picketing or sitting-in is a professional act. There is, then, generally no basis for limiting consideration of it to one's professional peers in the determination of tenure. In such matters one has no call for more or less protection from employers than employees of other kinds have. (It should be obvious, though, that criteria relating the broader issue of free speech to discontinuation of employment will be subject to limits due to social context just as criteria for professional academic work are.) On this I tend to concur with William W. Van Alstyne's admirable contribution to this symposium, "The Specific Theory of

[23] Cf. Staughton Lynd, "Academic Freedom and the First Amendment," *The Radical Teacher*, New University Conference (1969), pp. 23–28.

Academic Freedom and the General Issue of Civil Liberty." The question, rather, concerns the changing of standards for the *specific* activities of academic study, writing, and teaching in order to make those activities benefit another class.

Taking on trustees, sitting-in at draft boards, and interrupting speakers will, normally, be beyond the scope of what would be considered academic activity, even in the academy of a society in which our narrow view of the relation of theory to practice has given way to a view that sees all theory as but a moment in social practice. But theoretical moments in social practice are still different from nontheoretical ones. Your teaching may be integrated into some group's practice of civil disobedience, but discussing it in a cinder-block classroom, in your den at home, or in a storefront classroom with students in respect to whom you are performing your functionary role is a quite different moment in your practice and theirs from sitting-in with them at the draft board. The distinction is no more artificial than is class society itself. The reason one wants standards to be broadened is not to put demonstrative actions beyond the judgment of academic employers and within the judgment of only one's professional peers, but precisely to allow for thought about problems that have a direct bearing on the amelioration of the conditions of lower classes to be considered part of the repertoire of what is professionally relevant thought. Indeed, demonstrative action, not being specifically academic, does not fall within the scope of academic internal policing. It is properly judged by the community, whose standards of judgment will vary as the balance of power between classes changes.

In a profession like philosophy, where the accepted problems are diversionary and hence not integrated with social practice, this change of standards would mean a radical shift away from formal analysis of contrived problems to a dialectical concentration on concrete subjects. In professions that have not been altogether diversionary but have directly contributed to the advancement of the system of exploitation, this would mean a radical shift away from an exclusive emphasis on ruling-class problems. In the case of philosophy and similar diversionary studies, this constitutes what critics who accept the myth of academic neutrality are fond of calling a "politicization" of the field. In the case of, for example, physics, the law, and political science, it either complements one politicization with another or, ultimately, sheds ruling-class politicization for working-class politicization.

Organizing functionaries around problems shared by the working class does not, then, set us solidly on the course to overcoming capitalism. It only destroys the myth of academic neutrality and makes some relief work for the lower classes academically respectable. Further tactics must be devised to make a change of the controlling-class part of the teleology of professional work. Academic freedom will not extend protection to those who do such work— their work will also be called political, not professional, and thus they will not satisfy tests of professional competence—even in the stage of mass white-collar organizing. Whether academic freedom ever will extend such protection will depend on whether the ruling class decides to allow sentiment for a change of the ruling class to be vented in the universities rather than in more sensitive areas of society, such as the place of production itself. Allowing radical scholarship while at the same time conducting an all-out campaign to alienate the working class from the intellectuals, the ruling class might succeed in staving off disaster. It could pride itself on the unprecedented degree of academic freedom it has made possible. On the other hand, should an attempt be made to destroy the formation of professional groups aiming at working out the details of a transformation of power from the capitalist to the working class, this attempt would be met with general resistance from the working and functionary classes combined. This would doubtless be the case if, as Andre Gorz conjectures, "the cooperation of technocrats is indispensable to the labor movement for the specification . . . of certain strategic objectives of an economically coherent antimonopolistic alternative."[24] The important thing is that beyond the stage of organizing that leads to identification with the labor movement, there are a number of alternative scenarios for the play of freedom of academic functionaries. A transitional program can do little more than specify the appropriate activity for the present stage. Beyond that there are multiple branchings.

But, however dimly the means are perceived, the goal is a reversal of power between the primary classes that will allow the needs of the great mass of people to define the standards of profes-

[24] Andre Gorz, *Strategy for Labor* (Boston: Beacon Press, 1967), p. 125.

sional competence that are used in policing internally the academic profession. Internal policing is important for the efficiency of the organic academics of the working class. This internal policing is one of the great advances that capitalist society has contributed to education, an advance not to be jettisoned by a reversion to a form of capitalism in which functionaries lack the elbow room to do their jobs well. However, I emphasize the futility of defining academic freedom in such a way that, given the present relations of production, it cannot be a genuine right. Such an absent-minded definition will mislead academics as to the true limits of their freedom. To extend that freedom more must be done than for academics to insist on rights they do not have. A change in the balance of power between the primary classes of society will be necessary.

2. *Academic Freedom, Academic Neutrality, and the Social System*

BY BERTRAM H. DAVIS

Professor Fisk believes that academic freedom is presently limited because American colleges and universities are dedicated to the "preservation of capitalism in its currently destructive form." Thus, while academic freedom is tolerated in colleges and universities because it serves the purposes of the ruling class of profit takers, it is restricted by the fact that the capitalistic system imposes standards for determining professional competence—that is, for deciding who will gain entry into and remain in the academic profession—which either never admit to the academic profession, or root out from it, those who oppose that system. Hence, a significant limitation is placed upon academic freedom.

In order to broaden academic freedom, as Professor Fisk would have us do, he asserts that we must seek a "reversal of power between the major classes that will allow the needs of the great mass of people to define the standards of professional competence." Professors, whom he thinks of as functionaries of the capitalistic system, must identify themselves with the working class and hence devote their efforts to removing the exploitation that characterizes the capitalistic system and to seeking the betterment of the great mass of people rather than the perpetuation and advancement of present social forms. For, he says, it is only through this identification, and thereby through the acceptance and retention in the profession of persons with this larger and more socially desirable view of their profession, that we can achieve an academic freedom that is not burdened with the limitations now placed upon it.

It seems to me a matter of simple truth that most social institutions, colleges and universities among them, reflect the societies in which they have been established; and inevitably the leaders of society will look to the schools and colleges, as seminaries of instruction and learning, to see if they cannot be shaped to advance the interests of society as those leaders perceive them. German universities were different during the Hitler years than they had been in the first third of the century, and they have been different since World War II than they were before it. The universities in the Soviet Union are doubtless very different than those in the United States, in part because of the different societies in which they find themselves. To admit this, however, is not to admit that the source of present limitations upon academic freedom in the United States can be as readily identified as Professor Fisk believes; nor is it to admit that the change he advocates will have beneficial results for academic freedom.

The limits of academic freedom, or the extent to which academic freedom is tolerated, reflects, it seems to me, the limits of freedom in society itself. In a society whose leaders are devoted to the repression of views that they consider inimical to their interests or the interests of society (which, of course, they are likely to equate), the professor is seldom able with impunity to voice opinions unacceptable to those with sufficient power to take action against him; and it does not take many acts of repression to stifle dissent. In a society where freedom of expression is tolerated and legally protected, the professoriate will itself have a high degree of freedom. As probably all of us are aware, however, one of the difficulties of preserving and enhancing freedom—even in a very free society—is to be found in the nature of the human condition itself. Many people resent a serious challenge to their beliefs and will repress it if they can. Those in power may resist any threat to their power. The wealthy may strike out against anyone who by word or deed might diminish their wealth. Indeed, it must be a sturdy libertarian who does not prefer his own interests to someone else's freedom of expression. In a repressive society there will not be many libertarians in power. In a free society, the authoritarian, or the unsturdy libertarian, may find a subterfuge to mask his repression of freedom, unless he is so muddled or imprudent as to signal to everyone exactly what he is doing and why.

Professor Fisk seems to think that there is a fairly high degree of academic freedom in our colleges and universities, at least within the limitations that he sees imposed by the commitment of our institutions to the capitalistic system "in its currently destructive form." He does not find, however, that all members of the teaching profession are protected against threats that may inhibit them "from freely discussing, teaching, or publishing" their opinions, and he notes in particular that the possible disapprobation of one's colleagues when the time comes for reappointment is a "threat that inhibits, or at least engenders anxiety about," teaching one's opinions freely. This is simply to say that nontenured faculty members do not have the same academic freedom as tenured faculty members, a statement I find unassailable. It is, in fact, very difficult adequately to protect the academic freedom of nontenured faculty members, a truth that one wishes could be driven home to those persons who assert their support of academic freedom while at the same time attacking the concept of tenure.

To be sure, it may be an act of prudence on the part of a young instructor or an assistant professor to withhold his most controversial views until the reappointment or tenure decision is made, but it does not follow that the nontenured faculty member must fear the disapprobation of departmental colleagues because they are functionaries in a capitalistic system. (Depending upon one's colleagues, in fact, it may be very useful to announce a radical, anticapitalistic position shortly before the reappointment decision—and I have no doubt that this has been tried, in reality as well as in Mary McCarthy's *Groves of Academe*—because one's colleagues are then placed in the uncomfortable position, if they give notice of termination, of seeming to give it in violation of academic freedom.) Much more often than not, I suspect, the anxiety of the young teacher is based upon considerations far more immediate and personal than those imposed by the capitalistic system: perhaps some doubts about his own abilities, about the extent to which in the rather free-and-easy academic environment information about his performance may have come to those who will make the reappointment decision, or about the ability of senior colleagues adequately to judge what he has done and is likely to do. Any conflict that he senses may be solely a scholarly one; if, for example, he is a Johnsonian in an English Department with a chairman devoted to James Boswell, he may be uneasily aware that he has let slip the thought that Boswell is vastly overrated—that as a writer he is inferior to Samuel Johnson, and that as a man he is a toady, a bigot, a bully, a lecher, and a drunken sot who does not much reward devotion.

Probably Professor Fisk would agree that this is not an untypical situation, for, after all, as he suggests, has not "the philosophy of capitalism . . . [become] well enough entrenched in the young mind by the time it reaches the campus"? And if this is so, the capitalistic system, I am sure he would argue, is as mindlessly accepted in departments of English as in philosophy departments, so that the statement of David Horowitz that Professor Fisk quotes is equally applicable to both: "Most academics no more perceive the ideological basis of their work than we smell air or taste water."

Of professors and departments of philosophy I know next to nothing; of professors and departments of English I know perhaps a little more, and I rather think that by the time the literary scholar takes up a position in a college or university he has come to some extent to share the poet Shelley's conviction that "poets are the unacknowledged legislators of the world." Thus he is likely to look upon the study of literature as indeed leading to social change, if not directly through his own teaching and writing, at least through the recognition that great writers do in fact change the world and that those who teach them make their contributions to change by increasing their students' critical acumen, their judgment, their articulateness, their intellectual integrity, their receptivity to new ideas, and their hunger for truth, beauty, and justice.

I do not myself know how many professors of English, or professors of anything else, are committed to capitalism "in its currently destructive form," and I am willing to remain ignorant on this point. It is difficult enough for the professor to keep his eye on his fundamental commitment to the pursuit of truth and the advancement of learning—and the more we as individuals emphasize other commitments the more we are likely to obscure the more important purposes for which we and our institutions exist. If the university cannot (and should not) avoid reflecting to a degree, and perhaps even to a large degree, the society in which it finds itself, I think that by focusing on these purposes it can avoid the rigid imposition of professional standards for appointment and retention that merely serve to perpetuate a social system in any form. That we cannot achieve a perfect neutrality seems to me no reason for abandoning the effort altogether, as Professor Fisk would have us do, for there are great benefits to academic freedom, and hence to the advancement of learning, that flow from that effort.

Professor Fisk would point, no doubt, to the difficulty of the radical in gaining acceptance within the academic community as evidence that the whole idea of neutrality is myth—that, far from being less than perfect, it is totally nonexistent. That the radical has had no easy time of it seems to me beyond question, yet the radical voice continues to be heard, perhaps in greater volume from the academic community than from any other segment of our society. But what about some of those conservatives whom Professor Fisk finds ready to "tighten the noose of exploitation" around the necks of the working class and who would appear from his description to be thoroughly committed to capitalism "in its currently destructive form"—have they not also had a difficult time of it? I rather think so; and yet if Professor Fisk is correct, one would have to conclude that their opportunities for academic appointment should be very bright indeed.

I am thus in part agreeing with Professor Fisk's comments about our professional standards and their implications for academic freedom and in part disagreeing. That the present social system influences many of our decisions seems to me patently clear, although I should add that I do not by any means consider all of that influence adverse. But I do not see our standards universally imposed by our commitment to the capitalistic system "in its currently destructive form." Standards—which I think come from a nearer ether than the sky—may vary from department to department, and from time to time within departments. Individuals differ widely in their ability to tolerate hostile opinion, and their attempts to root it out, like departmental standards, may not have a political or social basis at all. Our institutions, in short, and the individuals who populate them are not quite so uniform as Professor Fisk would have us think.

Indeed, I find in Professor Fisk's remarks a tendency to capsule analysis that, while permitting conclusions suited to his purposes, seems to do damage to the facts. Citing the AAUP's 1956 statement on academic freedom and national security as an example of an "old one-vs.-many theory that is operative in the literature on academic freedom," he says, "it is suggested [in the statement] that the Communist is engaged in activities subversive of education itself and is thus unfit to teach." The argument, he adds, "would seem to run as follows: The Communist is an enemy of society— that is, of corporate democratic society—but it is by serving the needs of society that the academic has the right to teach and study without threat of discontinuation. Thus, as an individual, he or she has forfeited the right of protection against the encroachment of society."

Neither in the passage cited by Professor Fisk nor elsewhere in the AAUP's 1956 report is it suggested that the Communist *is* engaged in activities subversive of education itself or that he *is* an enemy of society. The suggestion is made that under certain circumstances he *may be* subversive of the educational process—not an unreasonable assumption in 1956, when one considers the abrupt about-faces in the Communist party line during the 1930's, 1940's, and early 1950's and the extent to which many Communists suddenly shifted their views to conform to the party line. The 1956 report is concerned essentially with the problem of intellectual dishonesty; and rather than asserting, as Professor Fisk says it does, that the Communist "has forfeited the right of protection against the encroachments of society," the report insisted that the professionally qualified Communist whose intellectual dishonesty could not be demonstrated had no less entitlement to an academic position than any other professionally qualified person.

Pointing to the hand of the foundation in setting standards for academic appointment and preferment, Professor Fisk says that "ever since the requirement of the Ph.D. for department heads was laid down for a college to be eligible for participation in the Carnegie Foundation's pension fund—ultimately TIAA-CREF— the requirement of the Ph.D. became unchallenged." Perhaps Professor Fisk is correct about the requirement laid down by the Carnegie Foundation, but I have not been able to determine that he is: even TIAA-CREF informs me that it has found no record of such a requirement. Assuming him correct, however, I think it altogether implausible to lay at the door of the Carnegie Foundation a development that had very much deeper roots. Nor can I accept the statement that, following the Carnegie Foundation's decision, "the requirement of the Ph.D. became unchallenged"; indeed it is difficult to think of any requirement that has drawn more challenges in recent years.

Turning again to the Carnegie Foundation, Professor Fisk states that "since an overeducated work force is a political threat to the capitalist class, Clark Kerr and his colleagues on the Carnegie Commission on Higher Education are devising a way of meeting the growing demand for higher education by severely limiting admission to the third and fourth years of college in a way that will meet economic needs and discourage 'experimentation in life styles.'" It has been my impression that Dr. Kerr was interested in a diversified system of education that would permit many more individuals to fulfill their potential for higher education and that this country's economy could support. I had not expected to find a capitalist under this bed whose real interest was to protect the capitalist class from an overeducated work force, and it seems to me that something more than Professor Fisk's unsupported statement is necessary for conviction on this point.

I suspect that among the many thousands of foundation efforts one could find enough examples to support almost any thesis. Not long ago, for example, when the federal tax bill was under consideration, some members of Congress seemed to think that certain foundation activities were inimical to the present social system. No doubt the foundations have encouraged and underwritten some ill-advised ventures, and no doubt we in the academic community— professors and institutions—have been at times only too willing to shape our interests less to the need than to the availability of financial support. If one considers only the fact that in some departments a high score in grantsmanship has become a major consideration for retention and tenure, it is impossible to take issue with Professor Fisk's contention that the foundations have influenced our professional standards.

With these comments, my areas of agreement with Professor

Fisk's central thesis come to an end. In particular, I am in disagreement with his proposition that an identification by the professoriate with the working class would broaden academic freedom. The identification he has in mind would stifle academic freedom, at least following its initial transitional stage, and the very arguments he has advanced to support his proposition seem to me to demonstrate why this is so. "Avoiding conflicts with the tendencies of groups on which one depends," he says, "is a motive that one has in order to raise a question as to what is right to do"; and, he adds, "The groups on which one needs to rely to realize one's interests as a group member may manifest conflicting tendencies." That this situation is fortunate for academic freedom seems to me apparent. For if, in deciding how to act or to speak, we must consider the reactions of various groups, including some that are in conflict with each other and may even have internal conflicts, inevitably some persons will make the decision one way and some another, and the result is a diversity of action and a diversity of viewpoint. If we remove this conflict among groups; if we, as professors, identify ourselves with the working class; if we set our sights relentlessly on what Professor Fisk calls a "classless society"—we have thereby eliminated much of the opportunity for a choice, and we have taken a giant step in the direction of total conformity and the suppression of academic freedom.

Professor Fisk, of course, would disagree, since under such a system "the tendencies of society as a whole become controlling" rather than the tendencies of the ruling class of profit takers. We shall thus have removed an obstacle in the way of "social amelioration for the working masses of mankind," we shall have destroyed the myth of academic neutrality, and we shall have substituted a broadened academic freedom for the current academic freedom, which, he says, "means more or less, according to how few or many capitalist goals are reflected in the standards" by which the internal policing of our colleges and universities is done. And we shall set ourselves "solidly on the course to overcoming capitalism."

One begins, in Professor Fisk's vision, with the universities; changing society itself is a long and uphill process, because even the unions, the instruments of the working class, "generally accept the supremacy of the capitalist class and content themselves with maintaining enough power to reduce exploitation." So they too will have to be jogged. And central to Professor Fisk's vision is destroying the "myth" of academic neutrality.

Academic neutrality, as I have said, may be imperfectly achieved: myth it is not. It is, in fact, a fundamental concept for all of us. Because of it we have an obligation to permit the expression of opinions, some of which may give comfort to the working class and some of which may give comfort, yea, even to the ruling class of profit takers. It places upon us the burden of not permitting our institutions to identify themselves with one cause as against another, with one group as against another, and in doing so it at least places a brake on any tendency to impose a stifling conformity upon the individuals who constitute those institutions. What Professor Fisk proposes would do exactly that: we would commit ourselves and our institutions to the working class and to the eventual defeat of capitalism, with the inevitable result that those not so committed would have no entry into the teaching profession.

I see no way in which such a transformation might serve to broaden academic freedom. It can only diminish academic freedom. To gird one's institutions for conflict is automatically to reject those individuals who have no heart for the fray or who stand on the opposing side. It is to make the exclusion of certain groups an objective to be realized rather than an error to be regretted. Perhaps Professor Fisk thinks that this is an essential price if our standards for appointment and retention are to be imposed by the needs of the working many rather than the desires of the ruling few, and if we are to devote ourselves to the betterment of the working class—if we are to make our dedication to the "common good" something more than a deceptive slogan. But the price, it should be perfectly clear, is academic freedom.

I do not know why the common good must be equated with the working class. Substitute "humanity" for "working class" and we have already a larger vision and one that avoids the politicization and the conflict inherent in Professor Fisk's. This broader vision avoids also the tendency to think of benefits in terms largely of material gains—of the control of the production and exchange of goods and the elimination of economic exploitation—though a pursuit of these ends is assuredly not excluded. Surely we might wish at times to benefit the ruling class of profit takers, even if only because, like the preacher, we may find ourselves more interested in the sinner than the saved. This, in fact, is the vision that most of us live by now and that motivates most of our institutions. Imperfect though it may be, to replace it with Professor Fisk's more limited vision would be to transform our universities into institutes and ourselves into functionaries indeed.

3. *Academic Freedom as a Moral Right*

BY HARDY E. JONES

In "Academic Freedom in Class Society" Milton Fisk challenges certain conventional, prevailing accounts of academic freedom in American universities. He appears to believe that as academics we are not nearly so free as we have led ourselves to believe. And he argues that the right of academic freedom we currently possess is inadequate and excessively limited. His argument for this thesis is based on a mixture of social observation and moral theory. The observations concern the way universities function in the United States and the ways academic "functionaries" function in them. The only academic activity allowed according to professional standards (the applications of which provide limitations on freedom) is thought to be that which serves the interests of the dominant, capitalist class. Fisk develops a general theoretical account of rights and applies it to claims about the right to academic freedom. I shall contend that this theory of rights is defective, even if he is correct that our freedom is weaker and more narrow than we have thought. In the second section I shall try to provide (at least the beginnings of) a moral justification for academic freedom.

I

The right to academic freedom is commonly regarded as the right of academics in their many disciplines to be left free from interference or punishment to teach and to publish what they sincerely believe to be true. As such it is very broad. Though he does not say so explicitly, Fisk is committed to the view that we presently have no such right. This position is implicit in his account of "normative moral realism," according to which "the very fact that an issue is a moral issue puts certain limitations on acceptable resolutions to that issue. In particular, I take it to be the case that, where the issue is over a right, acceptable resolutions are such that one never has a right to do what conflicts with the tendencies of the groups on which one must rely." A further feature of this view of rights is that "avoiding conflicts with the tendencies of groups on which one depends is a motive that one has in order to raise a question as to what is right to do. If one were not so motivated, then there would simply be no question of what one has a right to do." From these remarks it is a rather small, easy step to Fisk's claim that the exercise of freedom is restricted to activities consistent with the tendencies of the ruling class.[1] Given this theoretical account of rights, together with the observation that faculty members are dependent on the capitalist class, the only way to get a broader right to academic freedom is to change the power structure in society. The class of academic functionaries will then no longer be subject to the tendencies of capitalists.

I do not wish to deny that many changes are desirable. The *right* to academic freedom is not dependent on such changes, however, even if the *protection* of the right does require the sort of progress Fisk envisions. It is simply false that one cannot claim to have a right to do something that conflicts with the interests or wishes of a group on which one is dependent. Slaves had a right to freedom and a right to humane treatment before their rights were generally recognized and defended. It was morally permissible for slaves to insist on the protection of their rights before it became possible for them actually to be free. The avoidance of conflict may often be a prudent means to getting one's rights recognized, but it is not generally required in order to establish that one does indeed possess them. Consider a similar example. Although many children are not treated fairly by their parents, surely they can legitimately raise questions as to what they have a right to do or to get. They

---

[1] The notion of "tendency" is not clear. I believe, however, that my points of criticism will not be affected by its unclarities.

can raise these questions even if they pose threats to what parents see as their own interests. Yet it is obvious that children must rely on their parents for the satisfaction of many needs. A child has a right to be treated fairly even if it can be shown that such treatment (requiring time and effort) would conflict with the tendencies of his parents.

Let us suppose Fisk to be correct in the assertion that academics are functionaries who must rely on the capitalist ruling class. I see no reason whatever to think we should conclude that, for example, no professor has a right to publish a book challenging the legitimacy of class rule. A faculty member has this right even if its exercise conflicts with the tendencies of the groups who pay his salary and furnish him a place to study. And there is no reason to believe that this professor's position would be either incoherent or disingenuous if he claimed both that he has a right to publish his book and that he has no motive to avoid conflict with these tendencies. Indeed, one of his main motives may be to stir up conflict and controversy.

These examples may serve to bring out another important point about rights. Often one wishes to insist that he has a right to be independent of groups on which he must presently rely. All slaves have a right to independence, as do all normal children at a certain level of maturity. Professors also deserve a large measure of independence in their work. I shall not attempt to establish the grounds for these points here, but it must be admitted that they are perfectly plausible and certainly coherent. This is enough to show Fisk's account to be defective. He has analyzed the notion of "having a right" in such a way that one can make no sense whatever of that which is obviously sensible. The analysis is such that, were we to accept it, we could no longer consistently make certain very important claims about rights. And Fisk's position renders the distinction between *having a right* and having that right *recognized and protected* unintelligible. His view of academic freedom in American universities suffers from these pervasive difficulties of the general account of human rights.

A serious error in Fisk's paper is the systematic confusion of the basis for a right with the conditions necessary for a right to be recognized or defended. Fisk says that in order for there to be a right, "the class on which one depends must be prepared to intervene to assure the exercise of the right." This is most implausible as a necessary condition for having a right. There are many unfortunates—many blacks, children, and professors—whose rights almost no one is prepared to protect. The claim that a right exists is often itself offered as a *reason* why certain persons (perhaps those on whom the holder of the right depends) ought to do whatever possible to assure its exercise. If one has a right, then he ought generally to be left free to exercise it even though there are cases, seemingly paradoxical, when it might be wrong to exercise some legitimate right. But Fisk's analysis would render us conceptually incapable of using the fact of our having a right as a reason for trying to get it protected or defended.

These implications are very undesirable, even dangerous. A condition for having a right, according to Fisk, is that the class on which one depends *ought* to intervene to provide protection for the exercise of the right. But when is this the case? Unfortunately, only in a very restricted set of circumstances: "If the class *ought* to intervene, then doing so will not conflict with its own tendencies but will, in fact and not just in its judgment, advance its tendencies." Under present conditions most academics are blessed with these favorable circumstances; for, "by and large these requirements are satisfied in the case of intervention to support the right of academic freedom," even though "at different times there will be variations in the degree to which the capitalist class through its top functionaries will support academic freedom." According to this view, we are fortunate to have aligned our own interests with those of the dominant class. But it is much more plausible to insist that we have the right of academic freedom even if intervention to protect it *would* conflict with capitalist tendencies. Individuals and classes have no general right to do whatever is in accord with their present tendencies, and sometimes they ought to do things in conflict with them. Many large companies, for example, ought to take measures to make the environment cleaner and healthier even though doing so would, sadly, be contrary to their main tendencies. The claim that they ought to perform these actions can, of course, be contested. In order to challenge it successfully, however, it is not sufficient merely to say that their tendencies lead them not to do them. The appropriate response to this is that they have the wrong tendencies and that these ought to be changed. If a person's (or a group's) tendencies are not in accord with what ought to be done, then those tendencies ought to be frustrated. Fisk's remarks suggest that a group can always justify not performing an alleged duty on the ground that its fulfillment would conflict with its tendencies. Again the implausibility of the general account of rights and obligations renders his more specific claims about academic freedom most dubious. His points may be correct as sociological or historical remarks about when and how the right of academic freedom is secured and protected, but they are either irrelevant or implausible as philosophical claims about rights and freedoms.

What is wrong with Fisk's analysis may be pinpointed still more forcefully by a consideration of two further remarks: "It [the right to academic freedom] is a right whose exercise is limited to its origin in a coincidence of interest with the capitalist class" and "academic freedom will be a right the exercise of which has greater potential for human advancement when it has its origin in a coincidence of interest between academics and a ruling working class." These points are, I think, mistaken. Even if Fisk is correct about the limitations on its exercise, the right of academic freedom does not depend upon a "coincidence of interest." It is not even obvious that academic freedom is in every professor's interests. It may be in the self-interest of some academics not to have academic freedom; they might be better off having their work laid out for them in a very restricted manner. But even if this is true and even if they will not profit from its exercise, they still have the right to academic freedom. If one denies that they have this right, he cannot be content to rest his denial on the simple observation that it is not in their interests to have it. Again, a different kind of example may be helpful: citizens have the right to vote even if some would be better off were it left entirely to others to select their governmental representatives. The connection between one's rights and one's interests is not necessarily very close.

Fisk contends that the way to broaden the right of academic freedom so as to provide for greater "human advancement" is to establish a new origin. This origin will consist of a different identification of interests—those of academics with those of the working class. What is ultimately required is to change the society so that the capitalist class will no longer be ruling or dominant. It is important to note that, on Fisk's assumptions, this prevents the attempted use of a right to academic freedom as a means of radically changing the society. The sort of "prevention" relevant here may be called "logical" or "conceptual." Fisk's analysis makes it conceptually impossible for the right to academic freedom to be exercised in conflict with the tendencies of the capitalist class. Academics and workers are deprived (ironically) of at least one potentially useful tool—academic freedom—for bringing about the longed-for changes. But surely it is not incoherent to say that a Marxist professor uses his right to academic freedom as an instrument for realizing radical social changes.

Another undesirable feature of Fisk's account is that he cannot argue that the working classes have a *right* to more power or authority—or even that the capitalists are *wrong* to exercise power as they do now. (After all, are they not merely following their tendencies?) An implication of the general theory is that rights depend on power relations. The right to academic freedom is dependent on a certain distribution of power, and its exercise is assured only because the activities of professors are not at odds with the controlling groups. By making rights and obligations depend on power relationships, Fisk rules out the idea of a proper distribution of powers and privileges based on rights and determined by principles of justice. Of course, he advocates radical changes in the power relations of society: he believes it desirable for there to be transitions away from capitalist rule and toward working-class rule. Presumably the ultimate goal is a classless society and the "withering away" of the state. He does not, however, have a theory of rights that can enable him to use claims to rights as bases for the desired changes. This sort of difficulty is present in all general approaches that make what is moral dependent entirely on the existing social order or the prevailing patterns of political power.

The changes that Fisk advocates have potentially serious consequences for academic freedom. I have noted already that he regards academics as functionaries for a capitalist society. One might think this undesirable and expect that in the new society professors would have a more honorable status—perhaps a status more in keeping with their traditional image of themselves as respected, independent professionals. But, alas, this is not to be. Consider: ". . . functionaries of a ruling working class would derive their right to academic freedom from their definition of professional standards in a way that would further the interests of the working class. Functionaries would still have a derivative status and that would be a source of antagonisms. But the choice of the major class on which the functionaries would be dependent is not one they, and in particular their academic colleagues, are free to make. The choice will be made for them in the struggle between the major classes themselves." The life of academics, according to this view, is going to be undesirable under any social arrangements. Apparently we are doomed to be functionaries. This status is not merely a condition foisted upon us as a result of oppressive capitalist domination but is rather a more basic, inevitable role. Fisk begins by saying that we are functionaries for capitalists, but he later informs us that we will be dependent on whichever class is successful in the struggle. I cannot see how this would bring about a "broadening" of the right to academic freedom. It certainly will not give us the sort of freedom we have traditionally thought desirable and even essential. Indeed, it is quite possible that in the new order we would have considerably less academic freedom than now— even on the assumption that Fisk is right about the dismal present. He can give us *as academics* no reason whatever to use our talents in the struggle for a working-class society. It may be that we should be willing to sacrifice our academic freedom for the sake of the deprived and the oppressed. Or it may be true that in the new society we will no longer need the freedom to which we now aspire. But Fisk does not argue in these ways. Instead he suggests, in an apparent appeal to our sense of self-interest, that we can have a broadened, more substantial right to academic freedom if we identify ourselves with the working class. I think we could be justly charged with self-deception were we to accept this. For on Fisk's account we will always be functionaries, and we are not allowed even to choose whose functionaries we will be.

Fisk believes that present professional standards are excessively narrow. They need to be broadened so as to allow academic activities that give support to noncapitalist classes and interests. He says, "The reason one wants standards to be broadened is not to put demonstrative actions beyond the judgment of academic employers and within the judgment of only one's professional peers, but precisely to allow for thought about problems that have a direct bearing on the amelioration of the conditions of lower classes to be considered part of the repertoire of what is professionally relevant thought." I most certainly agree that such thought should be allowed. But is not such thought and writing already regarded as professionally relevant? Who would deny that it is? Of course, in many institutions it may not actually be allowed. This, however, is not because present standards are too narrow, but because they are not honestly accepted and applied by, among others, various deans and presidents. Let us suppose that some faculty member has been denied the freedom to teach and write about problems of the lower classes. Suppose further that it can be shown that such activity has been prohibited because it is damaging to the interests of a higher class. Can the professor protest that his right of academic freedom has been infringed? One would think so, and apparently the AAUP would agree. On Fisk's account, however, the professor cannot make this claim (unless he is either naïve or disingenuous), for there is no general right to academic freedom to which he can appeal. Fisk's conception of rights and his characterization of present standards rule this out as a sensible, coherent mode of protest. But it is clearly just the sort of protest we would expect and approve, and we need not go beyond present professional standards in order to invoke an appeal to academic freedom. This is only one of many counterexamples to the view Fisk advances.

II

A fundamental mistake in Fisk's paper is the confusion of the theoretical justifications for a right with the practical or social conditions necessary to a right's protection and recognition. I think it is clear that these are distinct. An acceptance of the distinction is an important step toward clearer thinking about academic freedom. But we are still in need of some account of the theoretical basis for the right to this freedom. What is the moral justification for this right claimed by virtually every member of the academic profession? Perhaps the most frequently offered justification is a utilitarian one. In his contribution to this conference, "Tenure and Academic Freedom," Rolf Sartorius says that "almost all statements on academic freedom that are explicit on the matter seek to justify it in terms of the interest of society at large in the free exchange of ideas. The right of the individual is depicted as deriving from the interests of society." Sartorius continues by saying that he finds it surprising "that those who are unsympathetic toward utilitarianism have apparently permitted this account of academic freedom to go unchallenged."

This is a serious challenge whose answer should be of interest to almost everyone concerned with the topic. I shall first indicate why I believe utilitarian justifications of academic freedom to be inadequate. According to one very popular version of utility theory, actions are justified in terms of their consequences for happiness. On this view one ought (and thus has a right) to produce the greatest total amount of happiness. Can such a principle be used to establish the right of academic freedom? The right to academic freedom can be justified only if it can be shown that its possession and exercise would lead to the greatest happiness. If it would not have this result, there is no good or sufficient reason for allowing academics to have the freedom they desire. On this utilitarian theory, academic freedom is depicted as important because of its usefulness for the production of happiness. It is valued merely as a means to a desirable end. But it seems obvious that in certain circumstances the exercise of a right to academic freedom could lead to more unhappiness than happiness. Or a violation of academic freedom could produce more happiness than a protection of that freedom. In such cases we (or rather deans, presidents, regents, and legislators) would be justified in taking academic freedom from professors or in never giving it to them in the first place. I do not wish to insist that academic freedom must be an absolute right in the sense that there is never any good reason for disallowing it. But the mere fact that greater happiness can be produced without this freedom is not sufficient to justify its denial. We must not think of academic freedom solely in terms of its instrumental value in the advancement of happiness. If the only reason for X is its usefulness for Y, then when X is no longer useful to Y or when not having X is more useful, there is no longer a reason for X. I doubt that many faculty members will be willing to stake their claims to academic freedom on such apparently shaky ground. Even Mill in *On Liberty* had trouble defending his famous principles of freedom on utilitarian grounds. Our own similar difficulties—especially if administrators and legislators reserve for themselves the right to determine the interests of and benefits to society—would seem to be at least as serious.

What else, then, can be said in favor of academic freedom? What sort of justification would be acceptable? I believe that academic freedom can be defended on the general ground that it is unjust for persons or groups to prohibit someone from doing, or to punish him for doing, what they have demanded or expected of him. It is prima facie wrong, for instance, for parents to prevent their children from brushing their teeth when they have let it be known that they expect them to do so every evening. Educational institutions expect, or say they expect, teachers and scholars to seek the truth in their various fields of inquiry. Academics are expected to discover and transmit—in research, teaching, and publication—what they honestly have found to be true. In a sense, this is their "job." Without academic freedom, academic men would not be able to do their work. If they perform these tasks diligently yet are rewarded with dismissal or recrimination, they have been treated unfairly.

This is a very general, sketchy account of a possible justification of the right to academic freedom. I want now to make some further remarks in the hope of clarifying and defending it. Someone might argue that the required expectation can itself be justified only on utilitarian grounds. This may be true, but I do not think it makes the justification of academic freedom utilitarian. The important points are that there is an expectation or demand and that it is unjust for the institution to punish someone for trying to satisfy it. However, even if the proposed justification is basically non-utilitarian, it could reasonably receive at least tentative acceptance by those who are sympathetic with utilitarianism. The principle stated above (the "expectations principle") can also be fitted into general theories of justice. In *A Theory of Justice* John Rawls views principles of justice as those that would be accepted by men in an original contracting position. It seems that the expectations principle could easily be accepted by such parties. The men in Rawls's situation do not know their own status, job, or social position; but they can adopt the general principle that the tasks expected of them should be accompanied by the full freedom necessary for performance. There may, of course, be exceptions to the principle.

I do not wish to say that an employee always has an obligation or a right to do that which his employer expects. We know that soldiers are sometimes given orders that they have no right to obey and that factory workers are sometimes asked to do things involving great risk of personal injury. Still, I believe it is a prima facie principle and that proposed exceptions require justification.

I have said that academics have a right to academic freedom because without it they would not be able to do that which is expected of them. Do most colleges and universities actually expect their faculty members to seek to discover and transmit the truth? Perhaps not. But most educational institutions pay lip service to the ideal of truth and appear to accept this view of the academic profession. If they do not accept it, then it is no longer clear what their purposes as *educational* institutions are supposed to be. And insofar as a university does not have professional academic expectations it is a strange place for academic persons to work. One might usefully consider an analogous case of a hospital administration that did not share even the minimal goal of the medical profession, namely, human health. Hospitals that did not expect their employees to seek to advance health would be odd and unfortunate places for dedicated doctors to try to work. Universities without the goal of attaining and disseminating truth are not institutions suitable for academics.

It is important to note the limited scope of the claims I have made thus far. I have said that one ought to be free to pursue, teach, and publish the truth if he is expected (as part of the requirements of his job) to do so. This is an expectation that I have assumed to be reasonable, and it is an institutional fact about universities that they claim to have it. I believe that the following may be accepted as generally correct: when X has the legitimate authority to require *a* from Y, and does so, then X has an obligation to allow Y to do *a*.[2] When university employers have the relevant expectations, they have an obligation to allow and to protect the academic freedom of faculty members. There are thus two obligations linked to these expectations. University authorities have im-

---

[2] The qualification in terms of "legitimate authority" is intended to rule out obvious counterexamples, such as demands to kill or injure persons. I assume that university authorities can legitimately expect faculty members to seek the truth.

plicitly committed themselves to allow professors the freedom to do that which is expected. They have an obligation to which faculty persons can appeal in defense of academic freedom. But professors also have an obligation. In accepting university employment they have implicitly committed themselves to fulfill the designated expectations. Academics thus have obligations to teach and publish what they honestly believe to be true. It is, I think, a conceptual truth that if X has an obligation to do *a*, then he has the right to do *a*. Their own obligations, then, are also ones to which they can properly appeal in protest against violations of their freedom. The right to academic freedom, on this account, has its source in two different obligations either of which is alone sufficient for it to be generally justified.

One may object that this proposed justification is very limited and that it does not apply to all academics. It does apply to a large number of professors but appears to break down when educational institutions fail to expect their faculty employees to pursue the truth. This is a serious problem to which I have already alluded, and what I have to say about it is admittedly vague and undeveloped. I do wish to suggest, however, that when universities do not have the desired expectations they forfeit their right to be called *universities*—or perhaps even *educational* institutions of *higher learning*. If this intuition is correct, the concept of academic freedom is linked to the concept of the university and to the notion of education. Of course, when confronted with this point, those who are antagonistic toward academic freedom can simply say that they do not care whether their institutions are *called* universities. Still, I believe it significant that a curious combination of arrogance and honesty would force many to admit this. The necessity of such admissions at least makes some of the issues clearer. It is also significant that we now have—thanks to Clark Kerr—a new term for many of our complex modern universities—the "multiversity."[3] Universities have become much more than places dedicated merely to truth seeking—and thus much more than mere universities. With the resultant multiplicity of goals, and with a more varied usefulness, such places have many more expectations than the pursuit

[3] I refer here to the now famous book by Clark Kerr, *The Uses of the University* (Cambridge: Harvard University Press, 1963).

and transmission of knowledge. And it is not surprising (though perhaps unfortunate) that these other demands sometimes assume a higher priority. But insofar as such institutions claim to be *universities*, they have an obligation to respect academic freedom. The multiversity can, one hopes, even in these bad times, still be a university.

The question remains: What if an educational institution does not have the expectations that I have emphasized? Suppose a college takes the position that the truth in certain fields is already known and that there is no need to allow its free pursuit. The administration may expect its faculty merely to pass on what is already deemed to be settled as correct. What can reasonably be said about such plans? Do not their faculty members have the right of academic freedom? It appears that one cannot rely on the expectations principle in order to provide a morally sufficient basis for such freedom. Of course, we are probably inclined to say that all educational institutions *ought* to demand the pursuit of truth. And it seems to be generally true that if X ought to demand *a* from Y, then Y ought to do *a* even if X does not in fact demand it. A shop foreman ought to demand safety precautions from workers under his supervision, but whether or not he actually makes the demand, the workers ought to act safely in handling equipment. In such a case the obligation of the workers would be dependent not on an expectation but on something else that would justify or require the expectation. But with regard to academic activity, what is this "something else" that would directly justify—without the intermediate link of an actual expectation—the free pursuit of the truth?

We are led to perhaps the deepest question yet considered. What is the basis for the view that men ought to pursue the truth? Many will insist that the truth is intrinsically valuable, or that it leads to happiness, or that it will make us free. Any or all of these suggestions may be promising. I do not, however, wish to argue along any of these lines. The argument I shall sketch is very simple but quite fundamental. The moral obligation to seek the truth, and thus the right of academic freedom to teach and publish, can be based on the significant fact that the circumstances and consequences of human actions are morally relevant and crucially important in deciding what ought to be done. One of the main sources of moral perplexity is that we do not know enough of what are commonly called "the facts." By seeking the truth and by giving professors the security and freedom to do so as a vocation, agents are put in a better position for knowing what to do. With greater knowledge they can more likely make wiser, fairer, more humane decisions. It may be objected that while freedom to pursue the facts is perfectly acceptable, professors should not be given the right to speak freely on moral and political issues. This would be based on the popular view that moral and political matters are not factual and that moral principles do not admit of truth-values. I think this is a mistake. Nonetheless, even if one is convinced that it is correct, he can still accept my justification of academic freedom. The basic idea is that such freedom allows us to determine better what we ought to do. The freedom to advocate and discuss moral and political principles should be allowed, then, because such principles are relevant and important in making such decisions. This is true even if one analyzes such principles as being neither true nor false and irrespective of whether or not there is a scientific methodology available for discovering them. I believe that the proponent of any reasonable ethical theory will admit that it is important to know the circumstances and consequences of actions. It may even be the case that one never knows enough about the act contemplated or described unless he knows something of its consequences and circumstances. If this is acceptable, then we have at least a start toward a nonutilitarian justification of the right to academic freedom. But it could also be easily fitted into general utilitarian theories. In a sense, it is a theoretically neutral justification: even though it is a *moral* justification, it is neutral with regard to many competing theories. It could become common to all standard theories, but its acceptance does not commit one to any of them.

The work of academics may be regarded as a way of contributing, albeit indirectly, to the doing of what is right. Their freedom is then of the greatest importance. From this perspective, academic activity is a heavy responsibility, though it need not always be felt to be burdensome. Virtually any item of knowledge is conceivably of moral relevance as providing knowledge of circumstances and consequences. Efforts to suppress what is honestly believed to be the truth, to stifle its acquisition or dissemination, are generally unjustified. A university that does not protect academic freedom is less worthy of its faculty's loyalty and service. And a society that does not sustain universities that do uphold academic freedom is neither as good nor as just as it might be.[4]

[4] I am grateful to my colleagues Robert Audi, Norman Gillespie, Martin Perlmutter, and Edmund Pincoffs for their helpful comments, especially on section II.

4. Comments on Hardy Jones and Bertram Davis

BY MILTON FISK

There is a social context for the pursuit of truth that affects the choice not only of subject matter but also of methodology. My paper emphasized this social context, and I identified the present United States context as a class society with a capitalist ruling class. My commentators have not emphasized the social context of the pursuit of truth. This enables them to see in the pursuit of truth a socially neutral basis for the right to academic freedom. But I insisted that the pursuit of truth is inseparable from its social context and is the basis for a right of academic freedom *only* in conjunction with the social aims it advances.

Jones's theory of academic freedom is, nonetheless, schematic enough to admit of an interpretation that places the proper emphasis on the class setting. His theory is that teachers, like other employees, should be given freedom to do that which they are expected to do by their employers. The pursuit and dissemination of truth is what employers in educational institutions should expect of teachers.

It should be noted, on the one hand, that by defining expectations educational employers will be accepting standards of academic performance that reflect certain social aims. My contention was that those standards will mirror the aim of preserving the relations that perpetuate the capitalist class as a ruling class. On the other hand, the right of teachers to freedom in meeting these expectations is based precisely on the tendency of the functionary class to improve its position by improving its functionary service. No source for this right beyond this tendency need be sought.

Taking these matters in combination yields precisely the view of academic freedom that I was espousing. This is a freedom to pursue and teach the truth in ways that stabilize the given class order. Teachers have a right to this freedom because of a general tendency of the functionary class. This is a tendency to improve its position through working to perpetuate the class order in which the capitalist class is a ruling class. Freedom to pursue and teach the truth in ways that stabilize the given class order provides an important respect in which functionaries work to perpetuate the given class order.

Davis denies my contention that in the service of stabilizing an order with a ruling working class academic freedom would have a broadened significance. He bases his denial on the fact that academic standards in an epoch of working-class hegemony would not only focus the pursuit of truth on the aims of the working class but also eliminate those who wished to pursue truth in another manner. This would, he contends, be antithetical to academic freedom.

Yet his denial is unsupported without the assumption that in the service of the currently ruling capitalist class academic freedom has not been limited by the definition of academic standards favorable to the continuation of the capitalist class as a ruling class. This assumption cannot be substantiated simply by repeating the uncritical, and I believe ultimately false, view that most of us currently enjoy freedom to pursue truth in a direction and by methods unaffected by social context. Thus Davis fails to support his denial.

The fundamental point in the theory of rights I relied upon is that one has no right to thwart the tendencies of one's class. If one is a functionary—a member of a class that works explicitly to continue the order in which another class has a ruling role—one's class will naturally have some tendencies that coincide with the tendencies of another class. If the ruling class has a tendency to preserve the system by which maximum private profits are extracted from labor, the functionary class will, overall, work to preserve this system. In this light, it can be seen that some of Jones's attacks on my view miss their mark.

Does my view imply, as Jones says it does, that slaves have no right to freedom? Insofar as the tendency of a class of slaves—as determined by their objective circumstances—is to break out of bondage, slaves certainly have the right to freedom. The difficulty here was my choice of the misleading expression "depends on." I said one has no right to conflict with the tendencies of a group one depends on. I wanted the expression to be so understood that the class one depends on is, primarily, the class to which one belongs, for one can and must rely on that class for the realization of interests generated by the conditions that make one a member of that class. However, if one's class has some tendencies that coincide with those of another class because the first functions explicitly to preserve the order in which the second is a ruling class, then—by an obvious extension of meaning—the first class, and its members, depends in regard to the existence of those tendencies on the second class. Functioning explicitly to preserve such an order involves being aware of the interaction of various classes. Slaves and paid producers of goods and services benefit their masters or employers without aiming at controlling class conflict in order to preserve the given class order. In neither my primary nor my extended sense of "depends on" are slaves and paid producers dependent on upper classes.

Does my view imply, as Jones claims it does, that one has no right to academic freedom if one attempts to disseminate views subversive of the given order? On my view, the question admits of no simple solution, though for Jones it is obvious that one has such a right so long as the subversive writing and teaching come under the pursuit of truth. The reason for the complexity is that within the functionary class there are tendencies that may conflict.

There is the tendency toward what I called the *internal* policing of the activities of the functionary class, for only by having a certain autonomy can that class do its job efficiently and thereby improve its position. There is, however, the tendency to preserve the *external* order, for the functionary class does serve the ruling class, whatever it is, by attempting to stabilize the order in which it is a ruling class. Putting these tendencies together gives internal policing by standards fitted to an external order.

Internal policing breaks down if the functionary class does not protect its members from direct external assault. In this respect the subversive has the right to academic freedom. But service to the external order is eroded if the standards of preferment, relevance, and method are not fitted to the external order. In this respect the subversive's right to academic freedom may be nonexistent.

This example points up the fact that in my paper I was not denying that academic freedom is a right. I was attempting to show that, because of the way in which that right is grounded, it is not as broad a right as my commentators believe. However, historical forces will change the character of the elements grounding the right and thus change its scope.

Part Two

◇◇

The central concern of the contributors to this volume is with the theoretical analysis of claims to academic freedom. In the following papers by William Van Alstyne and John Searle, two conceptions of academic-freedom claims are distinguished: those resting on an appeal to constitutionally guaranteed forms of freedom under the Bill of Rights, which are freedoms available to all citizens and not only to academics, and those resting on consideration of the special function of university scholars and teachers. Van Alstyne and Searle differ not only on the relative importance of these two conceptions, but also on the question whether the constitutionally protected extramural utterances and activities of professors fall within the scope of academic freedom.

William Van Alstyne, president of AAUP, is professor of law at Duke University. John Searle is professor of philosophy at the University of California at Berkeley. Although he offered comments on Van Alstyne's paper during the conference from which this book results, Searle prefers to be represented here by a section of his chapter on academic freedom in *The Campus War*. Amélie Oksenberg Rorty is professor of philosophy at Livingston College, Rutgers University, and fellow of King's College, Cambridge University. Richard Schmitt, who offers a radical critique on both Van Alstyne and Searle, is professor of philosophy at Brown University.

5. The Specific Theory of Academic Freedom and the General Issue of Civil Liberty

BY WILLIAM VAN ALSTYNE

INTRODUCTION

Gresham's law, that "bad money tends to drive out good money," applies equally to catchwords as it does to currency. Bad usages tend to drive out good usages, and by much the same sort of process. The process begins in the ordinary human impulse to seize upon certain significant phrases in an altered context, trading upon those phrases to improve an argument that might otherwise fail to impress those to whom it is directed. The process comes to its end when the constant overuse of such phrases becomes so very apparent that we are made to feel apologetic for having to use them at all—even when we believe them to be crucial in what

NOTE: Reprinted (with slight modification) from "The Specific Theory of Academic Freedom and the General Issue of Civil Liberties," by William Van Alstyne in volume 404 of *The Annals* of The American Academy of Political and Social Science. © 1972, by The American Academy of Political and Social Science. All rights reserved. Because portions of this essay bear directly on certain standards of the AAUP, it is of more than customary importance to stress that my statement of views is wholly personal.

we mean to convey. In short, the process begins with the inflation of rhetoric, and it ends with the debasement of meaning.

We are perfectly aware of Gresham's law in the rhetoric of politics, but we are far less conscious of it when the phrase happens to be one of our own. Most especially is this true when a promiscuous usage has become so much a habit of speech that it no longer sounds strange. Rather, the secondary meaning that was questionable at the time of its introduction gradually acquires its own natural currency until, at a later time, we are so accustomed to the secondary meaning that we become skeptical of those who may be doubtful of its accuracy.

I start with these very general observations because I have no illusions about the problems of this essay on "academic freedom." It, too, is a catchword of our profession, and I am well aware that there are a number of thoughtful people who see no corrosion or debasement in its expanded usages but rather an evolution of usage and the enlargement of a "special" theory into a more "general" one. (See, e.g., the careful, reprinted essay by John Searle in this volume.) My own view is that there is no suitable general theory of academic freedom at all, and that the one that is commonly urged is inadvertently a classic instance of Gresham's law. Even worse, I am convinced that our sheer success in having obscured the difference between academic freedom *simpliciter*, and freedom of speech as a universal civil right irrespective of one's vocation, has made it exceedingly difficult for the courts of this country to recognize an authentic academic-freedom case when they have had one. Additionally, I am persuaded that the overgeneralization of academic-freedom claims has contributed a great deal to our estrangement from others whose jobs are as often placed in jeopardy by their political utterances as our own but who, alas, not being academics themselves, realize no benefit from our protean exaggerations. Finally, I hold the view that we have done ourselves a disservice by heaping up so much in reliance upon "academic freedom," while saying so little about freedom of speech as a universal civil right irrespective of one's vocation, that we now find ourselves committed to a view that logically allows to academics less ordinary freedom of speech than other persons may be entitled to exercise. I doubt seriously whether this consequence was truly intended (although I believe some recognized it well enough and thought it quite proper as an appropriate ethical constraint unique to professional educators), but institutional employers have not hesitated to take full advantage of it from time to time.

Ultimately, my suggestion comes down to this: that both academic freedom *and* the nonacademic civil liberties of professional academics are far better defended in squarely recognizing a difference between the two principles than in continuing to overuse a single phrase that frankly cannot bear the strain. The difference I shall urge is not between a special theory of academic freedom and a general theory of academic freedom, however, because I do not think that this is at all where the difference lies. Rather, the difference lies in the specific theory of academic freedom and in its relationship to a more universal civil liberty of political expression without respect to one's vocation, a liberty that is not subject to some of the constraints that validly apply to academic freedom.

Gresham's Law and the Overgeneralization of Academic Freedom: "Any Old Port in a Storm"

Nearly eighty years ago, the First Amendment was construed in our courts in a manner that openly invited all levels of government to use the leverage of public employment to suppress political criticism. Insofar as the free exercise of political liberty was tied to one's job, neither professors nor policemen could presume to speak without fear of being fired. The insecurity of freedom of speech, when the government was the employer, was placed in bold relief in 1892 by Oliver Wendell Holmes, Jr., several decades before he revised his views in the 1920s as an Associate Justice of the U.S. Supreme Court. In 1892, sitting as Chief Judge on the Massachusetts Supreme Court, Holmes affirmed a lower state court judgment dismissing the complaint of a policeman who had been fired after venturing some public criticism in violation of a police department regulation. Holmes thought that the regulation was itself a reasonable one at the time, but going beyond the immediate requirements of the case he added the following dicta, which became utterly disastrous: "The petitioner may have a constitutional right to talk politics, but he has no constitutional right to be a policeman. . . . There are few employments for hire in which the servant does not agree to suspend his constitutional right of free speech, as well as of idleness, by the implied terms of his contract. The servant cannot complain, as he takes the employment on the terms which are offered him."[1] The point was not lost on the academic profession. In the dismal outcome of the Scopes Monkey Trial in 1927, the Tennessee Supreme Court seemed positively pleased that Scopes could gain no support at all from the Constitution: "Scopes had no right or privilege to serve the state except upon such terms as the state prescribed. . . . In dealing with its own employees engaged upon its own work, the state is not hampered by the limitations of . . . the Fourteenth Amendment to the Constitution of the United States."[2]

It was exactly during this same period that American professors, familiar with the tradition and values of *Lehrfreiheit* in German universities, began to domesticate it and to propound the concept of "academic freedom" as a principle worthy of general respect to fill the void of the positive law in this country. Given the circumstances—given the surprising success of the infant AAUP (founded in 1915 and at once startled by the extent to which its good offices were sought by aggrieved faculty members)—it is not remarkable that a tendency at once developed to expand upon the meaning of academic freedom to make it perform a larger service. From the solid and fortified arguments sustaining academic freedom as a logical imperative if academicians were to fulfill the critical functions of their profession, the principle was pressed into the larger field of civil liberties whether or not such liberties were professionally linked. In the absence of any other source of employment security that would protect professors from dismissal in pursuing conventional political activities off the job and on their own time, or entering into ordinary public assemblies and taking personal positions on social issues simply as private citizens and not as professional scholars or researchers, "academic freedom" offered itself as a possible way out. Gradually, the phrase slipped away from a close association with protection of the academic in his professional endeavors and assumed a new synonymy with the general civil liberties of academics (and especially their general *political* liberties). Accordingly, the protection of an academic in respect to the exercise of

[1] McAuliffe v. Mayor of New Bedford, 155 Mass. 216, 220, 29 N.E. 517, 518 (1892).

[2] Scopes v. State, 154 Tenn. 105, 111–112, 289 S.W. 363, 364–365 (1927).

his aprofessional political liberties was argued into position as a subset of academic freedom. The effort succeeded so much that it has long been routine for AAUP Committee A reports to describe the dismissal of professors on account of aprofessional political activity as a violation of their "academic freedom." Professor Fritz Machlup accurately reports the situation in the new *Encyclopaedia of Higher Education*: "Academic freedom (in its modern conception, though not in the past) includes the right of the academic individual to engage in political activity."[3]

Far from being helpful to the profession, however, the continued use of academic freedom in this expanded and indiscriminate sense has been damaging to the professor in three important ways.

First, the ubiquitousness of indiscriminate academic-freedom claims in respect to aprofessional political activities has provided substance to a widespread belief that the professoriate sees itself as an extraordinary elite, since we tend to associate our claim to such protection not with the general case for civil liberties but rather as a special case or subset of academic freedom. As implied in the following observation by Glenn Morrow in his effort to rationalize the defense of academic freedom, the sprawling claim seems, without reason, to be indifferent to the indistinguishable predicament of other citizens:

> The justification of academic freedom cannot be based merely on the right to freedom of thought and expression enjoyed by all citizens of a liberal society, for academic freedom implies immunity to some natural consequences of free speech that the ordinary citizen does not enjoy. An ordinary citizen who expresses unpopular opinions may lose customers if he is a merchant, clients if he is a lawyer, patients if he is a physician, advertisers or subscribers if he is the editor of a newspaper, or suffer other forms of social or economic penalty resulting from disapproval of his expressed opinion. . . . The justification of academic freedom must therefore be sought in the peculiar character and function of the university scholar.[4]

The point is the obvious one that others who work for a living may, as often as we, wish to affiliate with unpopular causes or to speak

[3] Machlup, *Academic Freedom*, 1 Encyclopaedia of Higher Education 6, 8 (1972).

[4] Morrow, *Academic Freedom*, 1 Encyclopaedia of Social Sciences 4, 6 (1968).

freely about political issues of the day without reference to their regular work or professional endeavors, sometimes even as in our own case, in sharp opposition to the known wishes of the same institutional employer. Manifestly, it must (and does) strike them as odd that professors nevertheless insist that professors have an *extra* right to be protected in these aprofessional pursuits and to do such things, a claim sublimely stronger than their own, insisting as professors do that such activities are part of their "academic freedom" and a special contribution to the social good, whereas such activities by others are merely an ordinary matter of common liberty to be tolerated in a liberal society but not, of course, of the same rank of special social good as the protection of academic freedom.

The consequent class cleavage and cost in good will that I wish to emphasize, however, is not simply the suspect elitism of our claim, for if the claim were well taken it would be a sufficient answer that we must simply try harder to persuade a larger public that it is indeed a correct one. Rather, the price we pay is the much greater cost of the lad who cried "wolf" so often when it was false that few would pay attention when it was true: an errant claim of academic freedom obscures the vital importance of academic freedom as more modestly conceived and thereby engenders public indifference even when an authentic issue of academic freedom is clearly and unmistakably involved. Were it not for the success of our own obfuscations, I believe it would be much more clear than it is that while a professor's exercise of ordinary civil liberties is not a special subset of his academic freedom, academic freedom is itself a distinct and important subset of First Amendment civil liberty. Its importance as a special subset is likely to be obscured and ignored, however, if we ourselves do not hold to the distinction.

Second, although I cannot prove the correctness of the impression, I believe that the earlier and errant expansion of academic-freedom claims beyond the boundaries of its core rationale has inadvertently delayed the specific assimilation of academic freedom into constitutional law. In 1958, the Supreme Court interpreted the First Amendment in a manner to provide separate and distinct protection for freedom of association, deriving the sense and substance of that freedom from three other clauses (those dealing with freedom of speech, freedom of assembly, and the right to petition for redress of grievances), but nevertheless marking it with a character of its own with certain instrumental features different from those of its parent clauses.[5] Nothing equivalent has yet developed in respect to academic freedom, however, in spite of the fact that the Court has often made highly honorable mention of the phrase in the adjudication of First Amendment claims. As a matter of interest, some of the Court's dicta may be quoted. In Keyishian v. Board of Regents,[6] the Court said, "Our Nation is deeply committed to safeguarding academic freedom, which is of transcendent value to all of us and not merely to the teachers concerned. That freedom is therefore a special concern of the First Amendment, which does not tolerate laws that cast a pall of orthodoxy over the classroom." In Griswold v. Connecticut,[7] the Court affirms that "the State may not, consistently with the spirit of the First Amendment, contract the spectrum of available knowledge. The right of freedom of speech and press includes not only the right to utter or to print, but the right to distribute, the right to receive, the right to read . . . and freedom of inquiry, freedom of thought, and freedom to teach . . . —indeed the freedom of the entire university community." In Barenblatt v. United States,[8] the Court tells us that "when academic teaching-freedom and its corollary learning-freedom, so essential to the well-being of the Nation, are claimed, this Court will always be on the alert against intrusion by Congress into this constitutionally protected domain." In the landmark case of Sweezy v. New Hampshire,[9] we learn that "the essentiality of freedom in the community of

[5] See Solter, *Freedom of Association—A New and Fundamental Civil Right*, 27 GEO. WASH. L. REV. 653 (1959); Emerson, *Freedom of Association and Freedom of Expression*, 74 YALE L. J. 1 (1964). The initial case was NAACP v. Alabama, 357 U.S. 449 (1958), which on its face required but the slightest extension of free speech and assembly precedents. By the time additional cases involving quite different interests had been decided, clearly it had become more useful and accurate to speak of a distinctive freedom of association. See, e.g., NAACP v. Button, 371 U.S. 415 (1963); Gibson v. Florida Legislative Investigation Committee, 372 U.S. 529 (1963); Brotherhood of R.R. Trainmen v. Virginia State Bar, 377 U.S. 1 (1964).

[6] Keyishian v. Board of Regents, 385 U.S. 589, 603 (1967).

[7] Griswold v. Connecticut, 381 U.S. 479 (1965).

[8] Barenblatt v. United States, 360 U.S. 109, 112 (1959).

[9] Sweezy v. New Hampshire, 354 U.S. 234, 250–251, 261–264 (1957).

American universities is almost self-evident. No one should underestimate the vital role in a democracy that is played by those who
guide and train our youth. To impose any strait jacket upon the
intellectual leaders in our colleges and universities would imperil the
future of our Nation. . . . Teachers and students must always remain
free to inquire, to study and to evaluate, to gain new maturity and
understanding; otherwise our civilization will stagnate and die. . . .
We do not now conceive of any circumstance wherein a state
interest would justify infringement of rights in these fields." In
Wieman v. Updegraff,[10] we are told that "by limiting the power of
the States to interfere with freedom of speech and freedom of inquiry and freedom of association, the Fourteenth Amendment protects all persons, no matter what their calling. But, in view of the
nature of the teacher's relation to the effective exercise of the
rights which are safeguarded by the Bill of Rights and by the
Fourteenth Amendment, inhibition of freedom of thought, and of
action upon thought, in the case of teachers brings the safeguards of
those amendments vividly into operation. . . . They must have the
freedom of responsible inquiry, by thought and action, into the
meaning of social and economic ideas, into the checkered history of
social and economic dogma. They must be free to sift evanescent
doctrine, qualified by time and circumstance, from that restless, en-
during process of extending the bounds of understanding and
wisdom, to assure which the freedoms of thought, of speech, of
inquiry, of worship are guaranteed by the Constitution of the United
States against infraction by National or State government. The
functions of educational institutions in our national life and the
conditions under which alone they can adequately perform them
are at the basis of these limitations upon State and National power."
In Shelton v. Tucker,[11] the Court says that "the vigilant protection
of constitutional freedoms is nowhere more vital than in the community of American schools." In Whitehill v. Elkins,[12] the Court
remarks that "we are in the First Amendment field. The continuing
surveillance which this type of law places on teachers is hostile to
academic freedom."

[10] Wieman v. Updegraff, 344 U.S. 183, 195–198 (1952).
[11] Shelton v. Tucker, 364 U.S. 479, 487 (1960).
[12] Whitehill v. Elkins, 389 U.S. 54, 59–60 (1967).

Despite these dicta of the Court, and despite the writings of those who have urged the judiciary to acknowledge a separately-identifiable First Amendment right to academic freedom,[13] it is clear that closure between the First Amendment and a distinct right of academic freedom has not yet been made. The current situation is summed up in Justice Holmes's observation about the work of a colleague: "I used to say that he had a powerful vise the jaws of which couldn't be got nearer than two inches to each other."[14] The lack of closure is illustrated by Epperson v. Arkansas,[15] invalidating a state criminal statute prohibiting public school teachers from adverting to any theory regarding the origin of man not consistent with the Bible. Despite the Court's many previous references to academic freedom, Mr. Justice Black saw no substantive difficulty with the statute and concurred in the result solely because he thought the statute to be impermissibly vague, that is, as a criminal statute it provided insufficient notice of the exact conduct teachers were expected to avoid.[16] While disagreeing that this was the sole fault of the statute, Mr. Justice Stewart suggested only that the statute raised a substantial question in light of "guarantees of free communication contained in the First Amendment," that is, a general free speech issue without any more specialized features peculiar to academic freedom. The Opinion for the Court went no further, moreover, than to hold the statute invalid as a violation of the religious establishment clause—leaving one to wonder whether the case has any significance at all beyond the religion-related novelty of the particular kind of statute involved in the case.

The prolonged gestation of "academic freedom" as an identifiable First Amendment claim, a special subset readily derived from but not simply fungible with freedom-of-speech doctrine in general, or

[13] See, e.g., Murphy, *Academic Freedom—An Emerging Constitutional Right,* 28 LAW & CONTEMPORARY PROBLEMS 447 (1963); Emerson and Haber, *Academic Freedom of the Faculty Member as Citizen, id.* at 525; Fellman, *Academic Freedom in American Law,* 1961 WIS. L. REV. 3; Van Alstyne, *The Constitutional Rights of Teachers and Professors,* 1970 DUKE L. J. 841 (1970).

[14] Quoted in EDWARD BANDER, ed., JUSTICE HOLMES, EX CATHEDRA 235 (1966).

[15] Epperson v. Arkansas, 393 U.S. 397 (1968).

[16] See also his dissenting views in Tinker v. Des Moines School District, 393 U.S. 503, 521–522 (1969).

First Amendment doctrine in respect to public employees at large, may ironically be the consequence of our own previous tendencies to blur the distinctions. In possession of a highly persuasive justification for the defense of academic freedom as a specific vocational necessity, but in also finding the general protection of other civil liberties hopelessly inadequate in respect to the security of employment and the exercise of free speech in general, we hastily seized upon the rhetoric of academic freedom to press for special degrees of protection that other kinds of employees were denied at the time. The cost of the campaign, however, has been the indefinite postponement of constitutional status for academic freedom as a separate, albeit limited, First Amendment right. The chances for the specific constitutional protection of academic freedom, as a subset of First Amendment rights, would very likely be improved if we ourselves had managed to respect the difference between academic freedom and freedom of speech as a more universal right.

Third, to return to my argument, there is marvelous irony in the fact that the condition of constitutional law has not remained static since Holmes's depressing dicta of 1892 or the *Scopes* case of 1927. Rather, the extent of positive law protection of public employees in general now extends fully to threats against their employment in retaliation for the exercise of freedom of speech and not merely to threats of fines or jail. The point was made by the Supreme Court again in 1972, clearly reiterating that even simple nonrenewal of an untenured faculty member by a public institution would violate the First Amendment if premised upon personal political activity otherwise protected by that amendment: "The first question presented is whether the respondent's lack of a contractual or tenure right to re-employment, taken alone, defeats his claim that the nonrenewal of his contract violated the First and Fourteenth Amendments. We hold that it does not."[17] Even more, the Supreme Court has recognized that a teacher would be so unequally inhibited vis-à-vis other citizens were he constrained by a strictly *professional* standard of care, accuracy, and courtesy in the rough-and-tumble of ordinary political discussion, that the First Amendment will protect his employment from jeopardy where his departure from that standard

[17] Perry v. Sinderman, 408 U.S. 593, 596 (1972). See also Van Alstyne, *The Demise of the Right-Privilege Distinction in Constitutional Law*, 81 HARV. L. REV. 1439 (1968).

relates only to his aprofessional political utterances as a citizen and is not a function of his teaching, research, scholarly publication, or any similar institutional responsibility of a professional character.[18]

Not only has the practical reason that provided the incentive (if not a compelling logic) for the earlier view that an academic's civil liberties are a specific subset of his academic freedom largely been removed,[19] but also the continued insistence upon that view may even work against the equal protection of professors as citizens. In having associated the right of the academic to pursue ordinary political activity with his interest in academic freedom, we have invited institutional employers to interest themselves in the "professionalism" that the academic employee reflects in his political utterances. The wooden insistence that academic freedom is at the heart of an academic's right to engage in political activity has repeatedly drawn the sharp riposte that, given this rationale, the political liberties of academics must be correspondingly reviewed by a higher standard (i.e., a professional standard) than the like activities of others. It thus presumes to make professors subject to a *greater* degree of overall employment accountability than others generally owe in respect to their private freedom, virtually as an elitist's concession of noblesse oblige given in exchange for the special academic freedom claim: that the claim of general civil liberty by academics is more important to society than the claim of general civil liberty of others. The instances in which educational institutions have acted on this concession are legion, as many of the

---

[18] Pickering v. Board of Education, 391 U.S. 563 (1968), and see discussion in text at footnote 16, *infra.*

[19] "Largely" is used advisedly in acknowledgment of the fact that neither the Bill of Rights nor the Fourteenth Amendment is applicable to institutions uninvolved with government. For a consideration of this issue, see Burton v. Wilmington Parking Authority, 365 U.S. 715 (1961); Pennsylvania v. Board of Trusts, 353 U.S. 230 (1957); Coleman v. Wagner College, 429 F.2d 1121 (2d Cir. 1970); Powe v. Miles, 407 F.2d 73 (2d Cir. 1968); Commonwealth v. Brown, 392 F.2d 120 (3rd Cir. 1968), *aff'g* 270 F. Supp. 782 (E.D. Pa. 1967), *cert. denied*, 391 U.S. 921 (1968); Grossner v. Trustees of Columbia University, 287 F. Supp. 535 (S.D.N.Y. 1968); Greene v. Howard University, 271 F. Supp. 609 (D.D.C. 1967), *dismissed as moot*, 412 F.2d 1128 (D.C. Cir. 1969); Guillory v. Administration of Tulane University, 203 F. Supp. 855 (E.D. La.), *vacated*, 207 F. Supp. 554, *aff'd*, 306 F.2d 489 (5th Cir. 1962). See also O'Neil, *Private Universities and Public Law*, 19 BUFFALO L. REV. 155 (1970); Schubert, *State Action and the Private University*, 24 RUTGERS L. REV. 323 (1970).

AAUP published reports of Committee A attest. Quite clearly, however, we cannot avoid some shared responsibility for this unhappy tendency, given our past practice of claiming so much for "academic freedom" and so little for "civil liberty." We may hope more swiftly to get out of this thicket, on the other hand, by returning to the fundamentals of academic freedom and simultaneously by insisting upon the uniform and robust protection of civil liberties.

The proposition that academic freedom is a special subset of First Amendment freedoms but that it is distinguishable from other civil liberties necessarily means that it is not uniformly available in defense of a teacher's or a scholar's purely aprofessional pursuits, including even some involving his general freedom of speech. The acknowledgment that this is so, however, does not imply that we lack a suitable forensic or constitutional basis to secure these other liberties from institutional or legislative abridgment, or that the AAUP should be less vigilant than it has been in reporting conditions in higher education inimical to those liberties. Indeed, I would argue that in certain important respects exactly the converse is more nearly true: that the special constraints of academic freedom cannot be invoked to arrest the latitude of general free speech and personal liberty that teachers are fully entitled to enjoy as citizens on equal terms with all other citizens, free from any intrusion of institutional or legislative power associated solely with their academic and job-related responsibilities. The legitimate claims of personal autonomy possessed equally by all persons, wholly without reference to academic freedom, frame a distinct and separate set of limitations upon the just power of an institution to use its leverage of control. In addition, more than the profession may generally know (and far more than an undifferentiated theory of academic freedom—with its excess baggage of general responsibility—may itself allow), the judicial recognition of these general limitations upon institutional authority has already taken hold. Part of this essay will attempt to make the case that the specific theory of academic freedom is entirely congenial to this welcome development in constitutional law, and that it may contribute far more toward the equal treatment of teachers and scholars in the enjoyment of their personal liberties than the less discriminating theory that treats an academic's political freedom as a subset of his academic freedom.

The Definition, Rationale, and System of Academic Freedom

Insofar as it pertains to faculty members in institutions of higher learning, "academic freedom" is characterized by a personal liberty to pursue the investigation, research, teaching, and publication of any subject as a matter of professional interest without vocational jeopardy or threat of other sanction, save only upon adequate demonstration of an inexcusable breach of professional ethics in the exercise of that freedom. Specifically, that which sets academic freedom apart as a distinct freedom is its vocational claim of special and limited accountability in respect to all academically related pursuits of the teacher-scholar: an accountability not to any institutional or societal standard of economic benefit, acceptable interest, right thinking, or socially constructive theory, but solely to a fiduciary standard of professional integrity. To condition the employment or personal freedom of the teacher-scholar upon the institutional or societal approval of his academic investigations or utterances, or to qualify either even by the immediate impact of his professional endeavors upon the economic well-being or good will of the very institution that employs him, is to abridge his academic freedom. The maintenance of academic freedom contemplates an accountability in respect to academic investigations and utterances solely in respect of their professional integrity, a matter usually determined by reference to professional ethical standards of truthful disclosure and reasonable care.

Academic freedom is a "freedom" (i.e., a liberty marked by the absence of restraints or threats against its exercise) rather than a "right" (i.e., an enforceable claim upon the assets of others) in the sense that it establishes an immunity from the power of others to use their authority to restrain its exercise without, however, necessarily commanding a right of institutional subsidy for every object of professional endeavor that might engage the interest of the individual professor. In cleaving to a limited program of instruction, for instance, or in husbanding its scarce financial resources short of every subject that might be worthy of investigation, the decision of an institution not to offer a particular subject or not itself to provide means for a particular line of research may be faulted as educationally unenlightened, but it would not on that account constitute an abridgment of academic freedom. At the same time, however, academic freedom would be abridged were any form of sanction threatened against a faculty member because of any of his professional pursuits, even assuming that the individual's interest pertained to a subject that the institution declines itself to support and may thoroughly disapprove. A principle of educational pluralism may excuse an act of institutional parochialism in what it is prepared to offer as an institution of higher learning, but the principle of academic freedom clearly condemns any act of institutional censure in respect to the professional endeavors of its faculty, assuming only no failing of professional integrity in the pursuit of those endeavors. Similarly, academic freedom protects the right of faculty members to conduct whatever instruction and research they may be retained to provide consistent with standards of professional integrity.

We may concretely illustrate the several foregoing observations by briefly stating three cases, all of which lie easily within the uniform protection of academic freedom:

Case 1. A faculty member is assigned to teach a course in biology inclusive of theories respecting the origin of man. A state law provides that a teacher may be fired and fined if he adverts to any theory of evolution or point of view respecting the origin of man inconsistent with the literal story of Genesis. The law is an infringement of the teacher's academic freedom insofar as it forecloses a professionally responsible treatment of the subject.[20]

Case 2. An English professor assigns a particular short story to give her students a better understanding of one genre of western literature. Conceding that the professor's ability and particular treatment of the subject are above reproach, the president of the college nonetheless admonishes her to discontinue the assignment because in his judgment the story is garbage, the philosophy of the story is destructive, and several parents have complained. Following her statement that she believes she has a responsibility to teach the story consistent with a professional treatment of the subject she has been engaged to teach, she is fired. Her dismissal clearly violated her academic freedom, assuming only that her selection of the story

[20] Compare Epperson v. Arkansas, 393 U.S. 97 (1968), discussed in n. 6 *supra*.

was not otherwise a clearly inappropriate professional means of fulfilling her academic responsibilities.[21]

Case 3. A professor of anthropology, interested also in genetics,
prepares a paper that he presents before an off-campus symposium
in which he reviews the basis for a particular hypothesis—that significant evidence suggests the inheritability of variable intelligence
linked to race. Although his utterances are extramural, they are
clearly academic in character. Assuming only that he has been guilty
of no failure of professional integrity in the manner in which he has
presented his hypotheses, his conduct is fully protected by fundamental principles of academic freedom. Accordingly, no matter how
unpopular, distasteful, socially destructive, or embarrassing his
extramural presentation may seem to the university where he is
employed, no action may appropriately be taken against him.[22]

The mechanism in common use in the United States for the protection of academic freedom reflects the political and institutional
circumstances of the academic profession in this country. Were
teachers and scholars sole practitioners, certified by licensure agencies in the manner of doctors or lawyers, we might expect that
questions of professional integrity would be reserved primarily to
these agencies—otherwise leaving to individual clients or educational "customers" the separate determination of whether each
teacher or scholar is good enough in his profession to warrant being
retained as an educational mentor or as an independent contractor
to engage in research. There are no such agencies in higher education as in law and medicine, however, and one will tend to starve as
a sole practitioner. Nor is today's academy at all like the original
Akademeia—simply a place on the outskirts of Athens where Plato
could be found by anyone interested in his views. Neither are universities under the benign protection of powerful autocrats, such as a
German prince or a powerful ecclesiastical organization that, while
brooking no academic freedom at all for criticism of themselves or
of the doctrines associated with their power, might otherwise offer
protection against the hostilities of all others. Nor are entire facul-

[21] Compare Parducci v. Rutland, 316 F. Supp. 352 (M.D. Ala. 1970), possibly the first decision clearly identifying academic freedom as a separate and
distinct First Amendment freedom.

[22] The similarity of this hypothetical to news accounts of Professor Arthur
Jensen's work is, of course, not accidental.

ties in this country endowed, as are Oxford or Cambridge, with sufficient assets that the faculties may largely control their own situation.

Rather, it is all very familiar that the academic profession is practiced in this country in association with public and private educational enterprises: that one's capacity for the exercise of academic freedom is inextricably tied to his university employment; that the ultimate financial resources of the institution are largely beyond the control of the faculty; that ultimate managerial responsibility is not lodged within the faculty; and that issues of professional integrity are resolved not by licensure or professional associations in the main, but within each institution—at least in the first instance. Insofar as public institutions are concerned, the power of the demos to force hemlock upon a modern Socrates is constrained by the Constitution —indeed, the power of the people even to secure an end to his academic freedom by having him fired is thus constrained. In the development of a more general mechanism within each institution for protecting academic freedom, however, no satisfactory reason has been given to distinguish between the two kinds of academic institutions—public and private. The fact that the Constitution makes such a distinction for purposes of positive law is largely beside the point.

In the absence of state, regional, or national professional licensure agencies composed of professional teachers and scholars, the mechanism of professional accountability common in the United States has gradually developed through the utilization of standing faculty committees within each institution in which the professional teacher or scholar is employed. Consistent with what we have already said about academic freedom, however, the charge of each such committee is strictly limited: it is to ignore the particular impact of any teacher's exercise of his academic freedom upon the institution and to concern itself solely with the question of whether the teacher or scholar has been guilty of such an inexcusable breach of professional ethics as to warrant his termination, the penalty of dismissal being appropriate only as a necessary means of vindicating the very functions that the system of academic freedom is itself meant to serve.

For several reasons, largely related to the practical necessity of using local review committees, the judgment of these standing committees is not final. Against the chance that the committee members (themselves nearly always drawn from within the institution) may show undue favor from too close an identification with a colleague, an authority of limited review is recognized in the hierarchy of administration. Against the chance that the committee members may show bias against him (as from fear for their own status, from a commitment to a given professional dogma, or from professional envy or sheer personal dislike), a more generous appeal may lie through the hierarchy of administration and thereafter to other bodies (like AAUP) and, on occasion at least, to the courts. Indeed, the academic maverick may sometimes need more protection against the entrenched dogmas of his immediate peers than against anyone else, thus necessitating some right of appeal from a local judgment to the judgment of others who have less of a vested interest in the maintenance of a given "truth."

This system does not always operate to accomplish the end for which it is designed, of course, as when a coincidence of prejudices (albeit often of different kinds) may operate against the faculty member at every level, but superior alternatives are not readily apparent. After all, no freedom, including even academic freedom, can claim exemption from some degree of accountability. Under current conditions of educational organization in the United States, we have yet to discover a safer choice than to entrust that accountability initially and primarily to professional peer groups within each institution, acting under the specific constraint of confining their review solely to an examination of the professional integrity of the manner in which the individual discharged his professional responsibilities.

This system, developed specifically for the maintenance of academic freedom, obviously differs from that which generally prevails in ordinary employment relations. Significantly, however, in respect to his academic freedom, the teacher or scholar is simultaneously under *more* constraint as well as under less constraint than would ordinarily obtain. Clearly he is under less constraint, of course, to the extent that the standard is more protective of him than were it the standard common to employment relationships in general, namely, did he perform his assignment as directed by management, did he avoid any indiscretions clearly forbidden by management, and has he otherwise conducted himself in a manner not injurious to the economic well-being of the enterprise? We have already noted that none of these considerations is permissible where the committee concludes that the professions or conduct for which the faculty member has been called to account were otherwise well within the prerogative of his academic freedom.

What is less obvious, however, is the one respect in which the exercise of academic freedom is also under considerably greater constraint than it would be were the conduct in which it is implicated governed only by ordinary standards of accountability to one's employer: as professional peers are admonished to be *less* concerned than the administration or trustees to consider any institutional repercussions resulting from what a given faculty member may have done professionally wholly consistent with the ethical use of his academic freedom, they are admonished to be far *more* concerned than others in making certain of that ethical use. The price of an exceptional vocational freedom to speak the truth as one sees it, without penalty for its possible immediate impact upon the economic well-being of the employing institution, is the cost of exceptional care in the representation of that "truth," a professional standard of care. Indeed, a grave ethical failure in the integrity of a teacher's or a scholar's academic representations, no matter of how little notice or coincidental concern it may happen to be to the particular institutional employer, is precisely the kind of offense to the contingent privilege of academic freedom that states a clearly adequate cause for a faculty recommendation of termination. The very reason for specially protecting the profession is itself frustrated, for instance, if experimental undertakings are knowingly falsified or positions of professional responsibility are sought to be gained through false representations of originality (i.e., plagiarism), and it is of no consequence that neither offense may violate any general law or that it may turn out to be a matter of indifference to a particular board of trustees. In either case, the trust of academic freedom has been violated and strict accountability is in order.

In this way, then, academic freedom speaks directly and distinctly to the special critical role of the professional teacher and scholar. He is encouraged in the development of all his professionally related activities to ply a bold and innovative critical acumen. On the other hand, he is accountable to those who share a like duty and a commitment similar to his own, to answer at a professional level for the ethical integrity of his work so as to establish by the fact of that integrity that he fully justifies the contingent privilege of academic freedom that he has claimed.

The distinction of academic freedom from the general protection of free speech is precisely located in its immediate and indissoluble nexus with the cardinal social expectation laid upon the particular profession with which it is identified—that there shall be a vocation to examine received learning and values critically, a vocation *expected* to do so and to make itself useful by the fact of disseminating its work. In this sense, the element of academic freedom specifically identifies the profession; it is simply contradictory to lay that expectation upon the profession and then to prevent its accomplishment by deterring its fulfillment through rules that punish its exercise. As Arthur Lovejoy, who helped found the AAUP, correctly observed: "It [i.e., the social function of academic freedom] is rendered impossible if the work of the investigator is shackled by the requirement that his conclusions shall never seriously deviate either from generally accepted beliefs or from those accepted by the persons, private or official, through whom society provides the means for the maintenance of universities."[23]

ACADEMIC FREEDOM AS A SUBSET OF FIRST AMENDMENT RIGHTS: A COMPARISON WITH THE GENERAL ISSUE OF CIVIL LIBERTY

As an identifiable subset of First Amendment freedom, academic freedom requires a significant modification in the standards of judicial review otherwise applicable to freedom of speech. Specifically, for instance, it clearly ought not be enough in a given case to uphold the discharge of a faculty member that the state may have generally criminalized any use of pornography, or that the university may have similarly presumed to forbid that use, even assuming that the material is not redeemed by standards the Supreme Court has otherwise developed in determining whether sex-related material is protected by the First Amendment.[24] If it were true that even the

[23] Lovejoy, *Academic Freedom*, 1 ENCYCLOPAEDIA OF THE SOCIAL SCIENCES 384 (1930).

[24] See Roth v. United States, 354 U.S. 476 (1957); A Book Named "John Cleland's Memoirs of a Woman of Pleasure" v. Attorney General of Massachusetts, 383 U.S. 413 (1966); Stanley v. Georgia, 394 U.S. 557 (1969); United States v. Reidel, 402 U.S. 351 (1971); United States v. Thirty-Seven Photographs, 402 U.S. 363 (1971).

hardest-core obscenity were being received, read, and shared with immediate professionally involved colleagues in what could be shown to be a professionally responsible study of the subject, the fact of the academic context is not irrelevant to a determination of the case and may, indeed, be controlling. Professionally related efforts directed in good faith precisely to fulfill the social directive of the academic profession, that is, to examine received learning and values critically and to report the results without fear of reprisal, will make the case appropriate for the constitutional protection of academic freedom when the absence of these elements might otherwise spell its failure.

There is, of course, nothing in this formulation that assumes that the First Amendment subset of academic freedom is a total absolute, any more than freedom of speech is itself an exclusive value prized literally above all else. Thus, the false shouting of fire in a crowded theater may not immunize a professor of psychology from having to answer for the consequences of the ensuing panic, even assuming that he did it in order to observe crowd reaction firsthand and solely to advance the general enlightenment we may otherwise possess of how people act under great and sudden stress. It is correct to say, however, that the context of academic setting provides an additional constitutional consideration (the specific consideration of academic freedom) that may well be determinative under circumstances where a free-speech claim would otherwise fail. Where other societal values are not so clearly conflicted by the particular manner in which academic freedom is exercised that the manner of that exercise can reasonably be described as professionally reprehensible (as would assuredly be true in the risking of human life in the "controlled experiment" to determine how crowds react to panic), the law or institutional rule that operates to abridge the exercise of that academic freedom should be held invalid as applied to the particular case. In this sense, then, it is proper to speak specifically of academic freedom as a subset of First Amendment rights and not to regard it as simply fungible with freedom of speech in general.

Simultaneously, we are bound to acknowledge that, when no claim of professional academic endeavor is present, neither can one lever himself into a preferred First Amendment position by invoking the claim of academic freedom. Granted that the proper characterization must sometimes be difficult and even elusive, we must admit that not all that a faculty member does in respect to his freedom of speech is a manifestation of professional endeavor. Indeed, a great deal of it is neither professional nor unprofessional (i.e., done under professional auspices but in a clearly unprofessional manner). Rather, it is simply aprofessional, and the distinction is not a trivial one: what is lost in respect to the special protection of academic freedom may be more than offset in a particular case by a different kind of gain—a gain in being freed from the special accountability of academic freedom.

We have hesitated to acknowledge the distinction between professional and aprofessional activity, even when the difference was abundantly clear, partly from an understandable anxiety that had we done so (i.e., had we dispensed with the academic-freedom claim), we might then have been without a place to stand in defending the faculty member or in reproving the institution that sought to dismiss him. In this, I think we have been mistaken and that the proper place to stand is the same place occupied by so many others —on the general issue of civil liberties and the just limitations on the relational authority of institutions. It was just this principle, for instance, that President Lowell reflected in risking the loss to Harvard of a ten-million-dollar bequest that was threatened to be annulled unless an openly pro-German professor was deprived of his chair. What is so instructive of the episode is that Lowell did not state his position in terms of claiming that what the professor had done was an exercise of academic freedom. Indeed, had Lowell done so, presumably he would then have felt called upon to say a great deal more, to justify the faculty member's utterances as sufficiently restrained, rigorous, and consistent with professional integrity, as not to call into question his ability to continue at Harvard. Eschewing this approach, Lowell declared instead:

If a university or college censors what its professors may say, if it restrains them from uttering something it does not approve, it hereby assumes responsibility for that which it permits them to say. This is logical and inevitable. If the university is right in restraining its professors, it has a duty to do so, and it is responsible for whatever it permits. There is no middle ground. Either the university assumes full responsibility for permitting its professors to express certain opinions in public, or it assumes no responsibility whatever, and leaves them to be dealt with like other citizens by the public authorities according to the laws of the land.[25]

It is perfectly clear that Lowell was himself making an implicit distinction between alleged abuses of academic freedom (for which Harvard would doubtless admit its responsibility of review of its own faculty) and alleged abuses of free speech and the general issue of civil liberty. The distinction is eminently correct and must not be placed in jeopardy by what may now be seen as the pyrrhic success of having extended the claim of academic freedom in a manner that invites more, rather than less, institutional monitoring of general civil liberties.

It is an altogether congenial development in our constitutional law that the Supreme Court has come essentially to the same conclusion in respect to the general civil liberties of those who teach: that at least where there is no affectation of professional endeavor in the aprofessional expressions of a faculty member (and no false trading upon his institutional affiliation), there is correspondingly no sufficient justification for the institution to presume to review the conduct of the faculty member by the more taxing fiduciary standard of professional care. Thus, should one be moved even casually to write a letter to the editor expressing his sentiment on some political issue of the day, it is entirely unjust for the institution that employs him to call his professional integrity into question according to that standard of carefulness and rigor that may appropriately qualify his professional undertakings and the contingent special protection of academic freedom. Indeed, to do so is in fact to disadvantage him in his prerogatives as a citizen:

What we do have before us is a case in which a teacher had made erroneous statements [in a public newspaper] upon issues then currently the subject of public attention, which are critical of his ultimate employer but which are neither shown nor can be presumed to have either impeded the teacher's proper performance of his daily duties in the classroom or to have interfered with the regular operations of the schools generally. *In these circumstances we conclude that the interest of the school administration in limiting teachers' opportunities to contribute to public debate is not signifi-*

---

[25] Recounted and discussed in R. HOFSTADTER & W. METZGER, THE DEVELOPMENT OF ACADEMIC FREEDOM IN THE UNITED STATES (1955).

cantly greater than its interest in limiting a similar contribution by any member of the general public.[26]

This First Amendment view of the matter seems to me to be entirely sound and desirably free from the false freight of special accountability that attached itself whenever we tried instead to justify the aprofessional expressions of faculty members as an act of "academic freedom," rather than as an unexceptional claim to the equal protection of freedom of speech. As a valid principle that is clearly to be commended as a reasonable standard of self-restraint for all institutions of higher learning, moreover, there is no basis for us to hold it less applicable to private institutions than to public ones.

THE RECONSTRUCTION OF THE 1940 STATEMENT OF PRINCIPLES

If there is any inhibition that currently restrains our profession from maintaining that the aprofessional activities of faculty members are not subject to institutional review by the same fiduciary responsibility for which they may be asked to account through academic due process in respect to their academic freedom, it may be thought to arise from the troubling ambiguity of the following paragraph from the *1940 Statement of Principles*:

The college or university teacher is a citizen, a member of a learned profession, and an officer of an educational institution. When he speaks or writes as a citizen, he should be free from institutional censorship or discipline, *but his special position in the community imposes special obligations*. As a man of learning and an educational officer, he should remember that the public may judge his profession and his institution by his utterances. Hence he should *at all times* be accurate, should exercise appropriate restraint, should show respect for the opinion of others, and should make every effort to indicate that he is not an institutional spokesman.[27]

If this paragraph were taken simply as a statement of professional

[26] Pickering v. Board of Education, 391 U.S. 563, 572–573 (1968). Emphasis added. For more extended analyses of *Pickering*, see O'Neil, *Public Employment, Antiwar Protest, and Preinduction Review*, 17 UCLA L. REV. 1028, 1040–53 (1970); Van Alstyne, *The Constitutional Rights of Teachers and Professors*, 1970 DUKE L. J. 841, 848–854.

[27] Reprinted in AAUP POLICY DOCUMENTS AND REPORTS 2 (1971). Emphasis added.

aspiration addressed to the good sense and esprit of the academic fraternity, it might well be thought to state a highly commendable view. If it is a statement that means to encourage institutional review (and possible dismissal) of faculty members because aprofessional utterances may sometimes lack the degree of accuracy and restraint not improperly expected of their professional endeavors, however, it is radically unfair to the equal civil liberties of academics and needs to be revised. As it happens, neither of the alternatives quite describes the present situation.

A clarification was provided of the critical "but" clause in 1963, in the course of a Committee A review of a case involving an assistant professor's letter to the editor of a student newspaper published and distributed at the University of Illinois.[28] The ad hoc investigating committee of the AAUP read the critical clause of the *1940 Statement* exclusively as an admonition addressed to the conscience of the faculty: "The ad hoc committee is of the opinion that . . . as applied to a faculty member having definite or indefinite tenure, making public utterances on matters of general concern to the community, the standard of 'academic responsibility' is not a valid basis for reprimand, dismissal, or other official discipline."[29] Nevertheless, the plurality Opinion for Committee A disagreed. From its assessment of the legislative history of the *1940 Statement*, it concluded that the "but" clause was not a precatory statement; rather, the clause was intended to recognize the legitimacy of university authority to discipline faculty members for violating norms of accuracy, self-restraint, and courtesy even in respect to professionally unrelated extramural utterances: "In light of Committee A's understanding of the 1940 Statement, together with the legislative history of the document and its 'interpretation,' the Committee disagrees with the authors of the report that 'the notion of academic responsibility, when the faculty member is speaking as a citizen, is intended to be an admonition rather than a standard for the application of discipline.' "[30] Left alone, this position would appear to embrace the most self-effacing (and simultaneously self-righteous) position of

[28] See *Report on Academic Freedom and Tenure: The University of Illinois,* 49 AAUP BULL. 25 *et seq.* (1963).
[29] *Id.* at 36.
[30] *Id.* at 41.

all. The fact that Committee A went on to stress the ameliorative influence of academic due process in such cases (and to disapprove the particular dismissal of the faculty member as "outrageously severe and completely unwarranted" under the circumstances) does little to relieve one's objection to the interpretation itself as a matter of sound principle. On the one hand, it appears to forswear any special claim of academic freedom in respect to a faculty member's personal prerogative of general public discussion "when he speaks or writes as a citizen," and not under pretense or claim of professional endeavor. At the same time, it appears simultaneously to accept the legitimacy of institutional restraint even in respect to such ordinary political rhetoric by the exceptionally inhibiting standards of accuracy, care, restraint, and courtesy identified with the individual's professional status (i.e., with his status "as a man of learning and an educational officer"). In this respect, the trade-off that the AAUP appeared to have accepted with the Association of American Colleges in 1940 (namely, to cultivate public confidence in the profession by laying down a professionally taxing standard of institutional accountability for *all* utterances of a public character made by a member of the profession) is substantially more inhibiting of a faculty member's civil freedom of speech than any standard that government is constitutionally privileged to impose in respect to the personal political or social utterances of other kinds of public employees.

Immediately subsequent to its *Report on The University of Illinois* in 1963 (but consistent with other portions of that report), however, Committee A adopted a more strict construction of the *1940 Statement*. This strict construction disarms that *Statement* to a considerable extent and brings it, as thus construed, much closer to the position the Supreme Court adopted on First Amendment grounds in 1969:

The controlling principle is that a faculty member's expression of opinion as a citizen cannot constitute grounds for dismissal unless it clearly demonstrates the faculty member's unfitness for his position. Extramural utterances rarely bear upon the faculty member's fitness for his position. Moreover, a final decision should take into account the faculty member's entire record as a teacher and scholar. In the absence of weighty evidence of unfitness, the administration should not prefer charges; if it is not clearly proved in the hearing that the faculty member is unfit for his position, the faculty committee should make a finding in favor of the faculty member concerned.[31]

Even conceding that this Committee A construction may go nearly as far as the AAUP can proceed in light of the phrasing and legislative history of the *1940 Statement*, it remains subject to criticism.[32] One step that may easily be taken is the more emphatic clarification of the *standard* of institutional review (assuming that such review is ever called for, or at least that the *1940 Statement*, unless amended, provides for the possibility) in cases where no claim of academic freedom is asserted and no willful trading upon professional status has been involved in the personal activity of a faculty member whose institutional position is thereby drawn into question by the character of the activity.

What needs to be done, however, is not merely to make clearer that a faculty member may not properly be held to answer to an institution for the integrity of his general utterances by the same professional standard by which he may have to account for his academic freedom, but to enlarge upon the implication of our position that his substantive accountability for such utterances will ordinarily not run to the institution at all. For an alleged abuse of one's ordinary freedom of speech, general provisions of law are available to provide for measures of redress and sanction as far as it has been thought both safe and just to allow. As a consequence, society may not expect, nor should the standards of the AAUP contemplate, that recourse for alleged abuses of ordinary civil liberty may be compounded by the gratuitous use of institutional disciplinary processes.

It may be conceded that circumstances will sometimes arise in which the personal conduct of a faculty member may so immediately involve the regular operation of the institution itself or

[31] Committee A Statement on Extramural Utterances (1964), reprinted in AAUP POLICY DOCUMENTS AND REPORTS 14 (1971). See also Advisory Letter from the Washington Office, 49 AAUP BULL. 393, 394 (1963), and the discussion in *Report on Academic Freedom and Tenure: The University of California at Los Angeles*, 57 AAUP BULL. 382, 394–400, 404, 405 (1971).

[32] See, e.g., Remarks by President J. W. Maucker of the University of Northern Iowa (on the occasion of receiving the Tenth Alexander Meiklejohn Award), 54 AAUP BULL. 251, 253–254 (1968); Schier, *Academic Freedom and Political Action*, 53 AAUP BULL. 22 (1967).

otherwise provide firm ground for an internal grievance that internal recourse, consistent with academic due process, is offensive neither to the general protection of civil liberty nor to the standards of the academic profession. Decisions like that in the *Pickering* case are instructive, however, that this exception is not nearly as broad as the presumption of custom has supposed.

BIBLIOGRAPHICAL NOTE

It is not possible accurately to credit the various sources that have helped to inform this essay, especially those that did so indirectly (i.e., in espousing quite different views of academic freedom than those offered here). Most especially helpful in thinking about the subject, however, were the many Committee A Case Reports scattered through the volumes of the AAUP BULLETIN, the brief essay by Arthur Lovejoy in 1 ENCYCLO-PAEDIA OF THE SOCIAL SCIENCES 384–388 (1937), the splendid volume by RICHARD HOFSTADTER & WALTER METZGER, THE DEVELOPMENT OF ACADEMIC FREEDOM IN THE UNITED STATES (1955), and Fritz Machlup's trenchant address, *On Some Misconceptions Concerning Academic Freedom*, 41 AAUP BULL. 753 (1955). Other very helpful materials include ROBERT E. CUSHMAN, ACADEMIC FREEDOM AND RESPONSIBILITY (1952); RUSSELL KIRK, ACADEMIC FREEDOM: AN ESSAY IN DEFINITION (1955); LOUIS JOUGHIN, ACADEMIC FREEDOM AND TENURE. A HANDBOOK OF THE AMERICAN ASSOCIATION OF UNIVERSITY PROFESSORS (1969); ROBERT MAC-IVER, ACADEMIC FREEDOM IN OUR TIME (1955); Ralph Fuchs, *Academic Freedom—Its Basic Philosophy, Function and History*, 28 LAW & CON-TEMPORARY PROBLEMS 573 (1963); Ralph Fuchs, *Academic Freedom*, ENCYCLOPAEDIA BRITANNICA (1965); Walter Metzger, *Academic Freedom in Delocalized Academic Institutions*, in DIMENSIONS OF ACADEMIC FREEDOM 1 (1969); Glenn Morrow, *Academic Freedom*, ENCYCLOPAEDIA OF SOCIAL SCIENCES (1968); Fritz Machlup, *Academic Freedom*, ENCY-CLOPAEDIA OF HIGHER EDUCATION (1972).

6. Two Concepts of Academic Freedom

BY JOHN R. SEARLE

Since academic freedom is such a favorite topic of discussion in university circles, one is somewhat surprised to discover that there is a scarcity of recent theoretical discussion of the subject. The literature tends to be polemical and historical rather than theoretical. Furthermore, discussions of academic freedom are often fogged by noble sentiments and high rhetoric. It is difficult for academics to express themselves in public about academic freedom in the abstract without striving for eloquence and the articulation of commencement-day emotions. A more serious reason, I suspect, for the paucity of theoretical examinations of the concept is that most professors simply assume none is necessary. Since they already know what academic freedom is, the problem is to defend it, not to analyze it or define it. The situation is somewhat like that of the famous judge in the obscenity case who said he could not define obscenity but he knew it when he saw it. Most academics would be hard pressed to define academic freedom, but they know violations of it when they see them.

Two Concepts of Academic Freedom

I think that the discussions one sees of particular cases of alleged violations of academic freedom reveal quite different underlying

NOTE: From *The Campus War* by John R. Searle. Copyright © 1971 by John R. Searle. With permission of Thomas Y. Crowell Co., Inc.

theories or concepts of academic freedom; and in this chapter I shall begin by adumbrating two of the most important of these. I do not know whether these two exhaust the field, but they will, between them, cover most of the cases of violation of academic freedom, and in my two years as chairman of the Academic Freedom Committee of the University of California—the faculty's institutional device for protecting academic freedom—they served me and the committee quite well in our numerous battles.

The Special Theory: Lehrfreiheit and Lernfreiheit

The classical theory of academic freedom, and the heart of any theory of academic freedom, is that professors should have the right to teach, conduct research, and publish their research without interference, and that students should have the corresponding right to study and learn. The justification for these rights derives from a theory of what the university is and how it can best achieve its objectives. It is important to emphasize at the very beginning that in the special theory these are not general human rights like the right to free speech. They are special rights that derive from particular institutional structures, which are created by quite specific sets of constitutive rules.[1] They are like the right of a defendant to cross-examine an accuser rather than like the right of all people to the free expression of opinion, in that they derive not from a general theory of man and society but from a special theory of an institution and the conditions of functioning of that institution.

The theory of the university from which the rights of academic freedom are derived is as follows: the university is an institution designed for the advancement and dissemination of knowledge. The purpose of the university is to benefit the community that created and maintains it, and mankind in general, through the advancement and dissemination of knowledge. This amounts to two axioms: knowledge is of value and the university is an institution for the furtherance of that value. But these two axioms are still not sufficient. To derive the rights of academic freedom, we need also a theory about how knowledge can be attained and validated; we need an epistemology, a theory of knowledge. And not just any

[1] For an explanation of the notion of constitutive rules, see J. R. Searle's *Speech Acts* (London and New York: Cambridge University Press, 1969), chap. 2.

theory will do; for example, if you think that knowledge is best obtained by looking it up in a sacred text, you will not be able to derive the classical theory of academic freedom. On this sacred-text theory, professors would be confined to scrutinizing and expounding the sacred text.

The full exposition of the epistemology that underlies our concept of academic freedom would require an account of the methodological and rationalistic assumptions behind the modern conception of science and scholarship. Indeed, it would require an account of the whole modern conception of rationality, for it is this conception that underlies the theory of the university. Suffice it to say, for our present purposes, that an important part of this theory is that knowledge is most likely to be advanced through free inquiry, and that claims to knowledge can only be validated as knowledge—as opposed to dogma or speculation—by being subjected to the tests of free inquiry. No proposition is so sacred as to be immune from these tests: every proposition derives what validity it has through surviving these tests. The university may be, as Rashdall tells us, an essentially medieval institution, but its contemporary ideology and methodology come not from the medieval period but from the Enlightenment.

Even adding this feature of a theory of knowledge to our axioms, we still do not have enough to derive the classical theory of academic freedom. The classical theory—and the theory of the university as an institution generally—accords a special status to the professor. The university is not a democracy where all have equal rights; it is an aristocracy of the trained intellect. The justification for according special status to the professor is closely connected with the epistemology. In virtue of his special competence in some area of academic study—and competence includes knowledge of existing results and mastery of the techniques of validation and investigation of some academic discipline—the professor is given special rights of investigation, of dissemination of knowledge, and of certification of students. To put it in less pompous jargon, because the professor is supposed to know more than the students about the methods and results of his subject, he, not they, is put in charge of the labs, the courses, the grades, and so on.

To derive the classical theory, then, we need at least the following elements:

1. A value claim: knowledge is valuable (both "for its own sake" and sometimes because of its "applications") and should, other things being equal, be advanced and disseminated.

2. A definition of the university: the university is an institutional device for the advancement and dissemination of knowledge.

3. Part of a theory of knowledge: knowledge is best acquired and can only be validated if subject to certain tests based on free inquiry.

4. A theory of academic competence: the professionally competent, by virtue of their special knowledge and mastery of techniques, are qualified to advance the aims of research and teaching in ways that amateurs are not.

Given these assumptions, one can, I think, justify most of the elements of the classical theory of academic freedom. Professors should have the right to pursue knowledge enjoying freedom of inquiry and should have the right to disseminate that knowledge in the classroom and through publication. Students should have the right to study and learn this knowledge without interference.

If one were to undertake a really rigorous analysis of the concept of academic freedom, this, I believe, would be the best way to proceed. One would state the axioms and carry out a derivation of the rights of academic freedom. However, there is still a serious problem left over. Not all the things we now call academic freedom and not all the violations of rights that we consider violations of academic freedom can be accounted for by this traditional Special Theory.

To illustrate this, I shall provide three examples of actions that I consider to be violations of academic freedom but that cannot be accounted for in any natural way by the Special Theory. Not everyone will agree that these are violations of "academic freedom," but the disagreement indicates that the boundaries of the concept of academic freedom are in dispute. First, imagine that a professor of physics is active in political work on behalf of the Democratic party. Imagine, also, that the board of trustees of the university, who are all Republicans, fire him or refuse to promote him because of his activities on behalf of the Democrats. Most of those who claim to be in favor of academic freedom would argue that this would be a violation of the physicist's academic freedom by the trustees. I entirely concur in this claim, but I fail to see how it is justified solely on the grounds provided by the Special Theory. How does the Special Theory, by itself, give a professor of physics the right to engage in political activity? One might, perhaps, argue that it gave him the right not to be fired or to have his promotion canceled on such grounds, because—so one would argue—implicit in the Special Theory is the principle that such academic decisions as terminating an appointment or making a promotion can only be made on academic grounds, not on other sorts of grounds. But it is not easy to see how this principle can be derived as part of the Special Theory without extra axioms; and in any case, stated as a general principle, it is violated all the time in ways that are perfectly consistent with the Special Theory. For example, it is not a violation of academic freedom to expel a student from the university for beating up other students, even though his grades may be acceptable and his beating up the other students was not a way of preventing them from studying (if, for example, he beat them up only as they were going to the movies). In such cases, we make a disciplinary decision that separates the student from the university, but we make it on nonacademic grounds. Now suppose the university authorities think it is both bad to beat up students and bad to work for the Democrats. Why is separation from the university a violation of academic freedom in the one case, but not in the other? I think the answer is that a professor or student has a *right* to engage in political activity, but he does not have the right to beat up other members of the academic community. But where does he get this right? It cannot be derived from the Special Theory, but only from a General Theory, which I shall shortly sketch.

This type of example is of considerable historical importance in the development of the concept of academic freedom. The original German conception of *Lehrfreiheit* did not include the right of the professor to engage in active politics. When the concept of academic freedom was imported from Germany to the United States, it was expanded to include this right of the professor to engage in political activity. In the United States it came to be regarded as a violation of academic freedom to fire a professor for his political activities (unless in some way they interfered with his professional work, in which case he could be fired for his professional failures and not for his political activity as such). Some authors believe that this American extension of the traditional concept of academic freedom derives from the more community-oriented, pragmatic role of the American university as compared with the German university.[2] They see it as deriving from an extension of the very concept of the university in the United States. But I find this explanation unsatisfactory. Even if one were to add a community-service axiom to the premises of the classical theory, it would still not authorize a *physics* professor to campaign for a political party. One could see how it might justify the political activities of a professor of social science; these activities could be regarded as an extension of his professional work, field work, as it were. But the American conception of academic freedom includes the right of all professors to engage in all sorts of activities that have nothing to do with their academic expertise. It is extremely difficult to see how this right can be derived from the axioms of the classical theory; I think it comes from a different and more general theory.

A second example: suppose a group of political fanatics disrupts a meeting of a private student club on the campus. I believe this is a violation of the academic freedom of the students, even though their club is not a part of the university's educational program and may even be engaged in activities unrelated to that educational program. It might be, for instance, an astrology club. Yet, though the club is unrelated to the university's official educational program, students have a right to hold these meetings, and any such political attempt to deprive them of this right is reasonably construed as a violation of their academic freedom as students. I do not see how their right to hold these meetings can be derived from classical theory.

A third case to show the insufficiency of the Special Theory: in 1960 the administration of the University of California, acting through a vice-chancellor, prevented me from addressing a law school club on the subject of the HUAC movie, *Operation Abolition*. At the time I was an assistant professor of philosophy. The administration announced that my criticisms of the film would be too controversial to be permitted without rebuttal, and at the last minute they canceled the speech and forbade the law students to have me at their meeting on the campus. In the end, a fraternity house off the campus gave us the use of its barroom, and I addressed the young

2 E.g., L. R. Veysey, *The Emergence of the American University* (Chicago: University of Chicago Press, 1970), p. 384.

lawyers there. I believe the administration violated my academic freedom (as well as that of the students), even though I am not a professional expert on the House Un-American Activities Committee, subversion, film criticism, or any of the other relevant aspects of the movie. I believe I have a right to address students on my own campus, if they want to hear me, even on subjects outside the area of my professional competence, but I do not believe that this right can be derived from the classical theory strictly construed. In order to deal with these—and countless other—cases we need a more general theory of academic freedom.

THE GENERAL THEORY OF ACADEMIC FREEDOM

The basic principle of the general theory of academic freedom is that professors and students have the same rights of free expression, freedom of inquiry, freedom of association, and freedom of publication in their roles as professors and students that they have as citizens in a free society, except insofar as the mode of exercise of these freedoms needs to be restricted to preserve the academic and subsidiary functions of the university. The justification for these freedoms under the general theory is exactly the same as the justification for those freedoms in the larger society. These justifications derive from a theory of society and of man's relation to society.

Where the Special Theory attempts to justify certain freedoms within the university, regardless of whether these freedoms are desirable in society at large, the General Theory assumes intellectual freedoms to be desirable for society and sets up academic criteria by which these freedoms may be both realized and regulated on the university campus. The Special Theory answers the question "What justification can we give for freedoms within the university?" But the General Theory assumes that the answer to that question is ultimately grounded in the desirability of intellectual freedoms generally, and it answers the question "What justification can we give for any restrictions of freedom in the university?" These are not competing or inconsistent theories. They are not competing answers to the same question but noncompeting answers to different questions. Both incorporate a theory of the university; but where the Special Theory sees academic freedom as deriving entirely from the theory of the university, the General Theory assumes the desirability of freedoms at large and asks how they can be realized and shaped in accordance with a theory of the university.

The General Theory incorporates the Special Theory because it includes the theory of the university, but it adds to it the following: students and faculty members maintain as students and faculty members the same rights they have as citizens of a free society. This means that not only can the state not interfere with these rights using its weapons, but also the university cannot interfere with these rights using academic sanctions; nor can the university tolerate interference by others, using ad hoc and informal sanctions. Interferences by the university have to be justified in terms of the theory of the university. Thus, for example, the student has the same rights of free speech on the campus that he has off the campus, but the exercise of his free speech is legitimately regulated by the educational needs of the university. He does not have free speech while the professor is lecturing; he can only speak when called upon by the professor to do so; and when the professor tells him to shut up so the lecture can continue, he is under an obligation to comply. The classroom does not entitle the student to "equal time" with the professor. Similarly, the professor does not have unlimited free speech in the classroom. He is only entitled to lecture on the subject of the course or lecture series, and he is not entitled to use the classroom for, say, political propaganda. If he reconstitutes his lecture series as a political indoctrination session, he both *violates* the academic freedom of the student and *abuses* his academic freedom as a professor. The General Theory is an extension of the concept of academic freedom because under it the academic role preserves the rights accorded the citizenship role, except insofar as those rights are regulated to realize the purposes of the university.

The General Theory really has two aspects. First, the university is an institutional embodiment of the general social values of free inquiry and free expression together with a theory of specialized scholarly competence. (This gives us all the rights of the classical theory together with the rights of the citizen extended to faculty and students.) Second, because the university is an institutional embodiment of free inquiry and scholarship, it is something quite different from such public areas as parks and streets. It therefore requires regulations of the mode of exercise of the general freedoms of a libertarian society in order to protect its special functions. (This gives us the sorts of regulations of the rights of students and faculty that are necessary to keep the university from turning into Trafalgar Square.)

Historically, these two theories are responses to different situations. Imperial Germany, where *Lehrfreiheit* was developed, was not a society committed to intellectual freedom, and in consequence the classical German theory of academic freedom was an attempt to carve out an area of freedom within the university and special to the university. The United States, on the other hand, is a nation committed to intellectual freedom in the community at large— however imperfect our realization of that commitment may be— and the General Theory of academic freedom is designed to cope with the problem of attempts to restrict those freedoms on the university campuses. The General Theory insists that the professor and the student both have their rights as citizens and that any attempt to interfere with those rights through university means must be justifiable in terms of the purposes of the university.

The General Theory of academic freedom deals with the three examples considered above as follows. First, professors, whether professors of political science or physics, have a right as citizens to engage in political activity, and as professors they have a right, under the General Theory of academic freedom, not to suffer academic penalties through the exercise of their rights as citizens. Second, students, as students, maintain their rights as citizens and hence have a right to form organizations and engage in free discussion on the campus on any topic they wish, provided they conform to rules designed to protect the special academic features of the university. If that right is violated by attempts to suppress their views through disruption of their meetings, their academic freedom as students, which under the General Theory incorporates their rights as citizens, is violated. Third, I have a right, as a citizen, to a free expression of opinion to such audiences as invite or care to listen to me. Under the General Theory of academic freedom, this gives me the right as a professor and hence as a citizen of the university community to address others in the university without interference by the authorities or the imposition of academic penalties.

Though most of the literature on the theory of academic freedom is cast in terms of classical *Lehrfreiheit* and *Lernfreiheit*, it seems to me many of the great battles of recent years in the realm of academic freedom have not been about the Special Theory but rather about the General Theory. Professors have been fired for being members of the Communist party; faculty members have been required to sign loyalty oaths; students have been disciplined for holding political meetings on campuses; professors have been prevented from addressing student clubs on political matters. Strictly construed, the Special Theory forbids none of these restrictions. It is confined to the rights of the professors and students in classrooms, laboratories, libraries, seminars, and other central university activities. Yet one feels—or at any rate, I feel—that each of the above actions involves a violation of the rights of students or faculties under some concept of academic freedom.

It is only in terms of the General Theory that the concept of student academic freedom really has very much meaning. Adherents of the classical theory are hard put to give content to the notion of academic freedom for students. In Imperial Germany it meant such things as the right of the student to wander about the country from one university to another—all the universities were run by the state —and to attend whatever lectures he liked in preparation for nationally given degree examinations. In the United States or England, where the educational systems are unlike those of Imperial Germany, it is hard to see how these conceptions of *Lernfreiheit* are supposed to apply. Academic freedom for students would have to be confined to such things as the right to be graded free of political considerations, the right not to be subject to political indoctrination in the classroom, and the right to go to class free of interference on political or racial grounds.

Under the Special Theory student academic freedom is at best a small territory, and some classical theorists even claim that students don't have academic freedom at all. For example, Ernest Van den Haag states: "Students benefit from the academic freedom of the faculty and perhaps from the atmosphere of freedom which should prevail on the campus. So does society at large. However, students do not have academic freedom."[3] And as Van den Haag defines academic freedom, in terms of a strict construction of Lehrfreiheit, that

---

[3] Ernest Van den Haag, "Academic Freedom in the United States," in *Academic Freedom*, ed. Hans W. Baade (Dobbs Ferry, New York: Oceana Publications, 1964), p. 85.

would certainly be the case. But, by contrast, under the General Theory the student has quite extensive rights, that is, he has the rights of a citizen of a free society, except insofar as those rights are restricted and regulated by the special educational objectives of the institution.

At one level the difference between those who accept only the Special Theory and those, like myself, who accept the General and Special theories, is purely verbal. It all depends on what one means by "academic freedom." But like most conceptual distinctions, it is crucial in all sorts of practical ways. For example, university administrations that are committed to the Special Theory but not to the General Theory will feel themselves justified in placing all sorts of arbitrary restrictions on the out-of-class behavior of students and faculty members, even though those restrictions cannot be justified as part of any coherent educational theory.

Why should we consider both of these theories to be theories of academic freedom? Why wouldn't it be less confusing to call one "the right to study and learn" and the other "civil liberties on the campus"? Any American constitutional lawyer would argue that the additional rights I am including under the General Theory are covered by the First Amendment, due process, equal protection, and the rest of the currently expanded legal conception of civil liberties. If constitutional rights include many features of the General Theory, so much the better for constitutional rights, but I think the two theories are logically related in ways that justify lumping both together as "academic freedom." In particular, both place a high value on knowledge and rationality. Both emphasize free expression, and both connect free expression and free inquiry to claims to truth in that both claim that free inquiry is necessary to validate claims to truth. Notice that almost all the rights under the Special Theory of academic freedom are also rights of the citizen qua citizen. He can investigate and state or publish his views as he sees fit. The additional rights that professors and students have under the classical theory do not derive from an independent conception of man and rationality—it is the same conception in both cases—but they derive from the fact that the university is a specialized institution dedicated to the advancement and dissemination of knowledge.

7. Dilemmas of Academic and Intellectual Freedom

BY AMÉLIE OKSENBERG RORTY

Van Alstyne believes that he must choose between a general and a specific theory of academic freedom, between one that derives professional rights and liberties from those assured to the population at large and one that treats such rights as derived solely from the nature of the profession. He also believes that the justification of such rights and liberties, however they are defined, must be either consequentialist or deontological. Rather than pronouncing on the merits of the arguments, I want to question the distinctions that seem to force a choice. Because I am not convinced that questions about the justification of professional rights and liberties—indeed questions about rights and liberties at all—can be raised ahistorically, I want to make some remarks about the political and social institutions that are presupposed in talking about the sorts of rights and liberties that we now call academic freedoms.

Van Alstyne argues that it is essential, if not actually necessary to the exercise of the academic profession, that its members receive protections not accorded to citizens generally; the essential activities of academic intellectuals would be undercut if they were not free to engage in research, to teach and to publish, being judged by their colleagues solely for their competence and their honesty. This is taken to mean that academics should be neither hired nor fired by considering the utility of their work in forwarding the ends of an institution, or any particular ideological program, or the interests of any particular class. Only the opinion of those qualified to judge the substance of a person's work should carry weight on appointments and promotions committees. Van Alstyne also wants to protect academics from being judged as professionals in nonprofessional situations; I shall not be concerned with this part of his paper. We would probably all agree with his general principle, though we would find considerable difficulty in applying it, since the line between professional and nonprofessional activities cannot be drawn sharply.

Whatever the justification for academic freedom may be, it cannot be claimed that the academic professions *cannot* be carried out without these protections, when it seems clear that they *were* carried out without them through a large part of known history. If Socrates, Galileo, and Bruno were feared, they managed to do something worth fearing. The argument must rather be that the intellectual life of teachers and scholars cannot be properly carried out *in a particular sort of polity* without these rights. Implicit in the analysis of academic freedom is a conception of society that roughly follows libertarian lines. Defenders of this view may recognize the naïveté of assuming that academic institutions are free of hidden economic or ideological interests and controls. They hold, however, that such controls are at work in every society and that they are less dominant, or at any rate more likely to be exposed, in a libertarian society than in others.

Van Alstyne believes that he and Searle disagree about whether the justification of academic freedom involves a consequentialist rather than deontological argument. He also thinks that they disagree about whether academic freedom is a strictly professional right, rather than an application of more general civil liberties. I think that there is less difference between them than appears on the surface; the interesting issues emerge not in declaring a winner, but in seeing why the controversy dissolves. The contrast between consequentialist and nonconsequentialist arguments is by no means as sharp as is generally thought. Furthermore, when we treat the justification of rights in their historical context, the contrast between general civil rights and specifically professional ones blurs.

Let me start by raising (and then letting fall) some tangential problems about the analysis of the function and nature of the academic profession. I have suggested that academic rights and protections are not entailed by the definitions of the professional activities of teachers and scholars. From this it does not follow that the justification of those rights can only take the form of consequentialist arguments. For the sake of the discussion, let us suppose that there are some purely professional rights and protections, such as the autonomy of academic appointments and promotion committees and the protection of tenure. But if the rights and protections of academics are theirs by virtue, and only in the exercise of their profession, then it is not obvious that all academics have the same rights and freedoms. It might be argued, for instance, that, as the duties and responsibilities of various types of teachers differ, so do their rights and freedoms. Those who are engaged in advanced research might be thought to have quite a distinct profession from teachers in elementary schools, high schools, or even junior colleges. They might, therefore, be argued to have quite distinct rights and protections. Teachers in an elementary school might be held responsible for not espousing views that may endanger what is thought to be a child's normal development; teachers in high school might be held responsible for not using the classroom to organize political movements. I do not wish to defend this position but rather to remark that, if we follow Van Alstyne's view that there are professionally defined academic freedoms, we may discover that there are diverse academic professions. The professional duties of academics engaged in research may be close to those of journalists and news analysts; the responsibilities of teachers in professional programs may be much more closely allied to other client-oriented professionals, such as lawyers and physicians. The responsibilities and rights of elementary schoolteachers may be quite different from those of college teachers. Obviously, extending academic freedom to nonacademic intellectuals and analyzing the varying responsibilities of distinctive types of intellectuals would require us to re-examine and possibly reorganize existing institutional structures. The nature and functions of the academic professions have varied considerably in the past and may usefully change in the future. Specific rights, such as the protection afforded by tenure appointments, may best be seen, and perhaps best be exposed, as contractual agreements that have been won by negotiation, under particular social and economic circumstances. They are outgrowths of a particular political and social order; they presuppose a set of assumptions about the definitions and functions of the various professions.

Lawyers and physicians also have, and clerics at one time had, rights specific to the exercise of their professions. Whether the members of a profession can be guaranteed specific rights, and whether they can be protected from being judged as professionals in nonprofessional situations, depends on the bargaining strengths of the institutions in which the professions are exercised and on the status and force of the profession in the society at the time. This is one of the reasons that academics were interested in defining themselves as professionals in the narrow sense: at one time, the universities and professional organizations sustained us. Academic intellectuals have been in a position to negotiate for their freedoms only when the universities acquired prestigious positions in society and were financed by sources that assured economic security while allowing them to remain relatively autonomous.

The contrast between the social and economic status of academics and journalists makes this evident; the security afforded journalists in the exercise of their profession is severely limited by the marketability of their writing: it requires courage and independence to exercise the simplest of civil liberties. In principle, "academic" freedoms are just as essential to the journalistic professions as to teacher-scholars. The reason that journalists have not enjoyed rights that might be thought "deontologically" theirs is that they did not work for institutions that managed to acquire independence from their owners or benefactors. If there had been foundations to establish institutional self-supporting magazines and newspapers as well as professional journals, then "academic" freedoms might have been extended to professions that are now regarded as para-academic. That universities became self-governing, even when they were not self-supporting, is a result of a complex set of circumstances, involving, among other things, a historical connection between scholars, educators, and autonomous religious institutions, and their eventual separation. When teacher-scholars were more closely allied with the teaching orders of religious organizations, the responsibilities and obligations that defined the academic professions were quite different from those we now suppose, and their rights and liberties were correspondingly different. It was, after all, still in the nineteenth century that university professors in England were required to subscribe to certain religious oaths and creeds and were expected to remain unmarried. Their religious or royal connections guaranteed them certain political autonomy, which they retained after separating from their religious orders or royal patrons. When the functions of a profession are thought to be well defined, there are nonconsequentialist and even deontological arguments to justify rights that are essential to the exercise of the profession as specifically defined. But extending or contracting professional obligations is a process that goes on continuously, and arguments about the proper definitions of the professions and their rights in relation to other professions require both consequentialist and nonconsequentialist moves. The justification of professional protections and rights involves appeals to the intrinsic worth of certain sorts of activities as essential to the development of moral or human values, as well as appeals to the consequences of restricting or expanding rights. All these arguments must, of course, take the form and substance of their time. Neither deontological nor consequentialist arguments are self-starting: both depend on appeals to accepted values. In the same way, the distinction between specifically professional rights and general civil liberties cannot be sharply drawn. The justification of what appears to be a specifically professional right may sometimes take the form of showing that they are necessary to guaranteeing more general civil rights. But in any case, when there are fundamental disagreements about the proper functions of the professions, analyses of their "deontological" rights, as defined at a specific time, cannot by themselves determine whether the professions ought to be changed. And that is frequently the very question at issue.

There are two concepts of social and political rights, and we see them both at work here. One is the view that rights grow out of existing responsibilities and obligations and that they are supported by the practices that define interests and the distribution of power. From this perspective, the justification of a right grows out of the necessity to perform an existing social function well; to be exercised, that right must be supported by the power to assert or preserve it. Academics' rights to special protection and to special liberties grew out of their professional obligations as these were defined in specific historical circumstances. Academics have succeeded in securing these protections as rights, rather than as privi-

leges, to the extent that it is in the interest of the larger society to
grant them or to the extent that academics have been able to secure
them, independently of the power of opinion.

The other view is that there are certain abstract rights, existing
independently of whether any society actually acknowledges or
protects them. On this view, there have always been both general
civil rights and specific rights for intellectuals; the trouble was to
get them recognized and acknowledged. No account of rights
would be complete without both perspectives; attempts to transform existing definitions and distributions of rights generally appeal
to an abstract analysis of justice. But such analyses can have little
weight in actually transforming conditions unless they can be
shown to appeal to the interests of the society. This does not pre-
clude arguments from moral or logical considerations; but these
considerations can only be effective if they are internalized. The
two conceptions of rights are intimately connected, dialectically inseparable, and mutually corrective.

The issues between Van Alstyne and Searle are not as cut and
dried as they may seem; it is not necessary to pick sides between
deontologists and consequentialists. Nor is it necessary to determine
whether academic freedoms are specific or general. It may be true
that at a particular period a set of rights and liberties follow from
a particular analysis of the functions and obligations of the academic professions. But historically, the networks of the various intellectual professions have involved shifting alliances and group-
ings, with a shifting balance of power and range of autonomy. The
justification of certain protections and rights, because they are
necessary to the exercise of the profession as such, often properly
takes the form of a deontological justification; but when we consider changing the place or function of a profession in the community at large, deontological arguments will seem question-
begging, and we turn to consequentialist arguments. But one move
in redefining the rights of a profession can also appeal to a
deontological argument about what is necessary for the exercise of
the profession *under a revised description.*

It might be objected that there is, and always has been, only one
central enterprise in the academic profession: the disinterested
pursuit of truth. *That,* it might be argued, is the center of the
matter, and all the rest is social service, which would indeed be

expected to vary historically. The various social services that academics perform as educators, scientists, or political theorists are all incidental to the heart of the matter: the search for the truth. All the various academic and intellectual professions require freedom of expression and publication, protection against unwarranted restraint on the freedom of expression. But these general rights are accorded to all citizens on the grounds that they are necessary to the working of a certain type of polity. If they are regarded as general human rights, it is on the grounds that a polity in which the freedom of expression dominates over civic conformity or unanimity of belief is a better state than one in which those values are reversed. To establish this, it is necessary to use both consequentialist and nonconsequentialist arguments.

Adjudicating disagreements about whether someone has violated the central standards of professional competence by slanting or directing his research to serve some interest or preconception will involve judging substantive questions, especially when there is considerable stress and disagreement in a society. If a man's interests are served by his research, it does not follow that he has done his research to serve his interests; judgments of disinterested competence are difficut to distinguish from judgments of truth and validity. Under such circumstances, no analysis of the nature of academic freedom will be of much use in arbitrating disagreements. Our dilemma is that, on the one hand, we want to assure academics and intellectuals freedom from external interference with their professional activities, while on the other hand, we want to avoid placing judgment in the hands of a self-perpetuating academic elite, which must form their judgments following existing standards of competence. This means that reforms or transformations of any kind, whether political or intellectual, are at an enormous disadvantage. The fate of the scientific innovator is the same as that of the political reformer or dissident: they are all judged by the theories they are attacking. It is a mistake to construe all such problems as political problems; doing so engenders the utopian idea that there may be political solutions to them. But it is built into the protective autonomy of the academic professions that intellectual revolutions, like political revolutions, suffer the devastating effects of the period when the burden of proof lies entirely on their shoulders. During this period, innovators are regarded as cranks, fakes, potential dangers to the standards of the profession. They suffer ignominy and poverty. And surely there is no doubt that many promising theories have died this way, as have many promising political reforms. Placing the burden of proof on change and transformation generally initially cripples all but the most rhetorically mellifluous or sophisticatedly ambiguous theories. Not only the weight of opinion, but also the whole machinery of existing institutions and the economics of research, make the conditions for receptivity to fundamental novelty unfavorable.

But what is the option? Putting judgments in the hands of an external group is obviously even more dangerous and restrictive. If, fearing the natural conservativism of academics, we turn judgment over to government agencies, we shall surely be worse off. Leaving judgment up for public grabs puts it in the hands of those who can exercise the greatest control of public opinion. It may indeed be naïve, as Schmitt has argued, to suppose that professional evaluations will be more neutral than nonprofessional ones. But it is important to distinguish the various senses in which the work of academics serves or betrays their interests:

1. Someone engaged in research may try to control the outcome of his research for the sake of personal gain, or to promote the interests of his employers or a group he wishes to serve, or for the sake of a belief or ideology.

2. A teacher may slant a presentation in order to induce students to form opinions and attitudes that serve the interests of his employers, or a group he wishes to serve, or for the sake of a belief or ideology.

3. Without controlling the outcome of his research, someone may take on a project in an area or a subject because he expects that developments in this area will benefit him, or his employers, or a group he wishes to serve, or a belief or ideology.

4. A person may get income, status, and power because the profession is structured a certain way and has a prestigious place in the society. Neither the outcome of his research nor the slant of his teaching need be affected by this, though his research may well be influenced (without being controlled) by the main lines of intellectual and social fashions. While he may be said to have an interest in the social structure and in current intellectual trends,

he may promote educational, intellectual, and social reforms. It is difficult to imagine any social structure or intellectual milieu of which this is not true. Members of an egalitarian society who might be expected to be disadvantaged by a change in structure also have an interest in maintaining the status quo. Of course, there are some inegalitarian polities in which the disadvantaged have a great deal to gain by a change in the social order, and the advantaged a great deal to lose. But in such situations it would be as unconvincing to argue that the disadvantaged are disinterested as it would be to argue that the advantaged are interested.

The defense of academic rights, like the defense of other civil rights, presupposes a general political theory. (Whether that theory is itself defended on deontological or consequentialist grounds is quite a distinct question.) If academics or intellectuals have an interest in maintaining a particular social structure and are committed to defending a specific sort of polity, it does not follow that they have the sort of interest in their work that would lead them to control the outcome of their research or distort their teaching. Even if there is a latent tension between professed interests and real benefits, it does not follow that academics cannot, in the appropriate sense, judge one another's work disinterestedly. And even if it is clear that there are some senses in which professional evaluations are not at all disinterested, it is not clear what policy for review and evaluation should be adopted. Certainly it does not follow that we should return to nonprofessional evaluations.

Suppose we accept, for the sake of the argument, what is implicit in Schmitt's analysis and grant that academics should also be judged by their services to society as a whole and, further, that what they do must (in the long run?) benefit the least advantaged. It is possible to subscribe to this principle and yet recognize that, if there is disagreement about the function and nature of academic professions, there will also be disagreement about what social interests really are and how they ought to be served. Pursuing this line, we come in practice very quickly to a distinction between what a society or an oppressed class believes its interests to be and its real or objective interests. This is especially true if the establishment or the ruling classes have successfully shaped public opinion to serve their own interests. For if, as is claimed, the minds of intellectuals have been formed by the interests of the ruling class, so also have the desires and judgments of the whole society, including the disadvantaged classes. If this is so, the evaluation of academics by citizens' committees composed of students, janitors, the town librarian, and the friendly neighborhood taxpayer will not reflect the real needs of the society any more than would judgments by other academics. We shall be back exactly where we started: with some set of intellectuals—now a different set, the group that claims to have analyzed the objective needs of the society—judging the competence, seriousness, and merits of the rest. We may indeed worry that professional judgments are in their very nature conservative—even radicals and revolutionaries are conservative in this sense. But it may well be that leaving judgment to the community at large increases rather than decreases this conservativism; it may also allow greater scope to the tyranny of fashionable and arbitrary judgments.

We are torn by intuitions that can in some cases lead to conflict. On the one hand, we think universities ought to be sensitive to the needs of a society, ought to direct attention to solving some of its major problems. On the other hand, we think that academics ought not to be at the service of any particular group in society or under any external control or direction. It would be pretty to think that this potential dilemma is resolved by the disinterested pursuit of truth, which enables one to judge genuine social utility. But even if, having carefully distinguished the various senses of "disinterestedness," we believe academics are disinterested in the appropriate ways, it is not immediately obvious that the sheer pursuit of truth, as defined by academics themselves, will serve the real needs of society. Of course it may be (trivially) true that, in the long run, this must be so, but that does not help resolve the immediate practical issues. On the one hand, we think that intellectuals ought to be the critics of accepted views about social needs and priorities; on the other, we think that they ought to reflect those needs and priorities. One might think there is no conflict here; universities must serve the real, and not the presumed or imagined, needs of a society. This is easy to say abstractly. But historically, in practice, universities have taken on so many quite distinct functions that their proper place in the society is quite difficult to assess.

I believe that the tensions between the various functions of the universities are wholesome and that it is better to have the universities balance out potentially conflicting aims than to have the universities represent only one set of functions or purposes, allowing other institutions to perform independent functions. On the whole, a system of checks and balances within one autonomous institution seems to protect more rights than a system that generates conflicts among distinct institutions, some of which may not be autonomous. For instance, if research institutions sponsored and financed by government agencies or private corporations no longer have a place in the universities, the standards that the universities have managed to impose on them will be severely weakened. What is perhaps even worse, people who do research will no longer be subject to the critical scrutiny of academic colleagues and students. Division of labor may increase efficiency at the cost of every other benefit. To put these functions or interests in distinct institutions accentuates their competitive and diminishes their cooperative enterprises. They will be in deadly competition for diminishing resources; being separated in distinct institutions, they are less likely to understand and protect one another's projects and rights.

The universities are the talent scouts and trainers of apprentices. In these functions universities tend to be conservative, accepting current criteria for ability and social utility. Because the machinery of universities is cumbersome and conservative, there is often a serious lag in this process: existing professional patterns are projected into the future without sufficient sensitivity to changes in the patterns. But universities are also supporters of "pure" research, and great libraries are settings for free and critical speculation.

The problems of balancing out these divergent functions emerge sharply in Schmitt's observation that universities and funding agencies can act as instruments of control. He argues that the logical form of the direction of research by the control of funds is the same as political interference. But though in practice the edges may get blurred, there is a great difference between penalizing someone for his views, on the one hand, and inducing him to pursue a line of research, on the other. We can at least distinguish important shades, if not kinds of differences in types of interference and redirection. Temptation or allurement is one thing, and force or coercion another. Both are bad, of course; but if we lump them together, we shall arm ourselves against the wrong thing, protect

ourselves in the wrong direction. The moves we make to protect
ourselves against allurement are quite different from those we make
to protect ourselves from force. If it were true that capitalism forces
consent to its principles, conformity to its practices, then it would
be idle to exhort academics living in a capitalistic society to turn
their allegiance to the proletariat or the exploited. Only a shift in
the economic structure could do that. And ironically enough, we
may see that happen, but it will come as a result of the arbitrary
unemployment of academics, rather than as a result of their realizing that their real allies are the exploited in a capitalist society. For
in a capitalist society, the real class interests of academics lie
neither with the oppressed classes nor with an elite as their functionaries. Rather, the class interests of academics lie in keeping
these two classes apart and in serving as their intermediaries and
go-betweens, the critical middlemen. It is only if one believes that
the transition to other forms of society are inevitable that one
might argue that the interests of the academics lie in an alliance
with the oppressed classes. If one does not believe that transition
is inevitable, the argument for the identification would have to be
a moral one. It would have to take quite a different form, and its
consequences on the analysis of academic freedom would be quite
different.

It is by no means clear, as Schmitt has claimed, that the logical
form of coercion and force (whatever that might be) is the same
as temptation to the sweettoothed. The two merge only when what
is withheld is *necessary* to the existence or identity of the person
under duress. There is no doubt that the funding agencies do direct
attention to some areas of research rather than others and that this
constitutes a problem and sometimes a danger; but the problems
and dangers are not the same as those of coercion and force, and
they cannot be corrected by the same strategies.

Balancing the desirability of preserving the autonomy of universities against their various (and often conflicting) social responsibilities is not something that can be done by formulating
principles. It would be surprising if we could draw up a list of
necessary and sufficient conditions for genuine academic freedom
or delineate the proper balance between autonomy and social responsibility. These matters require a climate of opinion, a relatively

benign economy, an ethos of fairness. We know of oppressive systems that nominally retain all the paraphernalia that are meant to secure freedom and rights, due process, and all the rest. Review of appointments and investigations into the sources and effects of research may go through academic boards without being genuinely free. When resources are scarce and employment limited, the principles we focus on to provide security are those that can be applied when there is enough consensus to assure fairness, but not enough to assure it automatically.

I have throughout this paper referred to the interests of "a society." It might be objected that, in doing so, I have presupposed that society is composed of homogeneous groups or groups whose interests are harmonious enough to be served by the same sorts of decisions. But it might be argued that politics are in fact internally divided: the politics of academic life is inevitably the politics of the ruling group who finances it and whose interests are reinforced at the cost of other groups. While this objection has considerable force, it does not seem to me to affect the argument. On the contrary, it seems to reinforce the claim that universities ought to remain as strong and antonomous as possible, retaining the variety of diverse functions that have, for historical reasons, accrued to them. Of course, when interest groups diverge markedly and when dissent is sharp and widely spread, there is likely to be conflict in the universities. This may endanger the rights of academics. I see no way to avoid this: since the protection of rights requires a benign climate of opinion, as well as a careful formulation of principles, the fate of academic freedom will depend on many social and economic factors. As Hume remarked, we require principles of justice when situations are not generous enough to provide for all; but if conditions are impoverished, then we cannot be assured that principles of justice will be applied.

Because many protective measures tend, as Van Alstyne observed, to have conservative effects, we ought to try to avoid being dogmatic about our views, whether they are political or professional, especially when they reflect our interests. We need to be sensitive to the hidden pressures of our interests, to understand them and their sources, being careful to assure the rights of those whose interests and opinions differ from ours. An analysis of our policies and institutions is incomplete without an account of their historical origins and functions. More than either of these, we need to find principles and procedures acceptable both to the established professions and to those who argue that academics are no longer serving their proper functions or that those functions should be redefined.

8. Academic Freedom: The Future of a Confusion

BY RICHARD SCHMITT

The controversy between Searle and Van Alstyne is familiar. It has been argued many times before.[1] It is just for that reason rather astonishing. For the controversy concerning the grounds on which best to defend claims to academic freedom (should we lay claim to this freedom by virtue of the civil rights that accrue to us, as to all citizens, or by virtue of our special status as scholars?) can get started only if all participants have a clear view of what the freedom is that they are arguing about. That clarity is within reach only if the concept of academic freedom is clear. But it will not be difficult to show that the concept of academic freedom is beset by many serious ambiguities. I shall deal with a number of them in this paper. But these ambiguities have, so far, been ignored. The same formulations of the concept of academic freedom have been reiterated by writer after writer, all of them professional academics, with rarely any attempt to clarify some of the serious opacities of the concept.

Once one begins to think about this, he soon stops being astonished, because he realizes that the effectiveness of the appeal to

[1] Russell Kirk, *Academic Freedom: An Essay in Definition* (Chicago: Henry Regnery Co., 1955); and William P. Murphy, "Academic Freedom—An Emerging Constitutional Right," in *Academic Freedom*, ed. Hans W. Baade, (Dobbs Ferry, New York: Oceana Publications, 1964), pp. 17–56.

academic freedom have been reiterated by writer after writer, all writer points proudly to the progress made in this field, since the founding of the AAUP in 1915, by such distinguished academics as John Dewey and Arthur Lovejoy. But much of this progress was due to specific confusions surrounding current formulations of the concept of academic freedom.

In the second section, I shall pay attention to some other serious obscurities in the concept. This will lead me, in the third section, to a sweeping prediction, namely, that full academic freedom will be available only in a communist society. Since that sort of society not only does not exist now but also is not in sight, I shall end by making some modest suggestions for mitigating the destructive influences of our present social arrangements on the academic professions and on the freedom to pursue the truth as we see it.

I

Searle and Van Alstyne formulate criteria for academic freedom very much in the way they are formulated by other standard authors.[2] In all cases, the central claim made by academics is this: There are two sorts of grounds on which one's work as an academic may be judged: professional and nonprofessional. The claim to academic freedom amounts to denying anyone the right to penalize an academic economically on any nonprofessional grounds. I may be refused promotion or continued employment only if I have been found to be deficient in my professional conduct. Professional incompetence or dishonesty warrants dismissal. Nothing else does. Only one's professional colleagues are competent to judge one's conformity to professional standards. That is the essence of the claim to academic freedom.

This notion stands and falls with the notion of the professional. To the extent that the notion is unclear, so also is the notion of

[2] Arthur Lovejoy, "Academic Freedom," *Encyclopaedia of the Social Sciences* (New York: Macmillan Co. and Free Press, 1930), I, 384; Fritz Machlup, "On Some Misconceptions Concerning Academic Freedom," *AAUP Bulletin* 41 (Winter 1955): 753; Sidney Hook, *Academic Freedom and Academic Anarchy* (New York: Cowles Book Co., 1969), p. 14; Robert MacIver, *Academic Freedom in Our Time* (New York: Columbia University Press, 1955), p. 6; John Searle, *The Campus War* (New York: World Publishing Co., 1971), p. 184.

academic freedom. It is easy to see that the term "professional" has, at least, four distinct meanings. I shall mention additional ones below. Persons are called "professionals" if (1) they are members in good standing of professional organizations in particular fields such as, for example, the American Philosophical Association; (2) they are in command of and use the specialized methods that are used by respected workers in the field; (3) they pursue truth impartially and disinterestedly; and (4) they have a mastery of a particular field by having acquired a certain requisite body of knowledge, produced by professionals, at least in senses 2 and 3. The thesis that the term "professional" is ambiguous amounts to saying that any person who is a professional in any one of these senses is not necessarily also a professional in all the others. I am not, of course, denying that there are many times in the lives of many academics when they can rightly claim to be professionals in each of these four senses. But there is no logical incoherence in claiming that someone who conducts himself as a professional in some, or one, of these senses is not professional in some of the remaining senses in some particular situation. Senses 1 and 4 are most closely associated. But it is not logically impossible that someone should be a member of a professional organization without reaching even very modest levels of professional competence.

The campaign for academic freedom in America has been very successful. Politicians have become wary of being labeled enemies of freedom for attacking academics. The benefits to be reaped from persecuting intellectuals have, as time has passed, become more costly. Given our political rhetoric, it is not good to be thought less than fully devoted to liberty.

The confusions surrounding the concept of academic freedom, particularly with respect to the central concept of the professional, have been extremely helpful in this campaign. Coalescing the four senses of the term "professional," we have portrayed ourselves as selflessly and disinterestedly pursuing the truth. As academics, we are not pursuing any interests of our own. We have no class interest. We have no limited perspectives. We are above the hurly-burly of the political arena where different interest groups battle with each other for more power. Thus, the attacks of politicians could be represented not as legitimate political struggles but as political attacks where such attacks were inappropriate. Being politically neutral, we had no political stance that could be attacked. We could thus easily portray our critics in statehouses as persecuting us simply because we had some intellectual freedom. Our claim to political neutrality was useful in the counterattack against our critics. But this sort of defense loses much of its plausibility once we distinguish the four senses of "professional" mentioned earlier. Once we admit that we are not always disinterestedly searching for the truth merely by virtue of being members of, say, the APA, or that we do not, just by virtue of that fact, always use specialized, professional methods even if we know how to use them, the politicians' attacks, except for the very crudest ones, may not look as radically inappropriate and gauche as we have been able to make them appear.[3] (At this point, as Searle remarks, the notion of political neutrality needs to be introduced and discussed explicitly.[4] I cannot do that here. Suffice it to say that it has given certain claims to academic freedom greater plausibility. But since it also is an extremely unclear notion, it only adds to the confusion of what we mean by "academic freedom.")

The confusions in the notions of the professional and of academic freedom have been extremely helpful in another, and more sinister, respect. The improved climate for academics that exists today is usually ascribed to the vigilance of the professionals and their associations, and perhaps also to the general growth of liberal sentiment in America. What is not usually recognized is that the professions have, for a long time now, been very careful not to give too much offense to possible enemies, particularly those that control the funds. This has involved rigorous self-policing on the part of the professions. In the 1950s that self-policing was very open. Many distinguished academics as well as their organization, the AAUP, concluded that members of the Communist party were not entitled to academic freedom, that they could be fired or, at least, not hired for being members of the party.[5] In its simplest form, the argument ran as follows: "Since academic freedom is a promise

---

[3] We shall see concrete evidence below that membership in professional organizations does not ensure the political neutrality of academics.

[4] Searle, *The Campus War*, p. 203.

[5] MacIver, *Academic Freedom in Our Time*, pp. 158 ff.; *AAUP Bulletin* 39 (1953): 91–97; Ralph F. Fuchs, "Academic Freedom—Its Basic Philosophy, Function and History," in *Academic Freedom*, ed. Hans W. Baade, p. 7.

not to dismiss professors for forming or professing independent views, it presumes that the professors themselves are committed to form and profess their views independently. But Communists are committed not to."[6] We do not hear that sort of argument very often any more. Once again, that is ascribed to liberalization—a "thaw" we might call it—since the McCarthy era. But a more realistic explanation is surely that the Communist party has lost much of its membership and importance, and, these days, radicals cannot be gotten at for being members of the party. That has made the elimination of radicals more difficult, but it has not prevented the professions from removing leftists of various colorations from their posts. That is usually done on the grounds that the professor in question is not professionally qualified. There is very little disagreement that this sort of thing is still happening. There is, however, considerable disagreement about the interpretation of the facts. The dominant view, held by Van Alstyne, maintains that anyone fired by his colleagues was subject to the judgment of his professional peers, and thus his academic freedom was not violated. Perhaps his peers erred. Professional qualifications do not render us proof against error. But even if the judgment against a professional by his colleagues was erroneous, it cannot be said to be political, for it was rendered by professionals, on professional grounds. An academic has his academic freedom violated only when the judgment against him is made on nonprofessional—for instance, political—grounds.[7]

This interpretation loses all plausibility as soon as we begin to see the ambiguities of the concept of the professional. A philosopher, for instance, who is denied tenure by his department on the grounds that his scholarship is poor (he introduces Marxist analyses in contexts where that seems inappropriate to his colleagues) is, indeed, denied tenure by professionals. But, in this context, they are professionals in sense 1 of that term. He is denied tenure by members in good standing of the APA. Nothing logically guarantees that they, in passing judgment, employed the specialized

6 Ernest van den Haag, "Academic Freedom in the United States," in *Academic Freedom*, ed. Hans W. Baade, p. 90.

7 William Van Alstyne, "The Specific Theory of Academic Freedom and the General Issue of Civil Liberties."

methods of philosophy,[8] that they searched for the truth impartially and disinterestedly, and that they had a modicum of competence in the relevant fields. Since Marxist scholarship is almost non-existent in America, scholars with Marxist leanings are almost inevitably judged by colleagues whose acquaintance with Marx goes back to reading the *Communist Manifesto* in college. Even membership in the APA does not protect us from becoming quite emotional when issues of promotion and tenure come up. An academic fired by his peers thus has no guarantee that they judged him dispassionately.

None of this goes to show that a distinction may not be drawn between professional and nonprofessional judgments of a person's work. What it does show, however, is that the common notion that all judgments of one academic by others are professional and therefore not political is false. There is no reason to think that Marxists fired by their academic colleagues are fired for any more professional reasons than Marxists fired by administrators or trustees. As a consequence, the confidence, which is widely shared at present, that any firing within a department cannot, logically, be political is clearly misplaced. Academics have their academic freedom violated by their colleagues as well as by nonprofessional persons.

Once we recognize this, our facile confidence—that all is quite well with academic freedom—evaporates.[9] The changes that have been praised as improvements consist in good part of professional academics now doing the job, formerly done by outsiders, namely, to maintain the public orthodoxy, whatever it happens to be. That this has been possible in spite of sincere dedication to academic freedom is due to the convenient obscurity of that term.

II

We have seen some ambiguities in the notion of academic freedom. We must now attend to some others. Much has been said

---

[8] The fact that philosophers, although devoted to conceptual analysis, have made use of expressions like "academic freedom" or "professional" without any attempt at analysis is a clear instance of the failure of professionals, in one sense, to be professional, in another, namely to use the specialized methods of their discipline.

[9] Van Alstyne writes that "superior alternatives are not readily apparent" to

in the last ten years about the increasingly large share of money for universities that comes to individuals and institutions from the federal government and large foundations for the purpose of supporting very specific lines of inquiry.[10] What seems to have escaped notice, however, is that, logically at least, such funding of specific projects has the same form as political interference in scholarly research, which is usually regarded as a violation of academic freedom. Where academic freedom is interfered with, the government, say, tells a scholar that he will not receive any more financial support unless he pursues certain lines of inquiry and not others. In the case of funding of specific research projects, the government tells a scholar that he will not, in the future, receive any financial support unless he pursues certain lines of inquiry and not others. The only difference between the two cases is that, in the recognized cases of interference with academic freedom, the work is already in progress, or has perhaps been completed, while government funding for specific research projects, more often than not, is refused for certain lines of inquiry before the work begins. But, in either case, the decision as to what work a scholar will pursue is not made on purely professional grounds but on the grounds of what sort of research the government wants to "buy." According to the now current notion of academic freedom, this constitutes a nonprofessional interference with purely professional concerns and thus is as clear a violation of academic freedom as many more familiar cases.

It may be argued that a scholar who does not receive a grant for a particular research project can, after all, apply for a grant for some other project. He is not in the same position as the person who is dismissed from his job for holding unpopular views. It is not clear to me that that argument is at all relevant to the point that funding particular projects constitutes a violation of academic freedom as currently defined. For his professional concerns still are not the exclusive determinants of his professional work. But, at any rate, there are cases in which entire fields have come into existence at

---

current practices in regard to academic freedom. Van Alstyne, "The Specific Theory."

[10] Charles V. Kidd, "The Implications of Research Funds for Academic Freedom," in *Academic Freedom*, ed. Hans W. Baade, pp. 183–194.

the instigation of the government and some large foundations. A notorious example is the field of Chinese studies, which was quite explicitly created in the late 1950s for the purpose of procuring the information needed to formulate U.S.-China policy.[11] No money was available, for instance, to study China as a major and very exciting experiment in socialism that might provide suggestions or even models for the transformation of our own society. Here, since the entire field was financed for a certain political purpose, anyone who did not want to do research along specified lines could not, as a matter of fact, find financing. It was not possible for such a person to go elsewhere and get grants for a different project in his field of interest. What is puzzling about this is the failure of the academic world to notice the clear infringement of academic freedom involved. We can only explain this failure to ourselves if we consider the different meanings of the professional.

The whole matter of funding for research and teaching brings up a totally different aspect of the concept of the professional, namely, that a professional is a person who makes his living by pursuing a certain kind of inquiry. A professional philosopher, for instance, is one who gets paid for being a philosopher. If I ceased doing philosophy for a living, I could not continue to call myself a "professional." One is a professional academic only as long as one finds one's livelihood in colleges or universities or comparable institutions. Add to that another aspect of the notion of the professional, namely, that in our society academic jobs and grants, like all other goods, are distributed in a market place. The trained academic sells his competence to institutional buyers of various sorts, depending on the particular competence that is his. This means that he needs to develop a competence for which there is a demand. It means that, as the demand changes, he must adjust to these changes in demand. Since he is a professional in the sense of deriving his livelihood from his studies and his teaching, he adjusts his work to the needs of those that have the money to pay him. A professional, in America, is an entrepreneur.

These aspects of being a professional are so familiar that one

[11] David Horowitz, "The China Scholars and U.S. Intelligence," *Ramparts* 10 (1972): 31–39.

would not think that they needed to be mentioned at all. But we read, again and again, that professional academics have the freedom "to inquire, discover, publish and teach the truth as they see it, in the field of their competence. It is subject to no control or authority, except the control or authority of the rational methods by which truths and conclusions are sought and established in these disciplines."[12] Here the notion of the professional is taken in three of the four senses mentioned in the preceding section. The economic aspects of being a professional have been conveniently forgotten. The same forgetfulness overcomes scholars when they accept grants from the government or from foundations. The fact that such channeling of research work by means of economic pressure actually violates academic freedom can be ignored only because we think of ourselves as pursuing the truth impartially and disinterestedly, without giving any thought to the economic aspects of being a professional. But, once we pay attention to those aspects, we encounter more serious problems with the current notions of academic freedom.

III

The demand for academic freedom stems from the experience that the new ideas, discovered or developed by intellectuals, have again and again come into collision with established ideas and the institutions erected on them. The people who have an investment in established ideas, and even more the people who have an investment in the institutions presupposing those ideas, have again and again used the power available to them to terminate inquiries that seemed, to them, to threaten the existing arrangements and their place in those arrangements. Experience has shown that such interferences are, in the long run, not useful. But whether they prove useful or not, intellectuals want to be free from such interferences.

Put in these vague terms, there is no objection to the demand for academic freedom. But we have seen that once the demand is stated in somewhat more specific terms, by invoking the distinction between professional and nonprofessional criticism of an intellectual's work, the ambiguity of the term "professional" has, in fact,

---

[12] Sidney Hook, *Academic Freedom*, p. 14.

served to make the demand for academic freedom into a cover for intolerance within the profession, at the same time as it urges tolerance on the part of nonprofessionals.

If we consider, in addition, the economic restrictions on research, it becomes even clearer that the criteria for academic freedom are not usefully formulated by means of the distinction between professional and nonprofessional considerations, as long as those terms remain as confused as they are now. For we have seen, in the preceding section, that it is a part of being a professional to have serious economic concerns and to follow one's inquiry not to whatever truth but to whatever lucrative position it leads us. The ideal of the free intellectual is indeed that of the person who follows his inquiry wherever it leads, guided only by the "rational methods" that are respectable in the particular discipline. But it is now clear that that notion of the professional intellectual is inconsistent with that of the professional who makes his living by offering his services to the highest bidder. In a capitalist society, however, where the market mechanism is employed to distribute goods, a professional must be an entrepreneur of some sort. Thus, the structure of the society forces roles upon the professional intellectual that are inconsistent with some other senses of "professional," notably that of "pursuing the truth impartially and disinterestedly." Insofar as academic freedom is violated by any nonprofessional, that is, a "partial and interested" interference with the search for truth, being an academic in a capitalist society is inconsistent with possessing *genuine* academic freedom. Such freedom is realizable only in a communist society.

This claim is no less important for being, at present, quite obscure. What is more, it cannot be fully clarified, both for lack of space and because some of the needed concepts are not available to us at present. The best I can do is to list some of the outstanding problems.

1. Current definitions of "academic freedom" are incoherent in that they depend on the notion of being a "professional." But by the present definitions of that term, no one can be a professional in all the relevant senses at one and the same time. What I suggested in the preceding section, but did not argue for lack of space, is that these confusions are an inevitable consequence of our socioeconomic arrangements. Hence what is not available to us in this

society is not "academic freedom" in the currently accepted sense but academic freedom in a sense yet to be clarified.

2. What we seek under the heading of "academic freedom" is freedom from irrelevant interference with intellectual work. But what makes interference "irrelevant"? The attempt to equate "irrelevant" with "nonprofessional" does not work. One wants to say that interference is irrelevant if it is "political." But the meaning of the term "political" shifts from social order to social order. We know what the term means in this society. But if the difficulties with the concept of academic freedom are, as I believe, not merely due to error, but are the result of our socioeconomic arrangements, then we need to know what "political" means in a communist society before we can use that term to clarify the concept of academic freedom. But until we have built that alternative society, all such clarifications will remain speculative.

3. A communist society, in the present context, must be understood as one whose members do not compete with one another for essential goods and services. This means (a) that in a communist society, essential needs are filled independently of anyone's performance as a worker. Intellectuals in such a society (assuming that they still form a separate class) need not orient their work by considerations extrinsic to their subjects, namely, the requirements of procuring a livelihood; (b) that a communist society can only be established where the productive capacity is large enough to satisfy everyone's basic needs. Few countries are presently in that position; (c) that none of the socialist countries in existence have established communist societies in the sense relevant here; and (d) that in a communist society resources are sufficiently ample so that time, library, and laboratory facilities will be available for everyone. Thus intellectual workers are free from interference on "nonprofessional" grounds because no one can threaten their livelihood or access to needed facilities.

This conclusion has implications for understanding our current practice, as well as for the immediate and the remote future. As to current practice, the conclusion makes it quite clear that the dedication of academics to academic freedom has been very qualified and, in fact, disingenuous. For academics to demand academic freedom has meant warding off interferences from persons outside the various professional organizations. The search for academic freedom has often been a well-disguised search for job security. For the defense was always against administrators who, legally speaking, do the hiring and firing and against politicians who can fire indirectly by refusing to appropriate money. The search for academic freedom has rarely included a defense of academics against the political prejudices of their colleagues or against the deformation of the search for truth by massive infusions of government and foundation money. In fact, in both these situations, it is the academics themselves who have violated their own and others' academic freedom, and they have done that with a minimum of soul searching or hesitation. Obviously, these two self-inflicted violations of academic freedom are intimately connnected. A good deal of purging of radicals from the various professions is fairly explicitly justified on the grounds that to keep them on as colleagues would jeopardize state appropriations, alumni gifts, and so forth, in the future.

Another implication of the preceding argument is this: The infringements on our academic freedom by ourselves are made possible only by our being very confused about the relevant concepts. Not only has this society forced us to violate the principles that it is in our interest to defend, namely, that the search for genuine knowledge should not be distorted by irrelevant concerns such as political and economic ones, but it also has forced us into refusing to seek the truth. Not only have we been forced into inconsistency, but also we have been forced, in specific areas, to abandon the dedication to truth altogether. Distinguished philosophers invoking the notions of professionalism or of academic freedom without ever inquiring into the meaning of these terms, or without seeing the glaring inconsistencies in crucial concepts, can hardly be a matter of innocent mistakes—for some of the people who have failed here possess very subtle intellects. There is no escaping the conclusion that they preferred not to ask questions when to do so would have been extremely inconvenient.

The implications for the distant future are simple: A capitalist society is incapable of allowing its citizens an untrammeled search for truth. Hence if we are, as professional intellectuals, interested in such a search, we must dedicate our efforts to overthrowing this capitalist society.

This conclusion seems paradoxical. For, as I noted earlier, one of the notions closely associated with—if not an ingredient in—the notion of a professional is that of political neutrality. But now we seem to find that being a professional, in the sense of being dedicated to the truth impartially and disinterestedly, involves us in being anything but politically neutral.

This conclusion raises very serious and very difficult problems, which cannot be discussed here for lack of space. But the preceding considerations have clearly shown that the claim made now by professional academics, that they are politically neutral, must be rejected. For the sake of their livelihoods, they have made themselves into supporters of existing arrangements. They have not fulfilled their traditional roles as critics and "gadflies" except in the most timid terms.

Once we understand this, it will be easier to see how, albeit very imperfectly, academic freedom must be defended in the present society. We can see now that the threat to the free, untrammeled pursuit of truth is much more widespread than is usually thought. Administrators and politicians are not by any means the only enemies of unhindered pursuit of truth. There are economic pressures of various kinds manifesting themselves in professional orthodoxies and in political orthodoxies. Unless a person does philosophy in certain accepted ways, he simply will not get a job.[13] Unless a person takes one of a number of approved political stances, he will not hold on to his job for very long. We have been unable to deal with these questions, because we have pretended that they do not exist. The first step toward realizing anything resembling academic freedom in America, as we know it, is to accept the fact that academics themselves are as guilty as anyone of violating academic freedom. The second step is to present to the various professional organizations, notably the AAUP, the task of studying these problems and providing a continuing forum for their airing. What is needed is full understanding of our position in a society that is on the defensive and that demands strict loyalty of everyone. Since we are subject to very direct economic sanctions, we find ourselves continually forced to take jobs that we cannot justify taking on intellectual grounds, or to harm colleagues whose work is intellectually defensible but politically offbeat. As long as this society

[13] See my paper "The Business of Philosophy," *Radical Philosopher's Newsjournal* 1 (1973): 32–52.

lasts, this situation cannot be remedied. The only choice we have is whether we are going to be willing tools of our employers or whether we shall resist. The first requirement for that is to practice what we preach, namely, to pursue truth fearlessly to where it leads. That requires, in the present context, that the professional organizations, as well as departments, become openly aware of the problems by making themselves into forums for political debate and for the analysis of the economic pressures on the profession. We may have to yield to these pressures. But if we are clearly aware of existing pressures, we may sometimes have, at least, a choice as to which pressure to yield to. As it is now, in our state of self-inflicted ignorance of our position, we bow to any pressure that comes along and only insult ourselves by doing so willingly while we praise ourselves for our disinterested professionalism. As long as this society continues, we shall remain unfree. But we can, at least, end the indignity of praising our own freedom while we cooperate in our own enslavement.

9. Reply to Comments

BY WILLIAM VAN ALSTYNE

The difference between Professor Searle's treatment of academic freedom and my own should become apparent upon further consideration of a hypothetical case advanced in his essay: "Imagine a professor of physics is active in political work on behalf of the Democratic party. Imagine, also, that the board of trustees of the university, who are all Republicans, fire him or refuse to promote him because of his activities on behalf of the Democrats." The hypothetical case implicitly stipulated two additional conditions: (1) that the activities the physics professor pursued did not involve an abuse of his university position (e.g., he was not attempting to collect party contributions from students or from others whose decision might be affected by anxieties arising from their institutional connection with him) and (2) that his political activities neither represented nor purported to represent an assertion of professional endeavor. They were, rather, indistinguishable from what any politically active person might do to advance the same cause.

Professor Searle believes that, although the professor acts under the circumstances simply "qua citizen," nonetheless the protection he deserves from trustee retaliation is grounded in a theory of "academic" freedom, albeit a "general" theory. Similarly, he says, the trustees are restricted from expelling a student under identical circumstances, in recognition of the student's "academic" freedom. The implication is given that no other rationale would provide as adequate an explanation as to why the hostile trustees properly lack authority to dismiss them. The analysis (and theory) is twice faulty. For reasons that become self-evident as the hypothetical case is sought to be extended and examined, moreover, it is ultimately unattractive as well.

Suppose that the person pursuing the stipulated activity is neither a student nor a faculty member, but rather a blue-collar employee of the same university, for example, a janitor, cafeteria employee, or typewriter repairman. Suppose also (as a next case), that such an employee may not work for a university at all, but rather in any of those capacities for the city or municipality in which the university is located. Under either set of circumstances, where the individual is not engaged in academic work and is neither an "academic" person nor even associated in any way at all with an "academic" enterprise, it gets us nowhere to defend the equal protection of his civil liberty by speaking of a general theory of *academic* freedom. The term will not stretch so far as this—and yet, no doubt, we are equally firm that retaliatory dismissal under the circumstances would be wrong. Indeed it would, as a clear abuse of relational leverage wholly without reference to the calling of the individual or the business of the enterprise. Moreover, a statement by the mayor, defending the refusal of city officials to act against such employees (exactly on the ground that President Lowell employed in the Harvard case noted in my paper), would be equally appropriate—all without reference to the special constraints or the special treatment of academic freedom. So, too, I have sought to argue, in respect to the personal, nonprofessional civil liberties of all persons, in whatever capacity associated, whether with institutions of higher learning or not.

Suddenly, then, to shift the ground and to treat the abuse of general civil liberty held equally by all those associated with educational enterprises on a different basis than the general case for civil liberty(i.e., on the basis that "academic" freedom explains the duty to forbear from retaliation), has at least the three critical shortcomings I have attempted to note in my essay.

First, by the selection of extraordinary label, such characterization implies an exclusivity of such protection (or, if not an exclusivity, at least a superior or additional right than others have) solely for those citizens associated in some dependent way with an *educational* enterprise. The claim implies a lack of equal protection for others that is false and a supererogation of elite status that is equally false, both inviting a general alienation and justified hostility by others. It is a fundamentally unsound approach; the protection to be granted proceeds not from a "general theory of academic freedom," but from a *specific* theory of *general* freedom and equal protection (see, for instance, John Rawls's *A Theory of Justice*).

Second, attaching the claim for protection to "academic" freedom unintentionally implies a duty of accountability by "academic" standards—that is, that even purely personal civil liberties are free from institutional sanction only to the extent that they are pursued in a "professional" manner, a manner not unbecoming an "academic" person. The result, under this view, is that the individual so situated is rendered *less* free in respect to his nonprofessional pursuits than others. This, after all, is the necessary logic of an indiscriminate theory that makes no distinction between manifestations of professional endeavor on the one hand and purely aprofessional pursuits on the other, implying a single norm of institutional accountability in respect to both and suggesting, moreover, that it is the more severe norm of academic accountability.

Third, and paradoxically, the pretense that abuses of civil liberties are really abuses of "academic freedom" leaves authentic cases of academic freedom without any standing room of their own. It subjects *that* freedom to the same explanation of employment accountability to which general civil liberties sometimes are made to yield, even when the case for protecting freedom of professional academic endeavor may be far stronger. The paradox is that, by weighting down its wings with every other kind of personal liberty, an indiscriminate claim that all freedom is "academic" freedom loses all possibility of giving academic freedom the power of independent flight.

Professor Searle concedes, for instance, that the "exercise of these freedoms," which professors have as citizens in a free society, is subject to restriction when it "needs to be restricted to preserve the academic and subsidiary functions of the university." But, consistent with the specific theory of academic freedom, that possibility can never arise in any case where a valid claim of academic freedom is authentically involved: not because the institution cannot be injured in a real-world sense by the exercise of that freedom (we know that it can!), but because the specific theory disallows taking such injury into account. The theory distinguishes the academic institution and the academic profession in respect to the definition of their primary function. What distinguishes that enterprise and that profession is their systematic establishment within a given society for the avowed purpose of subjecting received learning to review and to criticism. The same institutional duty is not specified in respect to General Motors, a city water department, or other institutions in general; nor are any of them expected to perform this task as an essential part of their business, however much one may hope that important services, ideas, or discoveries may arise from their work. Where published criticism of the conventional wisdom is part of the acknowledged social function of the very profession and enterprise, however, any injury which may befall the university is the *cost* of protecting academic freedom, rather than a justification for restricting that freedom. The valid exercise of academic freedom is never inconsistent with the primary duty of an academic institution.

To be sure, a society may end its commitment to the academic profession and to academic institutions. Society may erect its own set of eternal verities, consider the matter closed for all purposes of professional attention, and thereupon refuse to countenance the support or subsidy of institutions or professions directed to the regularized re-examination and critique of knowledge. It may do so, moreover, consistent with full freedom of speech generally, simply by leaving such investigations entirely to adventitious forces of personal curiosity and to the tolerated market of free speech in general. But the very practical prospect of that possibility takes nothing whatever away from the specific theory of academic freedom. Rather, it simply marks the society that is unwilling to accommodate and to nourish it.

In sum, I would say again that all who are associated with universities (whether as coaches, janitors, students, or faculty members) are entitled to the equal protection of their civil liberties on the same robust terms that should characterize the equal freedom of all persons everywhere in respect to their freedom from the abuses of relational leverage: not by claim of any special right peculiar to themselves, but as a matter of general right in a liberal society. To the extent that universities should be exemplars of humaneness, moreover, they may well, on that account, appropriately strive to do better in this regard than other institutions have done. We injure the common cause of freedom by resting that case on any special ground, moreover, and ought not articulate its defense through any special pleading.

This large and important general matter to one side, however, it is also true that the academic institution is meant to be different from other institutions in respect to its very raison d'être, as a place established for the primary purpose of the critical review of received learning, retaining a faculty professionally committed to that obligation. It is to that professional endeavor that the claim of academic freedom attaches, and it is to the protection of that endeavor that the specific theory of academic freedom applies.

Professor Schmitt's essay is less a comment on the subject of my paper than a brief introduction to a vision of academic freedom he evidently means to develop at greater length in writing, to appear elsewhere. In his haste to commend a view that "full academic freedom will be available only in a communist society" (albeit a kind that "not only does not exist now but also is not in sight"), however, he has simply misstated propositions in my paper. Specifically, he says: "The dominant view, held by Van Alstyne, maintains that anyone fired by his colleagues was subject to the judgment of his professional peers, and thus his academic freedom was not violated." To the contrary, my paper observes :

Against the chance that the committee members may show bias against him (as from fear for their own status, from a commitment to a given professional dogma, or from professional envy or sheer personal dislike), a more generous appeal may lie through the hierarchy of administration and thereafter to other bodies (like the AAUP) and, on occasion at least, to the courts. Indeed, the academic maverick may sometimes need more protection against the entrenched dogmas of his immediate peers than against anyone else, thus necessitating some right of appeal from a local judgment to the judgment of others who have less of a vested interest in the maintenance of a given "truth."

An equal error appears in confusing the position of Professor Ernest van den Haag and Sidney Hook with that of the AAUP on the matter of political affiliation as a test of academic fitness, it not being the case at all that the AAUP would thus restrict the profession—as its frequent participation in Supreme Court litigation to oppose loyalty oaths, and its very recent censure of the Board of Regents of California in regard to Angela Davis, among other things, make perfectly clear.

Since Professor Schmitt does not, in his comments, blueprint the communist society in which there are no longer any scarce resources but everything exists in such infinite abundance as to eliminate all issues of resource allocation (and correspondingly, all possibility of ulterior economic pressures that doubtless must, as Professor Rorty correctly remarks, be recognized for their bearing upon the *uses* of academic freedom as well as for their more direct threat to its very existence), I must forbear from commenting on the adequacy of that vision. Some brief remembrance of the current state of academic freedom in existing societies purporting to be animated by the spirit of communism, however, may surely give us pause before concluding that the true destiny of academic freedom lies in that direction.

Professor Rorty's paper seems to me to offer wise and excellent counsel on a number of dilemmas where I welcome her comments and believe they very usefully complement the consideration of academic freedom. Again, however, there may be small margins of misunderstanding even here. I did not say "that academics should be neither hired nor fired by considering the utility of their work in forwarding the ends of an institution," for that might imply that even considerations of basic teaching or research incompetence cannot state valid grounds for termination pursuant to full academic due process, even assuming that the transmission of knowledge is among the identified ends of the college. Rather, the suggestion was the more limited one that, where it is clear that the professor's actions are protected by academic freedom, the possible economic disutility of his actions to the institution (e.g., hostile legislative action in cutting the institution's budget in retaliation against the conclusions the professor may have reached in a professionally rigorous and scrupulous study) cannot state grounds for his dismissal. I think Professor Rorty did not mean to disagree with this, however, and I mention the matter only to avoid misunderstanding.

Part Three

It is nearly inevitable that discussion of the nature of academic freedom will turn to questions about the nature of the academic community—the academy. What is it about the academy that requires or demands freedom of inquiry, debate, and teaching? If the academy is a special sort of community, then what sort? How is it to be organized? What are the ground rules its members must obey? The rules adopted for the academy must be informed by a conception of its nature, but also they help to form that nature. The relationship is a reciprocal one. We cannot therefore set aside the question of tenure rules as having nothing to do with the concept of academic freedom. The tenure rules we adopt will help to shape our conception of the academy and of the rights that obtain within it. The discussion of Part Three, then, keeps turning back to the question of the ideal nature of the academy.

Rolf Sartorius, author of the principal paper, is professor of philosophy at the University of Minnesota. Alexander Ritchie is professor of philosophy and dean of the Faculty of Arts at the University of Newcastle, Australia. Graham Hughes is professor of law at New York University. Amélie Oksenberg Rorty is professor of philosophy at Livingston College, Rutgers University, and fellow of King's College, Cambridge University.

10. Tenure and Academic Freedom

BY ROLF SARTORIUS

Introduction

Academic tenure might be—indeed, has been—defended on a variety of grounds; my concern in this paper will be primarily with what I take to be its central defense—the claim that it is necessary for the protection of academic freedom. Not only is this claim the one constantly recurring theme to be identified in the literature on academic tenure, but also it is often explicitly said by proponents of tenure that considerations of academic freedom are the *only* reasons that justify support of a system that has many admitted disadvantages. In a leading paper on the subject, for instance, past AAUP President Fritz Machlup quotes with approval the following passage from Clark Byse and Louis Joughin's book-length study *Tenure in American Higher Education*: "Academic freedom and tenure do not exist because of a peculiar solicitude for the human beings who staff our academic institutions. They exist, instead, in order that society may have the benefit of honest judgment and independent criticism which otherwise might be withheld because of fear of offending a dominant social group or transient social attitude."[1] Machlup's own statement on the centrality of the

[1] Fritz Machlup, "In Defense of Academic Tenure," *AAUP Bulletin* 50 (1964): 112–124. Reprinted in Louis Joughin, ed., *Academic Freedom and Tenure. A Handbook of the American Association of University Professors* (Madison: University of Wisconsin Press, 1969). The quote is from p. 327 of

academic freedom defense of tenure is even more explicit: "All the disadvantages of a strict tenure system, whether they are borne by the institutions, by the individual teachers, or by the entire academic profession, are outweighed by one important advantage, accruing chiefly to society at large. This one advantage—really the only justification for the system of academic tenure—lies in the social products of academic freedom, a freedom which in many situations . . . can be guaranteed only by the instrument of tenure."[2]

I shall proceed as follows: In the remainder of this section, I shall briefly indicate what I take the relevant concepts of *academic freedom* and *tenure* to be and then attempt to render more precise the claim that is being made when it is contended that the latter is a necessary condition of the former. In the second section, I shall discuss some of the obvious disadvantages of tenure and seek to indicate how they are in large part due to the double standard of professional competency that a tenure system requires in order to be workable. In the third section, I shall attack the only arguments I have been able to find in support of the claim that tenure is necessary for the protection of academic freedom. In the fourth section, I shall sketch the ways in which academic freedom might be protected if tenure were to be abandoned. Finally, in the fifth section, I shall call attention to some of the practical difficulties that might confront attempts to replace or drastically modify current tenure principles and practices.

As a *status* that an individual may enjoy, tenure is the assurance of continued employment that may be given an academic after he has served a specified probationary period. As it will be understood here, this status must have a legal basis in contract or statute; tenure by grace or by moral commitment is not what is at issue. The assurance of continued employment is of course to be understood to permit of dismissal for "adequate cause," but only in terms of a relatively minimalistic standard of professional conduct, the discussion of which I shall defer until the next section.

Understood this way in terms of individual status, tenure could

---

the latter volume; all quotes from Machlup's paper will be from this volume. The work quoted by Machlup is Clark Byse and Louis Joughin, *Tenure in American Higher Education* (Ithaca: Cornell University Press, 1959).

[2] Machlup, "In Defense of Academic Tenure," p. 326.

conceivably be granted to all members of the academic profession, and the probationary period could in theory be null. As an institutional *practice* of the sort with which we are familiar, though, tenure demands a relatively long probationary period, with only some of those who receive initial appointments at a given institution eventually being granted tenure by that institution. The result of this practice is that at any given time only some members of the academic profession will be tenured, the rest—perhaps the majority—being prospective candidates for a status they do not yet enjoy.[3] I take it that it is the practice or system of tenure as characterized above that is at issue. For the rest of the details, I shall assume a shared understanding of AAUP principles and approved institutional practices.[4]

As a *status* that may characterize a given individual, academic freedom is the freedom of a member of the academic profession to engage in research, teaching, publication, and other such pursuits without fear of reprisals for the expression of unpopular opinions. As with tenure, there is here, too, an institutional analogue in the notion of a *climate* of inquiry that is relatively free from such threats to most individuals. Understood in either way, academic freedom is clearly a matter of degree. As with tenure, I am assuming a shared understanding of what academic freedom is,[5] although I shall not have anything to say until much later as to whether or not there is anything peculiarly academic about it. I turn next to the question of why it is viewed as desirable.

Almost all statements on academic freedom that are explicit on the matter seek to justify it in terms of the interest of society at large in the free exchange of ideas. The right of the individual is depicted as deriving from the interests of society, rather than as rep-

---

[3] More on this below, under the argument for academic tenure. The data gathered by Byse and Joughin here are not very helpful, for they do not distinguish between institutions having an approved tenure system and those that do not. What they report is that in the sixty-eight institutions surveyed in 1955, 31 percent of the *total faculty* was tenured; 53 percent of the *full time*. It is not clear whether responding institutions counted teaching assistants in calculating total faculty; the questions gave them no directions on this. See Byse and Joughin, *Tenure in American Higher Education*, p. 170.

[4] See the various statements in Joughin, *Academic Freedom and Tenure.*

[5] Again, see the various statements in Joughin, *Academic Freedom and Tenure.*

resenting a natural or human right, the protection of which is morally and legally obligatory regardless of the consequences for society of protecting it. Although I think such an approach pays insufficient attention to the fact that for some individuals freedom of inquiry has such great intrinsic value that, other things being equal, it ought to be respected for just that reason, I am in accord with the frankly utilitarian approach to the justification of principles of individual liberty in general, and to academic freedom in particular. What I find surprising is that those who are unsympathetic toward utilitarianism have apparently permitted this account of academic freedom to go unchallenged. What we all should find disappointing, if not surprising, is that the society in whose name academic freedom has been defended has so often shown so little respect for it. But more on this later.

The claim, then, is that tenure is necessary for academic freedom, which in turn is desirable primarily because of the interest of society at large in the products of this freedom. But given that we have distinguished two senses both of academic freedom and of tenure, there are now in principle four ways to interpret that claim:

1. For the protection of the academic freedom of each member of the academic profession, it is necessary for all members of the academic profession to have the status of tenure.

2. The practice of tenure as we know it, with only some members of the academic profession having the status of tenure at any given time, is necessary for the protection of the academic freedom of each member of the academic profession.

3. For the protection of the general climate of academic freedom, it is necessary for all members of the academic profession to have the status of tenure.

4. The practice of tenure as we know it, with only some members of the academic profession having the status of tenure at any given time, is necessary for the protection of the general climate of academic freedom.

The claim that has been made by proponents of tenure has been, of course, not only that it is *necessary* for the protection of academic freedom, but also that, at least other things being equal,[6] it is *sufficient* as well. But this means that we must also consider:

[6] I shall not try to spell out here what these other things might be.

5. For the protection of the academic freedom of each member of the academic profession, it is sufficient that all members of the academic profession have the status of tenure.

6. The practice of tenure as we know it, with only some members of the academic profession having the status of tenure at any given time, is sufficient for the protection of the academic freedom of each member of the academic profession.

7. For the protection of the general climate of academic freedom, it is sufficient that all members of the academic profession have the status of tenure.

8. The practice of tenure as we know it, with only some members of the academic profession having the status of tenure at any given time, is sufficient for the protection of the general climate of academic freedom.

Claims 5 and 7 seem to me unassailable,[7] but we need not consider them here for the same reason that we need not consider claims 1 and 3. For they are all in terms of each member of the academic profession being given the status of tenure immediately upon initial appointment to an academic position. In an academic world having professional and graduate degree programs quite different than those with which we are familiar, it might be possible to satisfy these terms without depriving educational institutions of adequate opportunity to assess the qualifications of their teachers and scholars prior to making a permanent commitment to them. In the academic world that we know, though, conferring the status of tenure at the time of initial appointment would clearly place totally unacceptable restraints upon most, if not all (possible exceptions being both the best and the worst), educational institutions.

What we must consider in our attempt to interpret the claims made by proponents of academic freedom, then, are claims 2, 4, 6, and 8, which are in terms of the familiar practice of granting the status of tenure to individuals only after a specified probationary period. Before turning to their examination, though, I would like to review briefly some aspects of the tenure system as we know it, with particular attention to the most important of its many admitted disadvantages. Such a discussion will reveal, it is hoped, some of the

[7] This is given the proviso that it is only in conjunction with certain other conditions that they are sufficient for the protection of academic freedom.

things that a tenure system requires to be workable and put us in a better position to evaluate the claims that its proponents have made for it.

TENURE IN PRACTICE

One would like to have some hard data concerning the average member of the academic profession who is eventually awarded tenure at some institution or another with respect to (a) the number of years devoted to full-time teaching prior to tenure being awarded; (b) the number of those years spent at the rank of instructor or above and which thus officially count as part of the probationary period; and (c) the number of years between the granting of tenure and retirement from full-time teaching. One also would like to know something about (d) the number of years the average graduate student devotes to part-time teaching prior to accepting his first full-time position.

Lacking such data, one might surmise that the number of years spent in the official probationary period—(b)—is about six; and that the total sum of years of actual probation—(a) plus (d)—exceeds it by at least a factor of 50 percent. However one cuts it, it is a long time; in all likelihood, probably somewhere around ten full years.

Assuming that the average individual who is granted tenure achieves this status around his mid-thirties, the number of years he will continue to teach prior to retirement—(c)—is probably around thirty or thirty-five years. A *very* long time.

At those institutions where tenure principles have been adopted, two quite different standards have evolved as the basis for determining continued employment. Roughly, but accurately enough: During the probationary period, anything at all is an acceptable ground for nonretention as long as its use does not interfere with the individual's academic freedom or civil liberties. He need not even be informed of such grounds, and they may range from his colleagues finding him unduly abrasive to the belief that an equally well qualified teacher and scholar is available on the market at a lower cost. Once tenured, grounds for dismissal are to be found in only the grossest forms of dereliction of duty; "incompetence" and "irresponsibility" are the terms most frequently employed to describe what the AAUP considers justified grounds for dismissal of a tenured faculty member. And although an individual may, in theory, be dismissed if his position is justifiably abolished, this is the sort of thing that simply almost never occurs. When a department or program is done away with, room is found elsewhere for its tenured members, often by creating new administrative positions that permit their occupants to continue to carry faculty rank. Even today, when many institutions are facing financial pressures that necessitate serious cutbacks, it is the untenured members of the faculty that are the first *and last* to go.

The above is put bluntly and without the customary niceties, for it is meant to remind us of the practice of tenure as it actually exists. I suspect, though, that this characterization will not go unchallenged. Professor Van Alstyne, current chairman of the AAUP's Committee A on Academic Freedom and Tenure, has recently suggested that tenure is consistent with the institutional employer applying a very high standard of professional performance in reaching decisions about the retention of tenured faculty. Van Alstyne's statement is worth quoting at length:

. . . the particular standards of "adequate cause" to which the tenured faculty is accountable are themselves wholly within the prerogative of each university to determine through its own published rules, save only that those rules not be applied in a manner which violates the academic freedom or the ordinary personal civil liberties of the individual. An institution may provide for dismissal for "adequate cause" arising from failure to meet a specified norm of performance or productivity, as well as from specified acts of affirmative misconduct. In short, there is not now and never has been a claim that tenure insulates any faculty member from a fair accounting of his professional responsibilities within the institution which counts upon his service.[8]

In theory, Professor Van Alstyne is, of course, correct. There are surely no legal obstacles to an institution and a faculty member reaching a contractual agreement that defines "adequate cause" so as to demand continued high performance from the employee. Indeed, I suppose a given individual could accept a tenured position with the contractual stipulation that *for him* "adequate cause" for dismissal would include failure to win a Nobel Prize at least once a decade, failure to demonstrate "competency" by publishing at least

[8] William Van Alstyne, "Tenure: A Summary, Explanation, and 'Defense,'" *AAUP Bulletin* 57 (1971): 328.

one journal article or book a month, or failure to fulfill his "responsibility" to teach his students in an amusing and untaxing way (as determined by student evaluations, say) while at the same time assuring their competency in a very difficult subject (as determined by objective tests administered by the administration).

I actually believe that Professor Van Alstyne is on the way to redefining tenure in a way that bears little relationship to current practice. Indeed, I think he may be right in doing so, and I shall turn later to a more serious discussion of his views. For the present, though, I think it important to keep our attention focused on the tenure system as it is and has been understood and practiced. A quotation from the "Report of the University of Utah Commission to Study Tenure," which appeared in the same issue of the *AAUP Bulletin* as did Professor Van Alstyne's paper, might serve to bring us back to a more realistic perspective: "Incompetence, indolence, intellectual dishonesty, serious moral dereliction, arbitrary and capricious disregard of appropriate standards of professional conduct—these and other grounds are fully recognized as 'adequate cause' for dismissal or other disciplinary sanctions against faculty members."[9] The language, I believe, speaks for itself.

The dual standard of conduct for the faculty members of those institutions that have a tenure system is the chief source of most of the disadvantages of the tenure system. Fritz Machlup was quite frank in acknowledging them,[10] but I think it important to review them here, if only because many of them take on an added significance during a period of financial crunch of the sort that we are now experiencing and are likely to continue to experience into the foreseeable future. Indeed, one wonders whether Machlup would have been so free in admitting the high price paid for tenure had he been writing in 1971 instead of 1964—the middle of a decade of unparalleled expansion and financial growth for educational institutions.

For many *individuals*, the probationary period has been nothing less than a brutalizing, dehumanizing, and discouraging experience. Especially in those universities that put a high premium on productive research, good young scholars have been forced to compete with

[9] "Report of the University of Utah Commission to Study Tenure," *AAUP Bulletin* 57 (1971): 422.

[10] Machlup, "In Defense of Academic Tenure," pp. 312–326.

their junior colleagues for the favoritism of the senior members of their departments with an eye to the inevitable tenure decision, a decision often made de facto at the time of the first or second renewal of an initial appointment. The extent to which such decisions have been arbitrary, uninformed, or otherwise unjust is difficult to estimate, but it is not only those who have come out with the short end of the stick that would in all candor admit that it is considerable. The department that hires twice as many first-rate individuals as it can keep is of course only one extreme; the department that with the support of an equally softhearted or incompetent administration tends to renew all initial appointments automatically, and eventually to grant tenure to anyone who stays around long enough and teaches his classes, is another. If too much competition is bad for at least some individuals, too little is equally undesirable for many others who, with a little healthy pressure, might have developed into better teachers or scholars than they do in an environment that exposes them to almost no critical standards. Now, I do not wish to claim that unduly harsh or overly lax critical assessments, or simply arbitrary and unreasonable ones whatever the standards, are the product of a tenure system. But they are clearly effects that the practice of tenure magnifies.

The way in which tenure magnifies the likelihood of such otherwise unjustified retention decisions is evident in the present very tight academic job market. It is a buyer's rather than a seller's market, and the department or institution that is out to upgrade itself faces a great temptation to adopt a revolving-door policy for its junior faculty. The individual who is unceremoniously dumped after three or five years is thrown onto a job market glutted by new Ph.D.'s and others in a position similar to his own. Whereas he might have gone from a first-rate graduate school to an equally prestigious department, he may now find himself forced to take a big step downward on the academic ladder in order to avoid unemployment. Others will find themselves dumped on the market after five or six years of more than satisfactory service at an institution just because the administration of the institution wants to cut down the proportion of tenured faculty in the light of an unstable and uncertain financial condition. Regardless of what AAUP principles say about financial exigence, the institution feels that it must either violate tenure principles (by keeping such individuals on without granting them tenure) or risk financial disaster, either by being overburdened with a relatively high paid tenured faculty that it cannot get rid of or by the lawsuits it fears would follow if it should at a later date try to cut tenured faculty. On the other extreme, knowing that nonrenewal of a junior faculty member will throw him onto such a market, some departments will be most tenderhearted, retaining, and eventually granting tenure to, someone whom (for his own sake as well as theirs) they would not otherwise have kept beyond an initial appointment.

There is another class of individuals who are hurt by the tenure system, one which is growing increasingly visible, and will continue to do so until cutbacks in graduate school enrollments take an effect. Those who are entering the academic market place for the first time are finding difficulties (an understatement for the plight of a well-trained Ph.D. who winds up driving a taxicab) that would not be as severe but for the fact that some out of a finite number of academic positions are occupied by incompetents protected by tenure. Again, I would not want to blow this consideration out of reasonable proportion, but there *is* a good deal of deadwood (see below), and it is *costly*. The removal of the incompetent, and the putting of some on less than full-time status in a manner reflecting whatever competencies they retained, would free a lot of money for the hiring of those younger members of the profession who are in search of employment.

To the institutions that have adopted tenure, and thus to the society they serve, the biggest problem clearly is that of so-called deadwood. This is perhaps an unfortunately broad term, and the pejorative connotations of it make the whole issue difficult to discuss in a fairly cool and objective manner. But those of us who have spent some years as academics (including student years) must admit that we have encountered quite a large number of individuals who are neither passably competent teachers nor scholars, although they continue to be paid as either or both. This is not to say that they might not at one time have been such; merely that they are no longer so, and thus that they are of no real service (if they are not a positive disservice) to their institutions, students, and colleagues. Where such individuals are in large number at a given institution, it is a good sign that recruitment and retention practices have over a period of time been less than desirable and that to some considerable degree incompetents have been engaged in the familiar practice of selecting their own kind. The barrier that a tenure system puts in the way of rapid institutional or departmental upgrading has been often noted. Today's buyer's market only increases the frustration for those seriously concerned with the improvement of educational quality.

The reply to this has typically been to acknowledge the existence of deadwood (and usually to underestimate it) but to pin the blame on the use of lax appointment and retention policies, rather than the tenure system. The lengthy probationary period that tenure demands is justified, it is claimed, because it gives the institution the *opportunity* to demand demonstrated competence before it makes the heavy commitment involved in a tenure decision. If an institution fails to avail itself of this opportunity and gives tenure to those who have not proven their worth, it has only itself to thank if it should later decide that it is burdened with an incompetent faculty. Indeed, it has been argued that a tenure system helps assure faculty quality by giving those with the responsibility good reason to take extreme care in making tenure decisions.[11]

Now, there is some truth in all this, especially where one has in mind a pattern of competency (or lack thereof) throughout an entire institution. But the reply is nonetheless far from fully adequate, for it seems to assume that an individual who has demonstrated his *ability* at the age of thirty or thirty-five, say, will both *retain* and *continue* to exercise it for the next thirty-five years or so. But this is simply absurd. For a great variety of reasons, an individual may lose his abilities as a scholar and teacher or else, while retaining them, fail to exercise them. Particularly given the demanding nature of serious teaching and scholarship, the latter especially calling for continued study and effort by which the former must be informed if it is to be really excellent, competency at one point in time is simply not a very reliable index to performance decades into the future. This is especially so where the granting of tenure removes the important motivational factor provided at least for some by a certain degree of competitive job insecurity.

The final chief disadvantage of tenure exists for all members of the academic *profession* and has to do with the security factor men-

[11] Ibid., pp. 313–314.

tioned above. It seems safe to assume that tenure is regarded as a fringe benefit by many who are attracted to the academic profession at least in part for broadly economic reasons. As Fritz Machlup noted, any marginal increase in the supply of academics created by the attraction of this fringe benefit of job security will depress the demand for academics, and thus their average salaries.[12] It also seems reasonable to suggest that the institutional disadvantages of tenure noted above are costs that are also borne at least in part by all members of the profession in terms of lower salaries.

Tenure, then, does have a number of quite serious disadvantages, most of which seem to be rooted in the dual standard of professional competence upon which it is based. What, then, has been said in defense of such a costly practice?

THE ARGUMENT FOR ACADEMIC TENURE

The claim that tenure is necessary for the protection of academic freedom may, as we saw in the first section, be interpreted in a number of ways. But in any sense that has to do with the practice of tenure as we know it, the claim, and the related claim that it is sufficient as well as necessary, is certainly not *obviously* true. As I began to read about the subject, I thus became increasingly uneasy at continually encountering the assertion without any accompanying argument for it. Optimistically, I thought at first that someone, somewhere—perhaps John Dewey in 1915—had given the knockdown argument for it, an argument of which everyone but I was aware. Certainly the tone of much that is written about tenure suggests that anyone who would dare question it today has in some way been remiss. To cite Professor Van Alstyne once again, his initial reaction to recent criticisms of tenure is: "Older members of the profession may well be inclined to shrug off these critical suggestions, having heard them more than once before and remembering the careful answers that ably replied to them. (It is in fact quite true that the issue has been joined many times, i.e., that the concept of tenure has never been allowed to pass unexamined, simply as part of the conventional wisdom.)"[13]

With all due respect, I must admit that I have not yet found an adequate defense of the claim that tenure is necessary (and suf-

[12] Ibid., pp. 325–326.
[13] Van Alstyne, "Tenure: A Summary, Explanation, and 'Defense,'" p. 328.

ficient) for the protection of academic freedom. Indeed, I have found little by way of argument at all. I have read Byse and Joughin's *Tenure in American Higher Education* from cover to cover, but all I find by way of a defense of the claim in question is this: "The principal justification for academic tenure is that it enables a faculty member to teach, study, and act free from a large number of restraints and pressures which otherwise would inhibit independent thought and action."[14] The 1969 Handbook of the AAUP, *Academic Freedom and Tenure*, contains many assertions to the effect that tenure is necessary for academic freedom. The only semblance of an argument it contains is found in Fritz Machlup's "In Defense of Academic Tenure." Let me quote at some length from the relevant section ("Tenure as an instrument of freedom"):

> I have heard it argued that permanent tenure is not an indispensable instrument for the guarantee of academic freedom; that freedom can be safeguarded without tenure rules.
>
> This argument is valid under two conditions: First, that all governing boards and administrators of institutions of higher education believe so strongly in academic freedom that every charge of abuse, and every suspicion of abuse, would inspire them with such a zeal to protect the offender that they would rather see the institution which they govern or administer impoverished or destroyed than allow the offender to be removed from his post. Second, that it is always possible to distinguish offenses that come under the heading of abuse of academic freedom from all other reasons for dispensing with the services of a teacher or scholar.
>
> Neither of these two conditions is satisfied. The difficulty of distinguishing between different reasons for "noncontinuance" is well attested to by the experience with nonrenewals of contracts of nontenured teachers. It is rarely possible to prove that the decision not to renew a contract was influenced, let alone determined, by some offensive or embarrassing publications or utterances of the teacher concerned. As a matter of fact, the persons who make the decision may themselves not know what motivates them: do they judge him to be a poor teacher, do they dislike him as a person, or do they dislike what he wrote or said? It is probably unavoidable that ineffectiveness in teaching and lack of scholarly publications are so readily noticed in a faculty member who has taken liberties and thereby embarrassed his institution; the same defects may go unnoticed in a pleasant chap who conforms and gets along well with everybody.
>
> To say that the first condition is not "realistic" would be the biggest

[14] Byse and Joughin, *Tenure in American Higher Education*, p. 2.

understatement of the year. Without strict tenure rules, the governing boards and administrative officers of the majority of colleges and universities could not succeed in protecting a faculty member accused of having abused his freedom. Many of us can, without long deliberation, recite a list of names of well-known scholars whose survival on the faculty of their institution has been possible only thanks to the rules of tenure. The president of the institution can say to those clamoring for the dismissal of the presumed public enemy: "I am sorry, much as I should like to get rid of Professor X, we cannot do it, for he has permanent tenure."[15]

You will recall that the first section left us with four possible claims that could be made for the *practice* of tenure: (2) that it is necessary for the protection of the academic freedom of each member of the academic profession, (4) that it is necessary for the protection of the general climate of academic freedom, (6) that it is sufficient for the protection of the academic freedom of each member of the academic profession, and (8) that it is sufficient for the protection of the general climate of academic freedom.

How, in these terms, are we to understand the argument presented by Machlup? His claim seems to be that the individual can only be insulated from bad motives and overt repression by having the *status* of tenure, obviously in terms of a standard of conduct minimal enough to prevent in most cases bad motives from disguising themselves from what are in principle acceptable reasons in terms of "adequate cause." But if that is the argument, it seems to lead to our original positions: For the protection of the academic freedom of each member of the academic profession, it is (1) necessary and (5) sufficient that all members of the academic profession have the status of tenure. Now this, the conjunction of claims 1 and 5, is clearly incompatible with claim 6, and thus in effect renders claim 2 irrelevant. The question must therefore be whether or not the conjunction of and argument for positions 1 and 5 are compatible with positions 4, the practice of tenure as we know it, with only some members of the academic profession having the status of tenure at any given time, is necessary, and 8, sufficient for the protection of the general climate of academic freedom.

Now, there seem to me only two ways in which one could interpret Machlup's argument so as to give the desired result. First, it might be said that the general climate of academic freedom that society

[15] Machlup, "In Defense of Academic Tenure," pp. 329–330.

has an interest in fostering only demands that *some* academics have their freedom protected. This would be like saying, quite correctly, that a region may have a fine climate if *enough* of its days are temperate, it gets *enough* rain, typically has low humidity, and so forth. All this is of course quite consistent with some days being as dark and nasty as you like. Those who have spoken of the "chilling effect" of attacks upon academic freedom and other individual liberties seem to have rejected this analogy, and I believe rightly so. Freedoms of speech, association, religion, and so forth do not produce socially desirable climates of freedom unless they are realities for all relevant individuals and groups. Likewise with academic freedom. One need only consider the following:

1. The proportion of tenured faculty at an institution having a tenure system may be only 40 or 50 percent of full-time faculty—seldom, I imagine, over 65 percent.

2. A substantial proportion of the academic community where it is deemed desirable that a climate of freedom prevail is composed of students and part-time faculty, two groups about which the AAUP has until recently shown very little concern.[16]

3. If the status of tenure is necessary for the protection of an individual's academic freedom, those who have it at any given time will be the ones who have been vulnerable during a prior lengthy probationary period providing ample opportunity to weed out mavericks and create habits of timidity among the rest.[17]

Surely, if the status of tenure is necessary for the protection of an individual's academic freedom, only some senior full-time faculty members being tenured is not sufficient to create or sustain a climate of freedom of inquiry and association in an academic community.

The second interpretation might be dubbed the "umbrella argument." If the tenured members of a faculty are and feel themselves free from intimidation, and if it is they in whose hands are placed the decisions about the retention of nontenured faculty and the ex-

[16] Machlup writes, ibid., p. 334: ". . . one cannot expect tenure status to be conferred on part-time teachers." Why not? On students, see the "Essay" by Walter Metzger in *Freedom and Order in the University*, ed. Samuel Gorovitz (Cleveland: Press of Western Reserve University, 1967), especially pp. 60–62.

[17] Machlup, "In Defense of Academic Tenure," p. 336.

pulsion of students, then the tenured can be relied upon to provide adequate protection for all. Only some will have the umbrellas, but a satisfactory (dry) climate is assured because those without umbrellas will find refuge in times of trouble under those of others.

This argument is not without merit, and it finds some recognition in standard academic practice. One feels that there is some such rationale lying behind the traditional practice of having tenured faculty serve on tenure committees, student conduct boards, and so forth. As the University of Utah Tenure Commission wrote, "the designation of tenured faculty members to serve on the faculty review committee provides a measure of protection against 'command influence' or other improper pressures."[18]

A *measure* of protection, yes. Adequate protection, no. Leaving aside the difficulty raised here by claim 3 above, this argument totally ignores the fact that threats to academic freedom may come equally well from within the academic community as from without. Although the average member of an academic community may be more politically tolerant than his counterpart in the nonacademic world, many of those who come under fire for their expression of unpopular political views find little sympathy among their colleagues. Given the argument (Machlup's) that bad motives may be concealed under the guise of reasonable principles, such a system of benevolent protection offers little security to the potential expresser of unpopular political opinions. And what about the individual who would be exorcised for the expression of heretical *academic* opinions. Or the young and vigorous teacher and scholar who fails to show sufficient respect for, and represents a serious challenge to, his or her tenured (and perhaps incompetent) senior colleagues?

The "umbrella argument," I therefore conclude, is no better than the argument previously considered, which contends that a climate of freedom may be preserved in the academic community even though it be admitted that only a minority of its members enjoy individual academic freedom.

The academic-freedom defense for tenure thus creates a genuine dilemma, for if the status of tenure is necessary for the protection of an individual's academic freedom, the practice of granting tenure only after a lengthy probationary period, which leads to only some

---

[18] Utah Commission, "Report," p. 423.

members of the academic community having tenure at any given time, clearly cannot be sufficient to protect the desired climate of academic freedom.

It is no way out of this dilemma, we have seen, to suggest that tenure might be granted to all upon initial appointment. Being as those who have tenure are held to only a minimal standard of competence, institutions must be able to employ a much more severe standard during the probationary period. Any suggestion that they might do otherwise would surely be met with dismay and outrage by administrators. Indeed, in the context of its report on the Angela Davis case, the investigating committee spoke of "the AAUP principle of equal standards of academic freedom and responsibility for all faculty members," which drew the following reaction from UCLA President Charles Hitch: "I am disturbed by what appears to me to be the view in the AAUP report that, if something in an appointee's record is not good cause for a dismissal, it cannot be a sufficient reason for nonreappointment. Unless a distinction is maintained between these two things, the whole concept of probationary appointments, as distinguished from tenure appointments, is in grave danger, and the consequences for an institution's ability to build a high quality faculty through screening and selective retention are most serious."[19]

ACADEMIC FREEDOM WITHOUT TENURE

It must of course be admitted that tenure, for those who have it, does provide some measure of protection for academic freedom. But being as it fails to protect those without it, the chief justification for it—that it provides protection for a general climate of academic freedom—fails as well. Given its other obvious and oft acknowledged disadvantages, one would hope that a workable and less costly alternative to it could be found. To continue to tinker around with the idea of in some way extending it to all upon initial appointment strikes me as a waste of time. But it does suggest what may be a fruitful line of approach, the notion of a common standard of continued employment for all, applied in such a way as to avoid the disadvantages of the present tenure system or the

[19] Charles Hitch, "Report of Committee A on the Angela Davis Case," *AAUP Bulletin* 57 (1971): 404, note 14. Hitch is commenting on paragraph 6 of the committee's conclusions.

even greater disadvantages of an extended one (which no sane academic administration would buy anyway). Might something of this sort be sufficient to provide an adequate degree of protection for academic freedom?

Two recent discussions of tenure, that of Professor Van Alstyne and the Utah Commission, come very close to providing an affirmative answer. For both discussions seek to ignore the fact that tenure is based on a dual standard of professional conduct and rather identify its salient features as (*a*) the provision of academic due process in cases where dismissal is disputed, with (*b*) the employer having to take the initiative to terminate the employment relation, and where (*c*) the burden of proof is upon the employer to show that "adequate cause" for dismissal exists.

Now the Utah Commission, as we saw earlier, understands the minimal standard used under the present tenure system, but much of its discussion focuses on just how crucial the burden-of-proof feature is. "The essential core of these [institutional dismissal] procedures," they write, "consists of the imposition upon the University of the burden of establishing to the satisfaction of a faculty committee the existence of adequate academic grounds for dismissal of tenured faculty members."[20] Their argument even suggests that the shifting of the burden of proof provides adequate protection of the individual's academic freedom as long as the standard used is a reasonable one, no matter how stringent. "Under the tenure system, where the burden of proof is squarely upon the administration, weak evidentiary support for charges of academic incompetence inferentially suggest the existence of unstated, and impermissible, grounds for the proposed dismissal.[21]

Professor Van Alstyne's discussion is the most interesting of all, for, as we saw earlier, he claims that "adequate cause" may involve as high a standard of conduct as one likes as long as it does not involve a denial of academic freedom. My reservations about his use of the word *tenure* aside, it turns out that, in spite of my frequent barbs at Professor Van Alstyne throughout this paper, I believe we are in substantial agreement. He, too, has noted that the academic-freedom defense of tenure is in grave difficulty; it

[20] Utah Commission, "Report," p. 429.
[21] Ibid., pp. 429–430.

"proves," as he puts it, "too much or too little: . . . if it is claimed that all members of a faculty are equally entitled to the free exercise of academic freedom, then it must be acknowledged either that tenure is not truly regarded as indispensable to the protection of that freedom or, if it is regarded as indispensable, that it must be provided for all alike."[22] His paper concludes with the comment that "the debate may rest . . . not on *whether* tenure, with its assurances of full academic due process, should exist at all, but rather on *when* it should appropriately be conferred!"[23] Why does he let it rest here, rather than reaching the conclusion that tenure (i.e., full academic due process with the burden of proof and the initiation of dismissal proceedings upon the employer) is demanded for all by the claim that it is necessary for the protection of academic freedom?

He gives what seems to me to be five separate reasons for pulling back from what would appear to be the inevitable conclusion:

1. The nontenured are given some protection and are entitled to full academic due process, but the burden of proof is upon them to show that their academic freedom has been violated or that the decision not to retain them was not made in a fair and informed manner.

Comment: He admits that this is not enough protection.

2. Those with long service are entitled to the added protections that tenure provides because their dismissal would typically represent greater hardship to them than would the nonrenewal of younger men with shorter periods of service.

Comment: This has nothing to do with academic freedom and is not responsive to the claim that the defense of tenure generates a dilemma. It is also a dubious empirical claim.

3. "To the extent that dismissal is more portentous than nonrenewal, the chilling effect on the individual's exercise of academic freedom may itself also be greater."[24]

Comment: This point is frequently made but is no defense of tenure if it is tenure itself that makes the distinction between nonrenewal and dismissal a significant one.

[22] Van Alstyne, "Tenure: A Summary, Explanation, and 'Defense,'" p. 332.
[23] Ibid., p. 333.
[24] Ibid.

4. "There is simply no basis to hold that the fact of one's first or second short-term appointment in teaching necessarily manifests an institutional presumption of excellence, which it would thereafter be the burden of the institution to overthrow when contemplating nonrenewal at the end of the term."[25]

Comment: This is inconsistent with Professor Van Alstyne's notion of tenure and the notion of adequate cause it may operate in terms of.

5. Where it is proposed that someone be dismissed whose service has been found satisfactory over a lengthy period of time, there is *more* ground for suspicion that bad motives are in operation than in the case of a younger man who has had a briefer association with the institution.

Comment: This appeals largely because it reflects current tenure practices. The grounds for suspicion are great enough in any case to justify making the institution carry the burden of proof in terms of the appropriate standard *should the individual wish to challenge.* (See below for elaboration on this qualifier.)

In short, I find no justification for Professor Van Alstyne's reluctance to accept the conclusion to which his (and my) argument seems to lead. But I suspect that he will have the reluctance until he is willing to abandon the description of the sort of *alternative to tenure* we are discussing *as tenure.*

Although it would take another paper—that I surely am not well enough informed to write—to elaborate upon it, let me sketch more fully what this alternative to tenure might be.

1. To the extent to which academic freedom is the assurance of the civil liberties of academics in their academic communities, more reliance must be placed upon the courts and legislatures. No one should be subject to dismissal on grounds extraneous to the nature of his employment, and where constitutional protections are not adequate, fair employment practices legislation and so forth ought to be fought for where such legislation does not already exist. Rather than claiming special privileges of the sort that present tenure practices rightly strike laymen as conferring, academics should join cause with others in fighting for the civil liberties that

[25] Ibid.

all ought to enjoy. If they would do so, perhaps they would have less to fear by way of attacks on their freedom from those outside the academic community.

2. Different institutions have different needs, especially with respect to differential emphasis upon teaching and research. Even within the same institution, quite different understandings may quite properly exist with respect to the terms of continued employment. Each individual contract of employment ought to spell out the terms of employment (in a way, of course, that does not infringe upon the employee's academic freedom). It ought also to indicate the conditions under which the contract will be renewed. The individualization of contracts that this would demand would surely be manageable and would force an institution to make clear to someone on an initial appointment just what was expected of him.

Although there is much loose talk of the "unknown quantity" that someone on an initial appointment represents, it should not be forgotten that someone with a Ph.D. is likely to have an educational record dating back some twenty to twenty-five years. Unknown quantities represent the kind of shoddy recruiting practices that the present tenure system encourages. An individual's potential as a teacher can be fairly well gauged in a year, if anyone really cares to investigate the matter. Thus, although an initial appointment of two years on fairly stringent terms might be fully justified, first renewal should perhaps be for five years in the normal case, with a second renewal for an even longer period.

3. Within the terms of the contract, and with the exception perhaps of initial renewal, renewal should be automatic unless the institution gives at least a full year's notice in writing, at which time it ought to specify the contractual grounds for nonrenewal.

4. If the individual who receives a notice of nonrenewal or dismissal wishes to challenge the grounds for nonretention, he is entitled to do so.

5. There should be an assurance of full academic due process.

6. The burden of proof to justify nonrenewal or dismissal within the terms of the contract should be upon the institution.

The assumption I am making here (along with the Utah Commission and Van Alstyne, *I think*) is that this is sufficient to provide adequate protection against bad motives concealing themselves in terms of good reasons. The criminal law, as I understand it, is viewed as having sufficient deterrent effect in spite of the fact that it deals with the notion of intent rather than motive and even though it permits of certain excusing and mitigating conditions that can be shammed.

7. Other protections could be added here, if they do not already exist. Uniform application of standards of professional conduct is important, and whether or not Jones's contract calls for "substantial contributions to the literature," his failure to publish more than one book review a year is not adequate cause for his dismissal unless the same standard is also being applied to his colleagues (where it is applicable) who are publishing nothing. Although an attempt to terminate the employment of one with long service may not be grounds for suspicion that an infringement of academic freedom is in the offing, choosing to apply to only one or a few a standard of professional conduct that applies to many surely is. The difficulties here, it seems to me, stem in large part from the nature of the present tenure system, where attempts to seriously review and perhaps terminate the status of those with long service are very rare. Were periodic and serious review of the qualifications and contributions of all faculty members standing institutional practice, there would be far less opportunity for infringements of academic freedom through the selective enforcement of standards of professional competence.

8. Where a dispute exists concerning the legitimacy of the grounds for nonretention, the faculty member is deemed to have the right to have the dispute adjudicated (if it comes to that and cannot be mediated in a less formal manner to the satisfaction of the parties) by a group of his *peers*. AAUP principles seem to me to have been overly insensitive to the need for making distinctions among possible peer groups, depending upon the nature of the putative grounds for nonrenewal or dismissal and contingent upon who it is that is calling for termination of the employment relation. In some cases, for instance, it would seem that an individual could only be assured a fair hearing from a group of fellow academics from without his institution. Something like an expanded version of the legal notion of change of venue is needed here.

There are two criticisms of such an alternative to tenure that are likely to be made on grounds quite directly related to considerations of academic freedom, and I should like to anticipate and attempt to answer them here.

First, there is the concern expressed in the Utah Commission report about the advisability of nontenured faculty being charged with the periodic review of contracts. Although they were discussing an alternative to tenure somewhat different than that proposed here, the point is surely relevant, not only with respect to initial decisions concerning renewal, but also with regard to peer-group adjudication of disputes over nonrenewal.

If all of the faculty were equally nontenured, as the proposal contemplates, those engaged in making retention (i.e., contract renewal) judgments would have a substantial conflict of interest, since they would be exposed to like review within a short period of time, possibly by the very persons whom they are currently reviewing. The inherent propensity of such a system to be tolerant of incompetents seems far greater than that of the present tenure system, under which faculty members who have achieved tenure and whose own economic security is thus not in jeopardy, are in a position to evaluate their colleagues according to objective professional standards.[26]

Under the alternative system sketched in this paper, it is clear that at any point in time a considerable proportion of the faculty would be under quite long-term contracts because of their demonstrated competency—many of them recently "recertified" and thus not facing renewal for a number of years. Those who felt that their security was due to their demonstrated abilities and who were confident that they would retain and perhaps improve upon those abilities, would, it is hoped, be inclined to make impartial and honest judgments of their colleagues. There are, in other words, grounds for arguing that the results would be just the opposite suggested by the Utah Commission.

Second, it might be claimed that the proposed system would encourage that proverbial "flood of litigation" against which all systems of adjudication must guard. Junior faculty members dismissed for adequate cause, but in a position to put the burden of proving that they had been upon institutional spokesmen within a formal adversary setting, could bring the system to a grinding halt by challenging justified nonrenewals. The incompetents who would

[26] Utah Commission, "Report," p. 430.

otherwise quietly leave would be encouraged by the proposed system to fight for their job security, especially in a tight academic market, by crying arbitrary treatment, uninformed judgment, or violation of academic freedom at every turn.

I find this parade of horrors unconvincing. Adjudication of disputes under clearly stated standards of competency (which we do not now have in most institutions) is a far cry from such things as jury determination of elusive physical injury claims in automobile accident cases. Even with the burden of proof upon the institution, an individual is risking a great deal when he lays down the gauntlet and challenges his employer to *prove* that there has been adequate cause for his nonretention. If he loses and seeks employment elsewhere, he will find himself at a real disadvantage.

If developed along the lines indicated above, it seems to me that an alternative to current tenure practices is not only possible, but also necessary and desirable. It is necessary to protect the academic freedom of those who cannot be protected (the untenured) by the present tenure system with its dual standard of competency. Not only would it protect the academic freedom of those who are tenured under the present system, but also it would have the desirable feature of no longer necessarily providing a shelter for the incompetent. It would avoid or sharply mitigate the other disadvantages of the present tenure system by abolishing the dual standard of professional conduct that, as we saw in the second section, generates them. In so far as tenure practices are grounded in considerations of academic freedom, such an alternative seems defensible in a way in which tenure, in spite of the claims that have been made for it, clearly is not. There might be other reasons for retaining tenure and rejecting the proposed alternative; I doubt this, but I am at least quite confident that, should they exist, they will have little to do with considerations of academic freedom.

REDEFINING TENURE

I think, and certainly hope, that Professor Van Alstyne will agree with my substantive proposals concerning "job protection" (to use a neutral term) and academic freedom. The real difference between us seems to be that whereas he is inclined to claim that he is speaking about tenure as it is, only "accurately and unequivocally defined,"[27] I have urged that what we are really talking about is the abolition of the tenure system in favor of a more desirable alternative. Is this anything more than a verbal squabble between us? I believe so.

None of us would like to see the years of effort expended by the AAUP and others go to nought. None of us would wish to risk sacrificing what protection tenure admittedly does provide by urging its abolition without being assured that at least as adequate an alternative would immediately take its place.

But Van Alstyne's implicit suggestion that what is needed is an extension of tenure to all at an early date surely will not do. For his notion of "adequate cause" is not the one reflected in current practice, and no suggestion of a universal tenure system could possibly get a fair hearing for just this reason. Such a system would be instantaneously prejudged as proposing that institutions be deprived of the opportunity to impose any sort of quality controls upon the selection of their own faculty beyond the stage of initial recruitment. Just consider what President Hitch's reaction would be (see quote and footnote 19 above). By suggesting that academic freedom may demand tenure for all, Van Alstyne would make it practically certain that the important reforms for which his paper points out the need would meet with the strongest conceivable resistance.

But to go to the opposite extreme of urging that tenure be abandoned would be to court a reaction that would be equally disastrous. Some administrators, putative friends as well as avowed enemies of academic freedom, might be too quick to conclude that it had finally been admitted that tenure was merely a shield for the selfish claims of the incompetent and that the suggested alternative system would not be nearly as efficient as a benevolent (and of course well-intentioned) administrative despotism.

Although it may be unlikely that the needed reforms will be brought about under the banner of tenure extended to all, it is equally unlikely that much good would be done by telling administrators, regents, trustees, and the likes of Governor Ronald Reagan and his constituents that we have now, after defending it

[27] Van Alstyne, "Tenure: A Summary, Explanation, and 'Defense,' " p. 328.

since 1915, decided that tenure is indefensible, either in general or in particular, as a protection of academic freedom.

It seems to me, though, that from *this* dilemma there is a way out. Let us perhaps speak of a "redefinition" of tenure, one more in accord with the growing realization that the rights of the un-tenured must be fully protected to assure a climate of academic freedom. And let us encourage the sort of arrangements for the untenured suggested above, using as a bargaining wedge the encouragement of higher standards of competence for all. In time, one might hope that a really new practice might gradually emerge, one that provided genuine protection for the academic freedom of all, while avoiding the disadvantages (for all) of the present tenure system.

Before plunging into attempts at reform, though, let us be sure that we have given the right answers to these questions: Is tenure as we know it neither necessary nor sufficient for the protection of academic freedom? If it is not, with what is it to be replaced; or, if you prefer, how is it to be redefined? Although I am less than confident that I have given fully satisfactory answers to either of these questions in the present paper, I do believe that I have presented sufficient evidence for concluding that they must be taken much more seriously than they usually are.

11. Tenure and Academic Freedom

BY ALEXANDER RITCHIE

I first agreed to be a respondent to Sartorius's paper before I had read it, basing my acceptance on a keen interest in the issues associated with the titular components and a fairly wide experience both of arguments that included them as topics and in managing a university's affairs in contexts in which tenure and academic freedom were key concerns. My first reaction to reading it, and other papers, was that I would find it easier to respond after other papers had been discussed and it had become clearer to me precisely what most at least of those present understood by "academic freedom." While on the face of it academic freedom is academic freedom, identical wherever it is found and discussed, and tenure is tenure, it seemed to me that discussion of the terms *simpliciter*, here as in Australia, tends to be at key points nebulous, and at other points uncertain, and at many points much discussion is certainly not common to both localities.

I suspected, too, that differences between conditions and institutions are in fact very relevant to this Conference, since a general term must be cashable in particulars, and I contemplated sketching out the conditions familiar to me so that differences and identities could be mirrored in the contrast, myself being able to pick up the mirroring as discussion proceeded. I decided against that as the pages mounted in number, and I got no closer to the detail of the paper.

I thereupon decided to do things the hard way and discover something of the requisite detail of the American situation for myself. So I spent some days immersed in the Joughin *Handbook*,[1] the Muscatine *Report*,[2] and a string of volumes of the *AAUP Bulletin*. Doubtless all of you are ahead of me in this detail, as you are in terms of knowledge of the detail and procedure in your own and other American institutions. All that I can be sure of, at the moment, is that there is an enormous variety of types of institution in this or these United States, in a variety of situations in relation to structure, aims, and sociopolitical setting, with varying types of de facto and de jure tenure conditions, with varying histories of how the structure and type of tenure was achieved, and that in some sense the actual differences and their history must be grasped if the discussion of actual relationships between academic freedom and tenure are to be intelligibly discussed.

The importance of the social, political, and historical background in making discussions of academic freedom intelligible can be illustrated, first, by a look at a foreign university. Consider, then, Mario Bunge's "The Argentine University: A Defense." Bunge was commenting on a 1960 article in the *Bulletin* by Samuel Shapiro,[3] which Bunge charges

draws an exaggeratedly gloomy picture of the Argentine university. . . . What is worse, the article overlooks the most important thing, which is not so much the present poor condition as the promising trend of Argentine higher education. One cannot forecast the evolution of a system on its initial conditions alone; its laws of development must be considered also. . . . the universities are in full growth, despite being under heavy fire by the armed forces, the Catholic church, the Ministry of Education, "nationalist" groups, and even some foreign press organs. . . . The continued growth of the Argentine university will need the help of foreign scientists, humanists, the technicians, as well as the support of foundations. But this help will be refused if people are misled by inaccurate and adverse infor-

[1] Louis Joughin, ed., *Academic Freedom and Tenure. A Handbook of the American Association of University Professors* (Madison: University of Wisconsin Press, 1969).

[2] C. Muscatine, chairman, *Education at Berkeley. Report of the Select Committee on Education* (Berkeley: University of California Press, 1966).

[3] Samuel Shapiro, "The Argentine University," *AAUP Bulletin* 46 (Winter 1960): 373–376.

mation. That is why I find it necessary to correct some inaccuracies in Professor Shapiro's article.[4]

At risk of boring you with familiar detail, let me extract the main claims of inaccuracy for what they reveal of the condition of the university.

First, it is not true that the 1955 revolution, which ousted Perón, expelled from the universities many able teachers, and that "the mere fact of having been appointed or retained by Perón was generally considered enough to warrant dismissal." Those who remained at the University after a certain moment—roughly 1953—did so upon joining the Peronist party and signing one or more manifestoes of abject and usually insincere allegiance to the dictatorship, thereby setting a regrettable moral example for their students. Yet, unless they had acted as active instruments of the regime and taken part in the persecution of anti-Peronists, they were retained after the revolution. Among those who stayed are some former deans and counselors, and a philosophy teacher who had proclaimed *ex cathedra* that Perón was the greatest philosopher of our era.

Second, the new regime did not suspend competitions for the professorships but, on the contrary, declared the previous appointments invalid because most of them had been marred by academic fraud and political pressures. New competitions were opened for all chairs, some a few months after the revolution. In this way most of the moral delinquents (unfortunately not all of them) were eliminated on purely technical grounds (i.e., because of lack of qualification) and an opportunity was given to teachers and investigators who had been doing odd jobs or had emigrated. Some of the latter, who had obtained secure positions in the United States and elsewhere, were persuaded to return to their country. As to the collaborationists, they found a place in the Catholic University. To maintain that competitions were suspended after the revolution is as insulting as it is inaccurate. On the other hand, it is true that during the brief *interregno* many incompetent anti-Peronists replaced equally incompetent Peronists; it is also true that some chairs were given on the basis of one or two original papers only. But such cases do not constitute a majority, and people are becoming more and more aware of the necessity of valuing competence above everything else.[5]

I cannot, of course, vouch for the accuracy of the corrections,

---

[4] Mario Bunge, "The Argentine University: A Defense," *AAUP Bulletin* 47 (Spring 1961): 53–55.

[5] Ibid., p. 53.

but I have no reason to doubt them, and have no reason at all to believe that the sort of conditions asserted to hold are not possible conditions. But how, and to what point, does one discuss the question of the necessity and sufficiency of all members having tenure for academic freedom in a way that is intelligibly related to the Argentine university as portrayed? Apart, perhaps, from making the obvious point that, if the picture of the Catholic University holds, there is a strong chance that absolute tenure is correlative with the absolute absence of academic freedom.

Nor do I think there is anything peculiar in claiming the absolute absence of academic freedom just on the grounds that there is not an academic institution concerned that could be said to be free or whose members could be said individually or collectively to be academically free. And this would hold even if no one of them ever wanted to say anything that would be objectionable and call forth sanctions and so found no restraint upon his freedom of speech.

I suggest that a brief characterization of the university as Bunge presents it is an institution with a vibrant academic spirit, an instance of academic strength freely exercising itself, in spite of a hostile sociopolitical environment (the armed forces, the Catholic church, the Ministry of Education, "nationalist" groups, and even some foreign press organs—all this adds up to a total opposition that makes anything I have encountered seem puny) and an academic-nonacademic split within the university itself.

That split comprises the political opposites within the institution, and the incompetent and competent within the institution. Bunge, identifying with the university, makes no mention of the administration as a separate entity, but whoever was administering was surely in opposition to the forces opposing the academic interests in the university, and my only suggestion is that what sustained it was something in the inertia of tradition, the sheer continuance of an established institution whose vicissitudes make us waver from tears to cheers.

In the luxury of retrospective phantasy I can feel an excitement, as an academic, of joining such a university and taking part in its fight for development and attainment. One is safe in retrospective phantasy; a present possibility may rather emphasize one's commitment to one's own institution, one's own department and subject, one's age, one's having given hostages to fortune by marrying and begetting a family. One might even indulge the phantasy of playing a significant role in the ensuing victory—at the level of principles and armchair strategy, ignorance of details hides the difficulty apparent in one's own fumbling with institutional problems. Yet it is good sometimes to reflect upon one's human limitations, one's human obligations, and to remember that academics are human, and sometimes all too human. If that humanity is lost then all may be lost.

But, to repeat, if we can propound universal propositions about academic freedom and tenure, those propositions must apply to all academic institutions; and if we limit our attention to the United States, guided by the *AAUP Bulletin* and reports on the difficulties that have been investigated and decisions taken in regard to tenure and freedom, the variety of types of institutions is to me, if not to you, breathtaking: Arkansas State (the *Higgins* case), Gove City College (the *Larry Gara* case), University of Illinois (the *Koch* case), Sam Houston State Teachers College (the *Koeninger* case), South Dakota State College (the *Worzella* case), the *Monmouth College* case, and the *University of Utah* case, which I want to outline because it was the first investigation and the first confrontation of the founding fathers of the AAUP.

These founding fathers were clear as to principle and saw nothing of the future role of the Association. Men of high status in leading universities, they saw the academic battle as a defense of the autonomy of disciplines against interested philistines, fundamentalists opposed to evolutionary theory, economicopolitical interests opposed to economic theory, and as already won. The "faculty" was united. "I do not know of any college teacher," said Dewey, "who does not hold that such infringement when it occurs, is an attack upon the integrity of our calling. But such cases are too rare even to suggest the formation of an association like this."[6]

From the logician Dewey, that was a remarkable statement. Against the background of a developing rash of institutions with professors, what Dewey did not know highlights the compatibility of enthusiastic agreement on principle and ignorance of what is

[6] Address to the Committee of Organization, quoted from *The Development of Academic Freedom in the United States*, by Richard Hofstadter and Walter P. Metzger (New York: Columbia University Press, 1955), p. 478.

going on in the world that gives sense to the terms of a principle.

Committee A had been established to formulate principles. No machinery for intervention or action of any kind was envisaged. And then, as you all know from Metzger, Arthur Lovejoy, a distinguished Johns Hopkins professor, went to New York on holiday and read a newspaper report of seventeen resignations at Utah over the firing of some colleagues.

Fifteen years before, Lovejoy had resigned with seven others from Stanford over the dismissal of the liberal economist, Edward A. Ross. The parallel was plain. He persuaded Dewey to back his immediate visit, and the *Utah* case became a case for the Association, which in consequence was committed to Colorado, Montana, Pennsylvania—and so on and on.

What Lovejoy found did not surprise him—a president more concerned with appropriation than principle, a faculty warned not to upset the Mormons, a suspect appointment, a dismissal because someone had crossed the governor, clear-cut cases of "academic freedom." What did surprise him was that the dismissals that brought about the resignations were not based on anything like this. Grounds for dismissal were specifically stated as speaking disrespectfully of the chairman of the Board of Regents, or having spoken in an uncomplimentary way about the administration. The president's recommendations were accepted, the professors dismissed without a hearing, and a principle enunciated—when friction becomes serious and irreparable, it must be eradicated. Investigation to find if the superior or the subordinate is most to blame does not stop the friction. The only practical course is to remove such causes of friction as are deemed least valuable to the work of the organization.

Compare this with the *1940 Statement*: "Institutions of Higher Education are conducted for the common good, and not to further the interest of either the individual teacher or the institution as a whole," and Dewey's presidential statement, "The defense of academic freedom and tenure being already a concern of the existing learned societies will not, I am confident, be more than an incident in the activities of the association in developing professional standards."[7]

---

[7] Joughin, *Academic Freedom and Tenure*, p. 156.

Lovejoy recognized the facts. He could scarcely avoid doing so. What he still failed to see was the Utah affair in its historical setting. That a president, that an institution, should demand the allegiance of the faculty was a long-established principle of structure and procedure in academia. It has its analogy in countless institutions. But academia had changed and was changing. Leading colleges were sometimes secular and public, the "executive" existed in many cases alongside professors with reputations based on research and intellectual position, as well as professors who had no such reputation. The former were not simply employees and followers. Academic professionalism had entered publicly, and unevenly, upon the scene, with freedom for some to move to other institutions at will.

Internal wrangling over precedence and procedure, over decisionmaking and power within institutions, not great intellectual combats, was the occasion of academic wars. Utah typified one form, and only one form, of trouble. And once committed to Utah, the Association could not refuse to accept responsibilities for which it, with its clear principles, was totally unprepared. And out of such situations emerged the need for the twins, academic freedom and tenure, as they grace the American scene today.

Lovejoy, the man of principle and proposition, discovered the institutional facts in Utah. He failed to see the history that made them intelligible and generally illuminating. He could not be expected to foresee what the *1940 Statement* indicates, a developing complexity of interests in the institutions of higher education, the indefinite "Common Good," the individual teachers and administrative personnel, the institution as a whole, and the unmentioned sociopolitical interests that come to bear with state funding— by the elected representatives of those who receive "the Common Good."

What Lovejoy had to discover and could not then have discovered may be indicative of what we, who discuss principles, need to know. The socio-political-historical background of the complexity of American institutions lacks the drama of the Argentinian case, but the condition of intelligibility of discussion is the same.

Let me conclude by making, in cursory fashion, seven points that to an interested and not unconcerned foreigner emerge from the paper itself. They are not the only points of interest, and I see no purpose in my discussing in detail the quite complicated analysis of the case for tenure or the proposed substitute; that task is yours.

1. I take it that Professor Sartorius, and at least many of the other contributors, are talking about academic freedom and tenure (where it is mentioned) in the local context, with their complex history and variety of institutions and institutional structures and conditions.

Part of the moral that I draw from the hasty work of the last several days is that the emphasis on tenure as it emerged historically was not preplanned but developed from and in relation to historicopolitical events, as a guarantee of certain basic conditions that made possible the development of a specifiable academic well-being *in* institutions as well as *of* individual university members. Both tenure and a conception of academic freedom appear to be now operative, however frustrating they are to a variety of social and institutional forces, in major academies and as accepted concepts of law. Nor is it open to anyone's extrapolitical decision to change this. Its change will, like its bringing about, involve the success of a political activity. Sartorius seems aware of this in the final section, though I am quite unable to work out to whom the "we" refers.

By contrast, I can suggest quite easily a whole range of interested parties, all of whom would be delighted to protest their dedication to universities, who would be eager to insist that tenure has dreadful disadvantages—look at the deadwood that clutters up the academies, look at all the brilliant young men denied tenure and ejected from the system after being used, at the sheer immorality of the double standard it breeds, at the hypocrisy and inefficiency of the so-called academics.

What might emerge from publishing the charges of dreadful disadvantages and awaiting reactions is a clarification, if such be needed, of what in the institutions themselves and in their environment is opposed to tenure; and a clear indication, if such be needed, of what tenure has made possible regarding the structuring and procedures and the developments of academies, the standing of teachers, and the possibility of their fulfilling their functions, including, as the details of attacks emerge, the *manifold new functions that have been demanded of universities*, especially over the last twenty years. This procedure is scarcely a way I could recommend for acquiring information. Even for Sartorius, tenure appears as a protection against disaster.

2. If I am right, much of the discussion of tenure and academic freedom in terms of "all members" and "some members," especially when tenure varies from institution to institution and academic freedom is said to have degrees, has to be both made more complicated and couched in terms of actual situations and conditions. The Argentine situation shows that tenure for all is compatible with academic freedom for none. The mythical community of scholars in which all who teach learn and all who are taught learn, and do nothing else—the essential, unstructured, unadministered, self-sustaining academy—excludes tenure as superfluous, by removing any counterconditions to freedom. But again, this is irrelevant to United States actualities. I note that in Sartorius's quote from Machlup, we find "a freedom which, in many situations . . . can be guaranteed only by the instrument of tenure"; and my impression is that "in many situations" does not figure in his discussion of the validity of the claim.

3. Data are lacking for years of probation, and so forth. Sartorious suggests ten years for probation, and thirty or thirty-five years for tenure, commenting that the latter is a *very* long time. Machlup, estimating the probationary as one quarter of the tenured career, regards the one quarter as excessive. I find it staggering; but I would (*a*) discount the period of completion of a Ph.D. and (*b*) like to know how many achieve tenure after a minimum period of, say, three years, and why others take longer. My belief is that originally the period of seven years maximum was set to cover cases of failure to satisfy some standards at one institution and the embarking on another full probationary period at another, or the same, institution. Here it was recognized that there were different types of jobs at academies and that forms of exploitation were rife.

4. The "deadwood" argument seems to rest upon assumption or claimed "agreement." Since this is a vital fact claim, it needs to be made out in detail—how much, of what types, in what institutions. The criteria would be interesting.

5. Somewhat the same applies to the "dual standard" argument. My emphasis on the *institution* goes against any reduction of the academic to "contractual teaching and research." That tends to obliterate the distinction between neophytes, apprentices or pro-

bationers, and journeymen or craftsmen—accepted full members of an institution with various roles to play and relationships to enter into.

It seems to me that the AAUP principles rely on tenure as a protection and leave enormous leeway for specific contracts, again conceived as contracts between "externally related" individual and employing institution. I am accustomed to think of universities as constituted primarily of human staff and students in special relations and with special responsibilities. Cooperative activity, embracing support, encouragement, assistance in a difficult common task that goes beyond taking classes at times and reading at other times are included. My experience in American universities is limited; but I know that many of my colleagues in this country agree with me.

6. There is no discussion of student rights and student freedom. These seem to me to require consideration. Surely "academic freedom" must range over all academic members of an institution.

Further, students do sometimes seem to assume a right to permanent membership in a university—to scholarships, Ph.D.'s, and appointments (i.e., tenure, with conditions of grades, etc.). At times I feel we are close to hearing a demand that refusal of an A grade is regarded as requiring "due process," with the responsibility on the part of the grader to justify his grading before a tribunal before the grade is determined.

Equally, some of them sometimes attack tenure as a barrier to the dismissal of staff to whom they are opposed, while some, and sometimes the same some, at another time support tenure to prevent anyone else dismissing staff of whom for their own reasons they approve.

All of this is relevant to the character of an institution in which the "general climate of academic freedom" is, I suggest, not a matter of number of staff on tenure.

7. Much of what Sartorius claims about conditions is to me surprising and, if true, disturbing. The conditions of probationary staff outlined suggest that they range from "brutalizing, dehumanizing, and discouraging," with "favoritism," and "arbitrary, uninformed or otherwise unjust" decisions, to life in departments "that with the support of an equally softhearted or incompetent administration tend to renew all initial appointments automatically, and

eventually to grant tenure to anyone who stays around long enough." Even if there are conditions in between, this is scandalous and an indication of the complete failure of academic competence and honesty in the matter of determining academic capacity.

But what point is there, then, in letting such academics loose on everyone at stated periods?

I think Professor Sartorius should inform the AAUP of this state of affairs, so that it can act or be prepared. No self-respecting board of regents can ignore the publication of details of such conditions in their institutions.

12. Tenure and Academic Freedom

BY GRAHAM HUGHES

Professor Sartorius has offered us a balanced and thoughtful analysis of the connection between tenure and academic freedom that more than half persuades me. In the end, I shall come out not too far away from his solution, but on the way there are some doubts and hesitations I want to express that will lead me to a modification of his proposed reforms.

I shall begin by accepting the description that Professor Sartorius offers of the present practice of tenure and by agreeing that it certainly constitutes a remarkable privilege shared by few other people in the working world. The assembly line worker has nothing like it, nor even the corporate executive, though he may have other contractual rights in the form of generous severance pay and, sometimes, the protection of a long-term contract. Most other professionals have no such shelter. It is true that the doctor or the lawyer cannot be divested of his professional license without a showing of gross impropriety that would have to be demonstrated in a full due-process hearing. But the doctor and the lawyer are protected only with respect to their license to practice a profession; they are not in the least protected with respect to their particular employment by a client or an institution, and certainly not in the sense of enjoying a right to continue to draw a salary or to perform services for a person or an institution that may wish to dispense with them.

Perhaps, outside the academic profession, the only other major example of a strong tenurial position to which one could point would be that of the judge, who, in many jurisdictions, can be removed only in the most difficult fashion by the most cumbersome procedures and after a showing of corrupt behavior. Certainly the legal profession in every common-law country can always produce a collection of horror stories about judges who are grossly incompetent or are sliding into senility but who cannot be removed, because of judicial tenure practices. There is no need to recite at great length the history of how we have come to accept that some price of this kind is worth paying in order to guard the judiciary from political pressures. Recent history in the United States will enable all of us to construct the hideous possibilities of what might have happened if judges held their office at the pleasure of the executive. But, before leaving the judicial analogy, two points are worth making.

In the first place, the incompetent judge, strange as the assertion may at first seem, is in some ways less of a threat than the incompetent tenured professor. For the actions of judges are always subject to review by appellate courts who operate in the glare of such publicity and public scrutiny that it is simply unrealistic to think that gross incompetence or mental degeneration could long be tolerated in one of their members. The student, unfortunately, cannot obtain appellate redress for the harm done to him by inept teachers.

Second, even in the judicial field, there are discussions in the air about the need to improve procedures for the enforced retirement of incompetent judges, though the discussions contemplate that such action would only be taken by a panel of appellate judges of the same jurisdiction. This has clearly a strong resemblance to a modified or diluted concept of academic tenure, which in a broad sense both Professor Van Alstyne and Professor Sartorius argue for.

The value of judicial independence is, I suppose, not only unquestioned in its importance but also would be thought by most to be one of the prime values in a just society. And there can be no doubt that judicial tenure does promote this value, though perhaps the full rigor of present judicial tenure is not *necessary* to its promotion and certainly not always *sufficient* for its full protection.

So one way to begin may be to ask whether what is customarily called "academic freedom" is a value comparable in importance with what is customarily called "judicial independence." This will clearly in turn depend to some extent on what we wish to include in the concept of academic freedom. Professor Sartorius defines academic freedom as, with respect to the status of an individual, "the freedom of a member of the academic profession to engage in research, teaching, publication, and other such pursuits without fear of reprisals for the expression of unpopular opinions." There is, too, he says, "an institutional analogue in the notion of a *climate* of inquiry that is relatively free from such threats to most individuals."

I think this puts it very well, except that I would want to expand on the statement in some directions. In the first place, Professor Sartorius does not say anything about *why* such a freedom should be a prime social value, and, indeed, at times one is not sure whether he takes it to be such a prime value. So let me hazard a few remarks in that direction.

The liberty of everyone to express unpopular opinions is presumably a fundamental value in our society, since it is given an entrenched status in the First Amendment to the Constitution. In the tradition of our culture, academics as a group play a definite role as critics of society, debaters of ethics, initiators of reform, and discoverers of knowledge. They have, of course, no monopoly in these fields and are often outshone by others outside academic ranks, but nevertheless it may be true to say that they have often represented the spearpoint of critical scrutiny of our institutions and practices. As such they are always likely to be, and historically often have been, in the front rank of those subject to attack by establishment institutions and by authoritarian persons in positions of power. For this reason alone, I believe that there would be some truth in the statement that academic freedom is a prime value in our social system—both because of the vital socially therapeutic ends that it serves and because it embodies the front-line defense against the forces of repression.

Then, second, academics are educators, and there is ample and, I hope, substantially unquestioned agreement about the dangers of allowing government to exercise an authoritarian position in education. Let me quickly interpose the concession that the present practice of tenure is not obviously a sufficient condition to fend off authoritarian government intervention in education, nor even obviously a necessary condition. But it may be suggested that there is historical evidence that the practice of tenure has actually contributed helpfully in this direction and that that in itself is a point of considerable importance.

Professor Sartorius might not want to quarrel with the way I have embellished his definition of academic freedom, but of course he does question the relevance of the present practice of tenure to the promotion of these values. I will turn to that main theme in a moment, but first I want to add that I do find something else missing in his definition.

He speaks of academic freedom only as freedom *to* act in certain ways, though I take it that there is implicit the notion of freedom *from* certain pressures and threats. I would like to suggest that freedom *from* a realistic prospect of dismissal is important in other ways that might be properly included in an enlarged concept of academic freedom. The academic community ought to be, I think, an example of a civilized minisociety. In many ways it very often is not that, but it ought to strive for that goal, and in some ways it has historically succeeded. Now, there is simply something harsh and inhumane about the prospect of terminating the appointment of a professor, aged, shall we say, fifty to fifty-five, because his standards of performance have deteriorated, even substantially. Of course, this may also be harsh and inhumane if the person in question is an advertising executive or a steel worker, but the duty of the academic community, as I have just said, is to set an example and not to conform to capitalist standards of production and efficiency. Perhaps Professor Sartorius and I are not in great disagreement here, because he may well say that his proposed scheme would not contemplate the dismissal of such persons simply because their performance is not quite what it was. He wants only to get at the "deadwood." But, up to a point, I would be willing to carry some deadwood, though I agree there must be a question of how dead the wood is and how much of the wood is dead. My reason would be that I think the gentleness and humanity of such a policy has a positive value that contributes to the master ideal of the university as the exemplar of a just and humane society. Very likely such a response will not turn away the wrath of students who make comparisons between the cost of their education and the quality of some of the instruction they get. I have already conceded that, after a point, gentleness and tolerance of inefficiency might too seriously threaten other values in the institution, but I would reach that terminus perhaps a good deal later than Professor Sartorius. As for the students, part of the task of educating them is, I think, to persuade them of the importance of values of kindness and gentleness so that they may see that some inefficiency is a worthwhile price to pay for being a member of an institution that practices such virtues.

But what has this to do with academic freedom? Quite a lot, I think, in an enlarged sense of that concept. I would like to think of academic freedom as including a freedom for academic institutions to be radically different in their practices from those modes and standards of performance that industrial capitalist societies have engrained into us. And not just a freedom to be different in this respect but also a duty to be different. For academic freedom may include freedom *from* the harsh practice of discarding people who are late in life to be judged as failures and the freedom *to* build a community in which a kind of efficiency is not given an inappropriate value. I think the present practice of tenure serves that value without often seriously damaging the general educational and research missions of a department or a university.

But it is now time to turn to Professor Sartorius's principal contentions that the present practice of tenure may not be necessary and also not sufficient to protect the narrower and more traditional concept of academic freedom that is his concern. Here I can agree with a great deal, perhaps the major part, of his lucid analysis, but not with all of his comments and conclusions.

Certainly it would be difficult to argue with his point that tenure for *some* academics is not a sufficient protection for the academic freedom of *all*. But there are two points here, to which I think Professor Sartorius does not give enough weight, though he acknowledges that they have some validity.

First, the existence of a large body of academics whose academic freedom is substantially unassailable does, I think, contribute in an important fashion to the general climate of academic freedom. It is true that a dilution of traditional tenure practices would not necessarily entail any concessions at all about the importance of the value of academic freedom. Dismissals that could reasonably be thought of as resting on the expression of unpopular opinions or the doing of unpopular acts could still be attacked as utterly reprehensible, as they can be today with respect to academics who do not enjoy tenure. It is also possible that the kind of due-process model that Professor Sartorius sets up would provide reasonable protection, though I doubt it. My experience in the courts and with university administrators convinces me that, helpful as a kind of due process may be, it is not as strong a shield as the present practice of tenure. The present practice of tenure does, I think, constitute a unique protection of the climate of academic freedom in that (*a*) it is a permanent institutional expression in the strongest possible terms of the paramount importance of that value and (*b*) it actually affords the most perfect protection for the academic freedom of a very substantial percentage of academics.

Second, I think Professor Sartorius does not give enough weight to what he calls very aptly the "umbrella" argument. I believe academics to be as malicious and given to establishment views as many other classes in the community, though not, in my experience, to the same extent as university administrators. I concede that the tenured faculty is hardly always to be looked to as the strongest defenders of the nontenured faculty member who defies convention. I speak from a good deal of experience in this area, since I have been a chairman of the Grievance Committee of the United Federation of College Teachers and have at times acted, at the request of the American Association of University Professors, as academic advisor to members of various faculties in dispute with their administrations. My experience has led me to conclude that university administrators are often thoroughly unscrupulous and grossly arbitrary in their dealings with nontenured faculty members and that an important weapon in opposing them, though certainly not always a victorious one, is the strong expression of disapproval by tenured faculty members. I am also convinced that many such faculty members would not join these battles and express these views if they enjoyed any protection less than the full present practice of tenure gives them. The umbrella may be leaky and sometimes does get blown away by the wind, but I have seen it keep out some heavy rain.

I have therefore come to the conclusion, for the reasons I have so far given, that the present practice of tenure has more to commend it than Professor Sartorius will acknowledge and that, on balance, it should be retained.

Indeed, it is not tenure that is the major problem but the lack of it for a substantial segment of the faculty, including most of its younger members. Professor Sartorius here proposes a most interesting new regime in which academic freedom would be protected for everyone by contractual provisions and presumably university regulations, under which faculty members would be engaged for contractual periods that typically, after an initial shorter contract, might be terms of five years. Termination of a contract would have to be preceded by written notice substantially in advance and would have to be for stated reasons, which might be challenged by the faculty member. Such challenges would be settled by a committee of faculty members in a proceeding where the general elements of due process would obtain and where the burden of proof would be on the university administration seeking nonrenewal of a contract.

Such a scheme is certainly feasible, but there are ways in which I think it provides both too little and too much. I believe it provides too little in the way that I have indicated above, namely, that there are strong reasons for preserving the present tenure practice for a substantial segment of the faculty. I believe it provides too much in that, without modification, it would place university administrators in a position where standards of excellence, of efficiency, and, indeed, of simple economic viability would be much more seriously threatened than under the present tenure regime.

We are all painfully aware of the financial crisis through which almost all private universities and most public ones are passing. In a society that has perhaps not thought through the nature of its commitment to higher education, it appears inevitable that many universities will for some time have to continue the budget-paring process on which they have already embarked rather vigorously. It is obvious that, even with the best will in the world (which regrettably is often not present), some reduction in the size of some faculties will be inevitable. I see nothing in Professor Sartorius's scheme that would provide for such a possibility, unless perhaps he implicitly meant to suggest that it would be a sufficient discharge of the administration's burden of proof merely for it to introduce convincing evidence that it could not afford to retain a faculty of the present size. But would there then be a further burden to demonstrate that those who were not to be retained were the least worthy?

It is true, of course, that decisions of that kind presently have to be made, and there is every reason to insist that they be made as fairly as possible. Perhaps the best existing practice is that in which decisions on promotion and status are made by committees, usually consisting of tenured faculty members, sometimes with advice from academics outside the department, school, or university. And, no doubt, when financial exigency requires the contraction of the size of a faculty, such committees must in fact try to decide who are the most worthy to be retained. But the concept of due process is, I think, only in part appropriate to such a proceeding, and the placing of a formal burden of proof on the administration is quite inappropriate.

In a nonlegal context, the introduction of adversary proceedings with the trappings of due process always has a tendency to inhibit decision making. If to this were added the burden-of-proof concept, then I believe that the administration, or faculty committee, would be in practice just about as tightly clamped to new faculty members as they presently are to tenured faculty members. The pursuit of perfect justice in decision making is simply not always a value to be pursued in institutional government at the expense of other important values. (I suppose the army is the perfect example of this, though I certainly do not want to press that analogy.) We must recognize qualifying principles of the pursuit of efficiency and the avoidance of the interminably time-consuming and also communally disruptive impact that I think hearings of the kind envisaged would produce.

At this point I may be laying myself open to the charge of wanting justice for older faculty members but not for young ones, but I do not think that would be a fair characterization of my position. The fact is that the demands of justice are relative to the claims one can legitimately make with respect to a practice or against an institution. Long service and the passage over initial hurdles build up proper claims that one's position should thereafter be disturbed only in extraordinary circumstances and in compliance with procedures that are deliberately made complex. But young people attempting to gain a foothold in a career can reasonably be asked to take some chances. And those who offer opportunities to young people to try out for a certain professional occupation can reasonably demand a fixed period of time in which to make judgments that are discretionary. This does mean that for such probationary candidates there will be less than perfect protection for academic freedom. But, while I suggested earlier that academic freedom is a prime value, I have never meant to suggest that it is an absolute one in the sense that a university must sacrifice every other interest in order to provide perfect academic freedom for everyone all the time.

My own model scheme for the retention or loss of academic positions thus differs in some important respects from that of Professor Sartorius, as shown in the following discussion, though it will owe a good deal to his constructive suggestions.

1. Initial appointments ought to be for a two-year period after which renewal would normally be for a further two-year contract. Termination of the initial contract or of its renewal need not be dependent on a due-process hearing with a burden of proof on the administration to demonstrate incompetence or lack of excellence.

However, I do wish to insist here that I am not endorsing a totally unstructured procedure even at this stage. I think it to be of the greatest importance that decisions here should be made either by faculty committees or at least with their advice and with the understanding that their advice should be departed from only after a statement of reasons to such a committee by the administration. It is also important that the faculty member should be warned in time that there is a likelihood of his appointment not being renewed and should be given an opportunity to appear before the appropriate committee, who should inform him of the reasons why nonrenewal is contemplated and give him an opportunity to present his position if those reasons go to his academic performance. And, of course, it should be understood that his expression of unpopular views or doing unpopular acts ought not in themselves to be a proper ground for nonrenewal.

2. At the end of a four-year period of the kind envisaged in the first point, it seems to me that in most cases the time for a tenure decision has been reached. American law schools have for a long time and for the most part given tenure at this stage, and the practice has generally worked well. In Britain tenure is generally granted after a probationary period of three years. But if tenure is not to be

granted at this time, then any further appointment should be for a period of three or four years with the understanding that tenure might be granted before such a period expires.

A decision not to confer tenure at the end of such a further contractual period ought to be an unusual one taken with some formality. The candidate should be given ample notice and warning and full opportunities to present his position before the appropriate committee. Most due-process notions, such as full particulars of charges of unsatisfactory performance, the right to call witnesses and to be assisted by counsel or an advisor, are, I think, appropriate here, though, again, the notion of a burden of proof on the administration or the faculty committee seems unwarranted to me. I would add, though, a further right at this point—to appeal from an adverse decision to the full tenured faculty of the school or of the department.

3. After the second stage I propose the conferring of full tenure according to the current practice.

In conclusion, I ought to say, in case it may not be apparent, that I share the view that there are disadvantages about the current tenure practice. For some, no doubt, tenure has meant a haven into which they have rowed after pulling hard at the oars during that probationary period that Professor Sartorius has said can be a brutalizing one. After such a labor, they may have felt that they have earned a thirty-year rest. Obviously they have not, and such people sap the strength of an institution. But I have suggested that there are gains here that outweigh the disadvantages.

In the end this may largely be an empirical question, turning on just how much deadwood there is. I think some commentators may have exaggerated this aspect. Academic people very rarely flaunt their laziness shamelessly, though they may be adept at disguising it. The general climate of academic opinion is usually sufficient to ensure that most tenured professors, even if they have little zeal left, preserve a decent minimum of activity. For those who do not, and who are patently guilty of a dereliction of duty, present tenure procedures do afford a process for removal. I would agree that such a process ought to be invoked more often than it generally has been in the past.

13. Some Comments on Sartorius's Paper on Tenure

BY AMÉLIE OKSENBERG RORTY

Rarely has any group given up established privileges voluntarily; even more rarely has any group abrogated its rights. The right to judgments by peers rather than by superiors, once a privilege of the aristocracy, was extended rather than abrogated. And it seems a counsel of prudence, if not actually a command of wisdom, that, if maintaining a right involves the sort of invidious comparison between classes and occupations that causes social conflict, it is better to extend rights than to abolish them.

Sartorius argues that periodic review of appointments, subject to due process, with the assumption to reappointment unless a case can be made against it, might spark greater productivity in the professions and avoid the problem of "deadwood" faculty. He thinks that perhaps a little job insecurity is a healthy thing, if sufficient safeguards are preserved to correct purely arbitrary nonreappointment.

As far as I can see, the best motive for genuinely good work, the one that least paralyzes, is loving one's subject, or at least being absorbed in it. The second-best motive is the desire for the esteem of those whom one esteems. Tenure in no way affects the operation of these motives, and there is good reason to think that abolishing tenure would affect them adversely. Those who are not moved by these motives and who write in order to preserve their jobs or get promotion tend to fill the journals with dreary duty pieces. The journals are already filled with the breath of the dead and dying. A person who is moved neither by his subject nor by the desire to contribute to the work of scholars in his specialty, but by anxieties about his reappointment, is unlikely to produce anything of great merit.

The measures of productivity in philosophy are subtle and diverse. Someone may be an exemplary teacher, or have a capacity for asking searching critical questions. But when there is pressure for review, the grossest of these measures, the most easily quantifiable, is likely to be used. We already suffer from this in making decisions about promotions and tenure appointments. Anything we can do to avoid channeling thought by current fashions for productivity would be an advance. Someone protected by tenure is not only assured of political freedom but also given breathing space to attempt uncertain, difficult, and speculative work.

Even if for a marginal number of people the practice of reviewing appointments would provide pressure for them to do work they might not otherwise produce, the number of people whose work and character is adversely affected seems to me to balance out any gain. We already pay a terrible cost for the three-to-five-year waiting period before a tenure decision is reached. This is a time when the thought and character of many scholars deteriorate badly: they take on fashionable projects with predictable outcomes; they become competitive instead of cooperative; they suffer all the damages of anxiety.

If there were academic review, agreement about the standards would be unlikely. The problems we now face with making tenure appointments would become far more severe. Let us suppose that the groups that now make tenure decisions would form the committees of review. This would probably mean there would be departmental committees in the first instance and committees composed of general faculty and administration as a second check. But whenever there are difficult decisions to be made, especially if they involve long-standing friendships and enmities, the tendency is to avoid trouble and pass the matter on or to turn to a measure that is relatively "objective." As long as review decisions remain in the hands of the faculty, the pressure of personal ties will tend to reappointment. The purpose of eliminating tenure will not be served, but there will be more work and agony for all. But if the decisions gradually swerve to the administration, then there is a danger that faculty will be inadequately protected in times of political and economic crises. The motto for the next few decades should not be "plan for the best of times." It should rather be "plan for the worst of times." It is only in fiction that the best of times and the worst of times coincide.

The people to whom one gives up a right may change; they may cease to bear good will, or themselves come under pressure to make decisions they would have preferred not to be in a position to make. Committees that make tenure decisions will be under severe economic and political pressure from administrators to trim faculty and ease out difficult faculty. When the members of such committees are themselves under review, they require protection to make decisions that may be unpopular with administrators.

It seems a council of prudence never to give up a right or a protection without knowing into whose hands it will fall. In the next few years we are likely to see the expansion of committees of appointment and promotion. Perhaps not only students, but also members of the community at large, will have a voice in such matters. Whether or not this is itself desirable, it would seem all the more important to protect faculty against external judgments based on popularity or political safety.

Far rather than introduce a system of review, I would recommend introducing tenure protection at a much earlier point. Seven years seems to me far too long a period of trial. Three years, especially in a small department, should be quite sufficient to determine whether a person is likely to be a good teacher and a good philosopher. In quite large departments, such decisions may require more time, and perhaps there might be a difference in the time allotted to small and large departments to make tenure decisions. The side effects of this—freezing the number of openings available for some time to come—may be the cost we shall have to pay. It is a cost that is likely to be borne in any case, with the sharp cut in university funds.

We ought to question, rather than to adopt "productivity" as a criterion of worth, a ground for continued employment. We are, to be sure, all too familiar with the phenomenon of "dead wood" in a department; when our most brilliant graduate students are forced to find jobs driving taxis unless we find a way of retiring some of our colleagues, its dangers loom large. But our undergraduates may well benefit more from the practices that assure the tenure of elderly scholars whose most productive qualities are their amiable waddles across the quad than they would from practices that treat individuals as dispensable when they no longer publish papers on fashionable subjects. The problem lies in securing suitable employment for the sprouting modal logicians of the world; we should concentrate on assuring that employment, without accepting the current assumptions that link hiring with tenure practices. Universities could be the testing grounds for theories and practices that reform the conditions for employment. We might encourage different sorts of universities to experiment with distinctive types of contractual conditions. For instance, small departments or departments whose members are expected to engage in advanced research might allow a relatively long period before granting tenure; large departments or departments in local community colleges might have a relatively short pretenured period. Or some universities might give tenure to part-time appointments, so that granting tenure does not reduce the number of available positions so sharply. The tenure system has helped to guarantee freedom for experimentation of this sort. To abandon it altogether, for the sake of providing a larger turnover in efficient and productive employment, seems like a rush of lemmings to the sea, also said to be a species-saving device in times of overpopulation. We do indeed need to re-examine the contractual conditions of academic employment: to abandon the tenure system is to limit the constructive experiments that could be safely carried out in redefining those conditions.

14. Tenure, Academic Freedom, and the Nature of the University

BY ROLF SARTORIUS

Rather than reply in detail to the comments of Professors Hughes, Ritchie, and Rorty, I shall take this opportunity to re-emphasize and elaborate upon some of the central themes that my paper was meant to suggest. In so doing, I shall attempt to identify, and relate my remarks to, some of the general issues that persistently emerged in the course of the discussion of most, if not all, of the papers presented at the Conference.

1. The chief thrust of my paper is to state that the argument for tenure in terms of academic freedom is broken-backed. I, of course, agree that academics must be protected against dismissal or non-retention on nonacademic (e.g., political) grounds. My contention is simply that present tenure practices, which provide that protection only for some, are not sufficient, even other things being equal,[1] to provide for a climate of freedom of inquiry and expression in institutions where a very large proportion of the research and teaching is being conducted by the nontenured.

The only really serious reply that I have encountered to this argument is what I called the "umbrella argument"—that is, that the

[1] Note 6 in my original paper seems to have been overlooked by Professor Ritchie.

tenured are both willing and able to protect the nontenured from encroachments upon their academic freedom. It seems that a number of the participants in the Conference agree with me that this argument ignores the fact that younger and nontenured members of the academic profession may need to be protected from, as well as by, their tenured colleagues.[2]

2. If I am right that present tenure practices are not sufficient to foster and protect a climate of academic freedom because they do not protect the untenured, how might the situation be rectified? Many seem to feel that the obvious answer lies in granting tenure much earlier than is presently the case. There are two objections to this proposal that are to my mind conclusive: (*a*) Understood in terms of the minimalistic standards of competency that accompany it, extending tenure downward in any appreciable degree would magnify the costs associated with tenure practices to the point where they would become intolerable; and (*b*) It is totally unrealistic to assume that administrators of academic institutions would be willing to accept such an extension of a practice that, even in its present form, is becoming increasingly difficult for them to defend.

3. My suggestion was rather that the protection of academic freedom afforded by tenure to those who now have it be afforded to all by the extension to all of the essential features of the present tenure system in so far as those features have to do with academic freedom. My proposals along these lines were meant to be only very tentative, but the basic ideas were the following: (*a*) The terms of continued employment should be as clear and explicit as possible, rather than tacitly understood (and frequently misunderstood) as is currently the case. (*b*) The probationary period during which a college or university is to be understood as having made only a minimal commitment to the academic employee should be dramatically shortened both in theory and in practice. (*c*) After an initial probationary period, an academic should be subject to dismissal only for "due cause" as understood in terms of a reasonably high and uniformly applied standard of competence. (*d*) The burden of proof should be upon the employer to show the existence of due cause for dismissal or nonretention if challenged to do so. This feature is of course

[2] See the papers by Professors Van Alstyne and Schmitt in this volume.

problematic and the details would not be easy to work out. I surely did not mean to suggest that the burden of proof should be upon the institutional employer within the framework of a formal hearing observing procedural due process whenever someone was unhappy with his nonretention. Perhaps it would do to require that the person seeking to challenge a nonretention decision first establish a prima facie case to the satisfaction of some peer-group committee operating in a quite informal manner. (e) I did not mean to suggest a system of fixed terms contracts, by now a familiar and to my mind not-very-attractive proposal. What I had in mind was this. Periodic review in terms of explicit and reasonably high standards of competence is not only necessary but also desirable. On the other hand, constant evaluation would produce an obviously undesirable level of insecurity. The proposal in broadest terms would be thus: After the probationary period, there would be periodic review (perhaps every five years) in terms of a nonminimalistic standard of academic performance, failure to pass such review constituting possible grounds for nonretention. In between reviews, dismissal would be justifiable only in terms of the present sort of minimalistic standards that demand (with the burden of proof of course upon the institutional employer) a showing of gross academic irresponsibility.

Details aside, I have not yet encountered any objections to this proposal that strike me as very convincing. To design and administer such procedures would admittedly be a demanding undertaking for many institutions and would, of course, demand considerable faculty participation in the inevitable committee structure that would be needed to adjudicate disputes. But surely this is a price well worth paying to support a system that—at least this is my contention—would *extend* the benefits of the present tenure system while avoiding many if not all of its obvious defects.

4. My concern with the so-called deadwood problem prompted charges of inhumanity and overemphasis. I shall speak to the former charge below; as to the latter, I would accuse some of my critics of overemphasis. It is they, not I, who attempt to place the consideration of this problem at the center of discussions of tenure. As reiterated in section 1 above, the chief source of my criticism of the present tenure system is of quite a different nature.

5. Throughout our discussions at the Conference, it became in-

creasingly clear that a central source of controversy with respect
to most of the questions discussed lay in the existence of possibly
competing conceptions of the nature of the modern university. As
the written comments on my paper indicate, some took me to be
urging the adoption of what might be called the "corporate model"
of the university, a model in terms of which the demand for efficiency would justify the inhumane treatment of those identified as
deadwood. To this was opposed a model of the university as a mini-
community,[3] acceptance into which carried a strong assurance of the
right to continued participation. Now, I am not too sure exactly
what this somewhat romantic image is meant to convey; to me, at
least, it seems to be somewhat at odds with the facts of modern university life, especially with high faculty mobility and the intellectual
isolationism that results from overspecialization. But it is of course
not for me to elaborate upon this model; indeed, I believe I can
avoid here the articulation of what model, if any, I would adopt
in its place. For whatever model one adopts, it seems to me that it
must indeed represent the university as committed to an ideal of
efficiency—not economic efficiency, of course, but the kind of efficiency that accompanies the ideals of free inquiry and the dissemination of knowledge. There is no room within any viable conception
of the university as an intellectual community, I would contend, for
the toleration of identifiable and demonstrable incompetence. To
tolerate such incompetence is to be more than inefficient; it is to
abdicate the function of the university. If the corporate firm tolerates
some marginal economic inefficiency as the price to be paid for the
sake of more humane treatment of its employees (gold watches at
retirement), its stockholders surely cannot complain that they have
been cheated. A student who is presented with an incompetent
teacher, on the other hand, seems to me to have the very strongest
kind of complaint. For what else can justify the existence of the role
(of student) in which he is placed unless it is the indefeasible commitment on the part of the university to provide him with the best
learning and scholarship of which it is capable? Although I agree
that the university should also attempt to present those who pass
through it, as well as its more permanent participants, with a model-

[3] In addition to the comments by Professor Hughes, see "Academic Tenure
at Harvard University," *AAUP Bulletin* 58 (1972): 62–68.

ing of a variety of virtues that are often lacking in other segments of American society, and while I agree that humane treatment is one of those virtues, it is the academic virtues of open and critical inquiry and of teaching informed by the best available scholarship, that are the central and characteristic features of the university. Unlike other institutional virtues, they are therefore not to be knowingly sacrificed in trade-offs for other values.

Part Four

◇◇

Hugo Bedau's paper is an attempt to understand sympathetically the radical claim that the disruption of speeches is sometimes justified. The paper raises a number of questions. Are there doctrines or policies that have no right to be heard? Can academic freedom possibly be reconciled with the notion that advocates of such doctrines or policies should be barred from the arena of academic discussion? One of the ways in which the radical argument can be understood, Bedau suggests, is as a move to shift the burden of proof onto the liberal. Does the liberal claim that there are *no* circumstances in which the right to listen to a speech can be overridden? Bedau shows that this is not plausible. But then, the simple appeal to the right to listen will not rule all disruption out of court. Alan Pasch points out, and Bedau agrees, that this is but a weak conclusion. It does not establish a right to disrupt. For that stronger conclusion, Pasch contends, additional arguments would be necessary; and they have not, he says, been provided by Bedau's analysis.

Hugo Adam Bedau is professor of philosophy at Tufts University. Alan Pasch is professor of philosophy at the University of Maryland and was, when he wrote his paper, executive secretary of the American Philosophical Association.

15. Free Speech, the Right to Listen, and Disruptive Interference

BY HUGO ADAM BEDAU

> "A distinction must be made . . . between the propaganda which a privileged group uses to maintain its privileges and the agitation for freedom and equality carried on by a disinherited group."[1]

> "Anti-Semitism does not fall within the category of ideas protected by the right of free opinion."[2]

I

In recent years, especially on college and university campuses, all of us have been made aware of attempts to disrupt, or to prevent by threat of disruption, meetings and speakers who are vulnerable to criticism from the New Left. Usually, these meetings have been arranged to present speakers who represent or are otherwise identified with the State Department or the military-industrial complex, or who have a history of racism. For example, at my own university in the spring of 1971, a visit by a U.S. senator under the auspices of the student University Lecture Series was cancelled prior to his arrival for fear of disruption of his talk provoked by his long identification with antiblack racist practices. About the same time, a meeting at Harvard University arranged by a coalition of

---

[1] Reinhold Niebuhr, *Moral Man and Immoral Society* (New York: C. Scribner's Sons, 1932), p. 245.

[2] Jean-Paul Sartre, *Anti-Semite and Jew* (New York: Schocken Books, 1946), p. 10.

student groups to hear spokesmen for the Saigon government was cancelled after a tumultuous disruption prevented the assembled audience from hearing the speakers. Nobel Laureate 'William Shockley and Professors Arthur Jensen and Richard Herrenstein—advocates, according to an SDS leaflet, of "Nazi theories" of black genetic inferiority—have suffered this kind of treatment on various campuses. Only a few days before this conference General William Westmoreland's scheduled address before the Yale Political Union was cancelled because the hall was filled with "loud and occasionally violent demonstrators," and the general's security men "estimated that he could be physically abused and shouted down by the crowd." The general's announced topic was "the Army's role in the search for peace."[3]

It is widely believed that such disruptions not only are in violation of ordinary decencies and constitutional liberties but also strike at the very heart of academic freedom, and that all defenders of these rights should rally round and work to prevent such assaults.[4] The litany of liberal objections to such disruptions is easy to recite. It goes like this:

1. On a college campus, whatever may be true elsewhere, disruption of speakers is like book burning. The denial of the right to listen and speak is like a denial of the right to read and write. It is directly incompatible with the purpose of the academic community to conserve, communicate, and create knowledge.

2. If the draft, urban renewal, the Vietnam War, the possible genetic inferiority of blacks cannot be discussed today, who knows what attitude, practice, doctrine, hypothesis, or theory will be condemned as beyond discussion tomorrow.

3. Radicals cannot plead the truth in justification of their disruptive conduct. For in disruption, as in libel and slander, the truth is no defense. Errors from the podium have the same right to be heard as does the truth. The disruptive posture of radicals is merely another case of presumptuous, not to say fanatical, claims to Truth monopolized.

4. In all such cases and especially on campus, the fitting rebuttal

[3] *New York Times*, April 6, 1972, p. 1.

[4] See, e.g., Sidney Hook, ed., *In Defense of Academic Freedom* (New York: Pegasus 1971).

for a false, outrageous, or insincere idea is its exposure as such. But this can be done only in patient, discursive, articulate counter-argumentative speech before an audience free to concentrate on the counterargument. Disruption irretrievably poisons the well of free debate.

5. No one can tell in advance of hearing, what someone will say. Therefore, to silence him on grounds that what he will say is intolerable is to prejudge the issue. Prior restraints, perhaps justifiably applied to certain persons given their probable actions, are logically absurd when applied to anyone's speech.

6. Disruptions by the dispossessed, slaves, and other victims of oppression can be excused and even justified. Disruptions by their self-appointed middle-class spokesmen are something else and are never excusable or justifiable.

7. To condone disruptions by the Radical Left would legitimate disruptions by the Radical Right, and in this direction lies chaos. Moreover, it is the Left that stands to lose most, because the Right commands the bigger battalions.

We all have heard these objections concerning disruptive interference with free speech on campus.[5] I tend to be persuaded by (some of) them myself. Nevertheless, I do not fully grasp the viewpoint of the disrupters, and before they are condemned by mechanical application of liberal Holy Writ, it is desirable to give a thorough airing to their argument. I am not sanguine that I shall succeed. Part of the difficulty is that the radical defense of disruption frequently blends with a very different, essentially liberal and reformist, position that tacitly adapts general arguments for civil disobedience to the specific circumstances of justifying violations of academic freedom and free speech.[6] I suppose I am myself more in sympathy with this view than with the more radical position I shall attempt to formulate, and this sympathy may distort my per-

[5] They have been most recently used in the attack on Professor Bruce Franklin of Stanford University; see Herbert L. Packer, "Academic Freedom and the Franklin Case," *Commentary* 53 (April 1972): 78–84. It is obvious from the article that the author and others believed Professor Franklin to be guilty not only of disruption of free expression on campus, but also of graver offenses against persons and property.

[6] I am indebted to my colleague David Israel for bringing this point forcefully to my attention.

ception of the radical argument. I would much prefer to examine the radical defense of disruption rather than try to invent that defense myself. Regrettably, I have nowhere found in print what I suppose must be the general or background argument on which the more sober and responsible disrupters rely.[7] No doubt it is inspired by Marxism, and it may even originate somewhere in that vast labyrinth of doctrine. I suspect its most popular recent academic influence is Herbert Marcuse's attack on "repressive tolerance."[8] No doubt it is at the mercy of corruptions and distortions in the hands of clumsy proponents and enraged critics. Still, there may be value in trying to do justice to a position that I do not accept and on behalf of advocates who still owe us their own coherent account.

My discussion will be in two parts. First, I shall try to set out the general argument alluded to above, in its own quasi-Marxist terms. Then I shall shift to criticism of the right to speak and to listen from within essentially liberal premises. As for criticism of either part of my argument (of which several possible lines have already been suggested in the preceding paragraphs), I shall leave that to others.

II

Suppose some professor or government official believed in slavery for the lowest intelligence percentile in the nation, or in extermination of the American Indian, or in apartheid for native black Americans. Expressing belief in and even advocating these things would not be in violation of existing law or the Constitution. But suppose you were a friend of some in that lowest intelligence percentile, or married to an American Indian, or a student or patient of a black American teacher or doctor, and you knew that an advocate for such views had been invited to present them in public on your

---

[7] I have found of some use "Free Speech at Harvard—an Answer to Various Deans," a Progressive Labor Party pamphlet (privately printed, Winter 1968). Conversations with my colleague Norman Daniels were a stimulus to me in the early stages of thinking out my views. After finishing this draft, I noticed the essay by Gary Shapiro, "The Ideology of Academic Freedom," in *Clear and Present Danger*, ed. Nicholas Capaldi (New York: Pegasus, 1969), pp. 205–211.

[8] Herbert Marcuse, "Repressive Tolerance," in *A Critique of Pure Tolerance*, by R. P. Wolff, Barrington Moore, and Herbert Marcuse (Boston: Beacon Press, 1965), p. 90.

campus. Is there anything—apart from the law—that imposes on you the duty of restraint or gives the speaker the right of expression and others the right to listen to him?[9]

No doubt it follows from his legal right to hold, express, and advocate such views that members of his audience are under a legal duty not to become tumultuous—to hoot, catcall, shout, whistle, clap their hands, stamp their feet—in order to prevent a speaker from being heard. There are, usually, ordinances that prohibit such conduct, at least in public places and buildings. No doubt it is true, under our law, that "the existence of a hostile opposition cannot be grounds for cutting off or curtailing expression. Rather it is the constitutional duty of the government to protect the person seeking to exercise the right of expression."[10] But why should university officials rely upon such ordinances in order to use campus or city police to arrest disrupters? Why should university officials use existing legal authority at their disposal to protect speakers who advocate slavery for imbeciles, extermination for Indians, apartheid for blacks? These ordinances do not place officials under any moral duty to exercise the police powers at their disposal to prevent disruption of meetings where such ideas are being advocated. Wouldn't it be better if in fact university officials permitted, or even encouraged, disruption of such meetings? That question apart, such ordinances do not foreclose the question of conduct for those in the audience who may be afraid of becoming victims of slavery, extermination, or apartheid, persons not themselves guilty of any crime but now under discussion as though they were criminals and deserving treatment accordingly. From the fact that speakers only believe in and advocate such outrages, and are not attempting to implement them (or to incite others to implement them—yet), nothing follows as to the duty of others to permit by their own acquiescence the propagation of such doctrines. Nor does putting the speakers into the sacred groves of academe secure for them a moral immunity they otherwise lack. Surely, their prospective victims have every reason to oppose such speakers to their face with tactics sufficient to stop further public discussion of the immoral practices they advocate. Why should the

[9] See the discussion in Thomas I. Emerson, *The System of Freedom of Expression* (New York: Random House, 1970), pp. 336–342.

[10] Ibid., p. 337.

friends of these victims and other decent persons be required to stand aside and lend no weight of their own to bring such discussions to an immediate stop?

Unless it can be shown, in the case of my examples above, that preventing speakers from advocating such doctrines is wrong, then it cannot be wrong in principle to prevent speakers from advocating only slightly more controversial and therefore less obnoxious doctrines—for example, continuing the war in Vietnam, throwing poor people off welfare, keeping profits up by cutting back on employment, contriving policies to keep nonwhite minorities as a permanently subjugated class. The rightness of disruption cannot be ruled out in advance of the particulars of each such case. I am not arguing that it is always right to cause disruption of advocates of slavery, aggressive war, and so forth. I forego appeal to any general right to disrupt and prevent advocates of such policies from presenting their views. I argue only that it is not always wrong to disrupt them, that there is no duty not to disrupt (except, of course, a legal duty), and that on some occasions, given the speaker, what he has said before and is likely to say on this occasion, the audience and their grievances, disruptive interference may well be the right course of action.

The background argument for such a conclusion can be put as follows:

1. In our society as it actually exists, there is no such thing as free public speech, speech free of social effect, free of social purpose, free from judgment under appropriate social criteria. All speech on issues affecting human life is interested speech, all speech has social effects, and the question that must always be asked in regard to any speaker seeking an audience is, Whose freedom and interests, and which effects of speech, do you—the speaker, your hosts, guests, visitors—support, in virtue of which this speech before this audience is to take place? Only someone utterly indifferent to social effects, or else culpably ignorant or cynically knowledgeable of them, will stand by and permit anyone to say whatever he pleases to whomever is pleased or curious to listen.

2. Universities and society in general do not in fact give equal opportunity and untrammeled freedom of expression to those who want to attack the established system of injustice, prejudice, and

class oppression at its roots. Therefore, it is hypocritical or cynical for their spokesmen to invoke a general and abstract right of free speech and right to listen in order to attack those who would prevent and disrupt certain meetings and speakers. The vaunted neutrality of the university is in fact false, and plainly so. The government contracts, tax subsidies, classified research, military and police training programs, economic interests of influential trustees and alumni all tell a different story.[11] The university's "hands off" policy on behalf of allowing anyone duly invited to use its facilities for purposes of speechmaking masks its tacit but wholehearted support of the existing social order.

3. We need to ask whose interests are served by extending toleration, courtesies, immunities, and privileges to the spokesmen for oppression. Surely, it is not those who are truly devoted to the creation, conservation, and communication of knowledge and the acquisition of the skills thereof—the traditional purpose of the liberal university and of those who are part of it. Surely, it is not the oppressed; it is in their interest to expose and render impotent their enemies. Cultivating the illusion of free speech and disinterested inquiry on university campuses does not do that. Yet it cannot be in no one's interest for industrial and government spokesmen to appear on campuses in search of receptive audiences; if it were in no one's interest, no one would have a motive to seek such invitations; nor would anyone else have a motive to extend them.

This leaves only one alternative. It is in the interests of the oppressors to gain access to platforms on university campuses and to defend their doing so by appeal to abstract rights of free speech.

4. Speakers who ought to be disrupted fall into different categories. Some are sincere believers in dangerous and outrageous doctrines. Some are suave and hypocritical servants of their masters. Others are pompous and arrogant elitists whose style is *Diktat* and pronunciamento. Perhaps a few are naïvely manipulated by superiors who know full well that their underlings are ignorant of the true

---

[11] See, e.g., the extensive documentation of counterinsurgency, chemical-bacteriological war (CBW), and other government-financed research conducted on university campuses in *Viet-Report* between 1966 and 1968; the pamphlet, "How Harvard Rules," mimeographed (Cambridge, Mass.: Action Research Group, 1969); and especially Dorothy Nelkin, *The University and Military Research* (New York: Random House, 1972).

meaning and purpose of the policies they defend. Thus, some speakers deserve to be disrupted in virtue of what they have to say. Others deserve the same treatment in virtue of whom they represent. Still others deserve disruptive response here and now because of what they have done or said elsewhere. Some disruptions are warranted by virtue of the purpose of the meeting or the intentions of the organizers. All such persons and meetings forfeit any right to an uninterrupted public audience, and their critics and victims who see through the sham should act accordingly.

5. Sincerity of belief, along with the motives and intentions of the believer, is thought by many to be a defense or justification of being allowed to express one's belief. But this is false. And it is a particularly dangerous falsehood when the sincerity in question is exhibited by those with the power of life and death over others. Disruption of the sincere public expression of their beliefs may be one of the few ways to show them that a militant, organized group of disbelievers is arrayed in opposition to them. Sincere fanatics, like sincere dupes, do not by virtue of their sincerity deserve an audience properly denied to the corrupt and insincere. The law and the Constitution in our society, in their majestic indifference to social realities, may provide a legal right of free speech for the sincere anti-Semite, the honest war monger, and their friends. But such persons ought not to have the unhindered use of university facilities to pump out their vicious doctrines. What they preach are lies and falsehoods of no redeeming social importance whatever. Their obscenities deserve to be crushed.

No one has any moral obligation to respond with decorous silence, courteous applause, patient rebuttal, or mere heckling when the platform offers spokesmen for mass murder, imperialistic exploitation, reckless military adventuring, benignly negligent racism, indifference to the plight of the unemployed and the poor, and the defense of the existing power structure that alone makes such violence possible and acceptable. On the contrary, one ought to silence all such talk at its source, exactly as the actions themselves should be prevented. Speakers ought not to want to say such things, audiences ought not to want to hear them. This is especially true of university campuses, for there, if anywhere, the truth should be left free to combat error in all its guises. It is important, furthermore, to teach racists and murderers that their audiences include their prospective victims and their friends, and that though oppressed they can and will fight back and have the confidence to do so to their enemy's face.

7. By allowing the spokesmen for undeclared war, racist education, and the like to present their views openly and without interference and to go through the charade of discussion afterward, decent people succumb to the illusion that factual issues on which these racist and militarist views depend are still in dispute, that not all the evidence is in, that there is room for reasonable men to disagree (or, even worse, that these issues are really matters of "opinion" or taste and thus beyond rational determination). The truth is precisely the reverse. There is nothing to discuss on the merits or justification of class oppression, imperialism, racism, or third-world exploitation, any more than there are two sides to murder, rape, theft, and other criminal conduct. Academic freedom—the freedom to teach and the freedom to learn—is not violated when the advocates of criminal ideologies are denied the opportunity to use the podium and lectern. For the university to permit such speeches and meetings to take place is to become complicit in the abuse of its own facilities. Students and faculty should prevent their university from lending legitimacy to the views of such spokesmen.

8. Speakers on campus who are not sincere seekers after truth or witnesses with their own personal story to tell free of ideological taint should not be confused with scholars and investigators. Instead, they thrust themselves upon the university community in the name of tolerance, free speech, rational inquiry, the market place of ideas —all freedoms and rights that they do not extend to their victims and critics except when they are forced to do so or when their own power is so immense that they run no risks from the rights granted to dissenting minorities. In such cases as these, what John Stuart Mill defended as "freedom of thought and expression" is not at issue. True principles of free speech do not extend to protect those who come in the uniform of Gauleiters, or who are on the payroll of international gangsters, merely because their true affiliations may be somewhat masked. Such speakers do not come to an academic (or any other) community with clean hands and for the purpose of conducting free and open inquiry. They are the advance guard of an oppressive ideology whose objective purpose is to secure the continued dominance of that ideology, whatever private motives or

intentions they as individuals may profess. They should be greeted with a response appropriate to the true role their presence has. Disruption is one kind of response they cannot ignore.

9. What is being defended is the correctness of disruption of certain speakers, on certain topics, in certain cases. In other situations, physical assault on speakers, intimidation by threats of violence, even destruction of their personal property and injury to their persons may be justified, too. All that is being defended here, however, is prevention by disruptive interference of certain speeches by certain speakers. The act of disruption can be viewed after the manner of thwarting a dangerous person about to injure an innocent third party, as an act of vicarious mutual aid, when it cannot (as it often can) be viewed as an act of self-defense. The act of disruption might better be viewed as a confrontation between representatives of the oppressive ruling class and the vanguard of revolutionary change.

10. Nonviolent resistance and other modes of decorous and passive response are invariably preached by the violent and the naïve to their helpless victims, by masters to slaves, by rulers to the oppressed, by governments to their citizens, by the haves to the have-nots, by those who are ready to use much greater violence whenever they judge it necessary to preserve their advantages. Nonviolence is reasonable as the mode of response to oppression, if at all, only on tactical grounds. Tactically speaking, it is not always a reasonable choice, for it tends to encourage oppressors into believing that their victims are weak and docile. Disruptive interference, in any case, is not destructive of property or injurious to persons and is a perfectly acceptable (nonviolent) tactic in many situations.

11. Measured on the scale of class warfare over the past century, or on the scale of the slaughter of the innocents practiced by governments against the poor, working-class people, and unpopular minorities, the disruptions the present argument would justify are laughably insignificant. A society, such as our own, that historically has employed every social institution to repress the oppressed—a Jim Crow constitution, underfunding of public education, neglect of social services, exploitation of women and children, ghettos for the immigrants, violent oppression for native Indians and imported blacks and orientals, corrupt justice under law, tax relief for the

rich, unemployment for the poor—such a society cannot complain without scandalous hypocrisy when its leaders, officials, apologists, hirelings, and hatchetmen are openly and publicly refused a hearing by those of their victims and their allies who know the social realities and the struggle needed to change them.

12. Therefore, some speeches ought not to be given, some speakers ought not to be heard, some audiences ought not to hear what they came for; and if the only, or the least violent, way to ensure these results is by disruptive interference, then disruptive interference is justified.

III

Have I argued, in effect, that protesters have a perfect right to disrupt lectures and speeches by Professors Arthur Jensen, Richard Herrenstein, and William Schockley, General William Westmoreland, the Dow and Army recruiters? No, I have not. "Perfect right" smacks of "never wrong" and "always right," and I have not argued for any such conclusions at all.[12] It is, rather, orthodox liberals who believe in perfect rights, the categorical, unqualified right to speak and to listen no matter who the speaker is and no matter what the topic, purpose, and effects of his speech. Short of verbal incitement to riot (which is not free speech because it goes beyond mere advocacy of riotous conduct), there are no limits to speech and speakers in conventional liberal doctrine. Thus, the American Civil Liberties Union, in its official policy statement on the subject, says that "students should have the right to . . . select speakers and guests . . . [and] the same right as other citizens to hear different points of view and draw their own conclusions."[13] The AAUP, in a resolution from an annual meeting, asserts that students have "the right . . . to listen to

[12] The impossibility of appeal, on Marxist theory, to abstract natural, human, or moral rights, originates in Marx's own polemics in his *Critique of the Gotha Programme*, ed. C. P. Dutt (New York: International Publishers, 1938), first section. Precisely what place, if any, contemporary Marxist theory allows for the notion of extralegal rights in a nonsocialist society is obscure; for discussion, see Maria Hirszowicz, "The Marxist Approach," *International Social Science Journal* 18 (1966): 11–21, and Istvan Kovacs et al., *Socialist Concept of Human Rights* (Budapest: Akademia Kolnai, 1966).

[13] American Civil Liberties Union, *Academic Freedom and Civil Liberties of Students in Colleges and Universities* (New York: American Civil Liberties Union, 1970), p. 14.

anyone whom they wish to hear."[14] A section of the American Bar Association has recently declared that "students should be allowed to hear any person of their own choosing for the purpose of hearing his ideas and opinion."[15] The first two statements do not explicitly include the faculty among those who have the right to listen, and the last statement is not explicitly the assertion of anyone's right. Still, it is plausible to read these and similar texts as an assertion of the right to speak and to listen for faculty, students, their companions, and guests. It is precisely such alleged rights that need closer scrutiny.

First of all, let us admit that the right to speak and the right to listen are not rights that everyone has, or rights without limitation on their possession and exercise, rights beyond forfeiture or alienation. Consider the case of prisoners who claim the right to listen to a course of lectures from fellow inmates who are experienced safecrackers, counterfeiters, burglars, and other "professional" criminals in their midst. The prisoners want to hear their coprisoners lecture on crime as a profession. I do not think that anyone (save some misguided convicts, perhaps) believes that prisoners have the right to solicit, arrange, advertise, and conduct such meeting without restraint and interference from the authorities. On the contrary, prisoners ought not to arrange such meetings. They have no right to do so; they have forfeited any right, by virtue of their prior felonious conduct, to give or hear such lectures. Quite apart from whether or not they have the right in question, it would be wrong for them to be exposed to such lectures and wrong for prison officials not to suppress them. Prior restraints by persons in authority against such lectures are fully justified. Patient rebuttal in argument after such lectures by social workers is an altogether inappropriate way to respond in the nature of the case. If such lectures were somehow arranged, but interrupted or otherwise prevented, including prevention by violent disruption, no one's right to listen would have been violated.

[14] Louis Joughin, ed., *Academic Freedom and Tenure. A Handbook of the American Association of University Professors* (Madison: University of Wisconsin Press, 1969), p. 112.

[15] American Bar Association, Section of Individual Rights and Responsibilities, "A Statement of the Rights and Responsibilities of College and University Students," *Human Rights* 1 (August 1970): 149–150.

I think this one hypothetical example could easily be supplemented with parallel examples involving children in a family, employees in a business, visitors in a library or museum, indeed, from almost every institutionalized setting with which we are familiar. There are some rights that some people simply do not have (so-called special rights),[16] either because they have not yet acquired them or because they have forfeited, waived, alienated them, and so forth. The right to listen and the right to speak, irrespective of who is speaking, who is listening, what the intentions are of the speaker, what the effects are upon the listener, are such rights—if they are rights at all. People in our society believe this, their conduct bears out this belief, and the alternative would be irresponsible and unreasonable.

Notice that this would not be true, given that our prisoners want to hear such lectures, if the entire source of their right to listen were their want, wish, or desire to listen. If this were the source, there would be no way to deny them the right to listen to the lectures by their expert fellow convicts. This point can be generalized. If the source of the right of anyone, including students and faculty, to hear whomever they pleased arose from the desire, wish, or want to listen, then people would have rights that in fact they do not have. To put it concisely, from (1) A wants, wishes, or desires to listen to B talk about x, it does not follow that (2) A has the right to listen to B talk about x, any more than it follows from (3) B wants to talk to A about x, that (4) B has the right to talk to A about x. We simply do not understand the idea of "has the right to" in such a way that it is correct to infer (2) or (4) given (1) or (3), respectively.

In this light, it is useful to return for a moment to those texts quoted earlier, which enshrine current liberal policy on the right to speak and the right to listen in our society. A true understanding of these documentary sources for these rights shows them to be far less sweeping than they at first appear. All that is really being defended by these liberal spokesmen is that the authorities—university administrations, trustees, and state legislatures—should not invoke the

---

[16] I rely here on the familiar distinction drawn between "special" and "general" rights by H. L. A. Hart, "Are There Any Natural Rights?" *Philosophical Review* 64 (1955): 175–192. Reprinted in A. I. Melden, ed., *Human Rights* (Belmont, Calif.: Wadsworth Publishing Co., 1970), pp. 61–75.

police power or other coercive instrumentalities of government to interfere with talk among students and faculty. It is comforting that the ACLU, AAUP, and ABA should be arrayed on the side of students and faculty and their freedom of communication when it is the demonstrated purpose of so many to challenge this freedom. By contrast, it is strikingly rare for these organizations or for academic authorities to insist that communists be hired by university faculties, or that racists and sexists on faculties be exposed as such, or that professors who mastermind the destruction of South Vietnam be fired. Given the massive conservative weight exercised by the authorities who rule the establishment of higher education in the United States, students and faculty need all the help they can get from liberal organizations. In any case, if these liberal texts are correctly construed after the fashion I have urged above, they amount to the assertion that (5) by virtue of being a university trustee or administrator, or a state legislator, one does not have the right to interfere with the freedom of students and faculty to communicate. In our society, I think (5) is true; but it does not entail that (6) students and faculty have a perfect right to listen to whomever they please and say whatever they like—even if the converse implication does hold.

From the argument so far, I think we can conclude three things of general importance. First, if there is a right to speak and to listen on campus, then it must be a "special" right that some persons do not have with respect to some topics. Second, those who do have this right do not get it from their desires, wishes, or wants; where they do get it remains so far an unanswered question. The burden is clearly on advocates of the right to listen to show what it is that is "special" about ordinary persons in their roles as students or faculty, or what it is about the setting of a college or university, in virtue of which this right arises. Third, the right to speak and to listen, which liberals profess to believe in and to protect, is best regarded not as a perfect right at all but as the denial of the right to interfere with the freedom of communication on campus by those in a position of legal authority who have the power (and a long record) of subversive interference.

Let us consider now the sense of "right" in which it may be correctly asserted on liberal assumptions that students and faculty have the right to listen and the right to speak. There are only two important possibilities for us to consider, one a weaker sense of "right" and the other a stronger sense. The first is that of a right in the sense of a *liberty* or *privilege*. (Notice that this question is independent of the prior question whether this right is a "general" or a "special" right. Some general rights are rights in the weak sense, e.g., the privilege against self-incrimination. Some special rights are rights in the strong sense, e.g., the right to specific performance under a contract.) On this interpretation, the right to listen is identical with being under no obligation not to listen. Thus, if students and faculty have the right to listen to whomever they please, this is identical with the absence of any obligation or duty on them to not listen to whomever they please. More loosely, in this sense of "right," the right to listen is simply the absence of any wrongdoing in listening.

If this is the nature of the right to listen, is indecorous reception and preventative disruption of a campus speaker a violation of this right? I think not. For in virtue of this right, no one in the audience has the duty to (or does wrong if he does not) listen without interruption. A right of this sort entails no duty of compliance, non-interference, or respect upon anyone. From (7) A is under no obligation not to listen to B speak about *x*, it does not follow that (8) C, D, (or even A) is under an obligation to listen to B and not to disrupt B. Of course, (8) might be true in certain cases. It might still be wrong in general for lectures ever to be disrupted on college campuses; there might even be a general duty of students and faculty never to disrupt; those who invited B to campus would be acting rudely and in bad faith if they were to disrupt his speech. But if this is true, it cannot be explained merely by reference to the right to listen when that right is construed in the weak sense of "right," as in (7).

The problem, therefore, for the defenders of the liberal doctrine of abstract and unqualified rights to listen and speak, is to show by argument precisely *why* the right to listen is not a mere liberty or privilege. Presumably, liberals believe it is not merely a privilege, since they denounce disruptive interference with speakers and listeners. Two bad arguments come to mind that might explain their view. One is this: Rights in the sense of privileges are not what advocates of the right to listen have in mind, because this idea of a right as a privilege is deviant, novel, unfamiliar, alien to the liberal tradition. Now, this simply cannot be correct. Decades ago, W. N. Hohfeld argued that the privilege sense of "right" is one of its standard senses.[17] Although Hohfeld does not mention it, it is this idea of right as privilege that is clearly contained in Hobbes's doctrine of jus naturale. More recently, H. L. A. Hart has pointed out that it is in precisely this privilege sense of "right" that liberals have understood the right to business competition and a free market.[18] Surely, liberals are in no position to attack the idea of a right to listen as a mere liberty on any such general grounds as this first objection contains. The second bad argument is this: Since the right to listen is a right shared equally by all, the right to listen cannot be merely a liberty. In so far as the right to listen is an equal right, this objection also has no force. Suppose we explain the doctrine of (9) A, B, and C each have the right to listen to M talk about x, as meaning (in the weak sense of "right") (10) A, B, and C each is under no obligation not to listen to M talk about x. This is fully consistent with (11) A, B, and C are not wrong if they disrupt M's talk about x in order to prevent D, E, and F from listening to M. Again, (11) may be false, but not because the right to listen cannot be an equal right unless it is a right in some sense other than the weak sense so far explored. I admit, of course, that I have not proved that the right to listen is a right only in the weak sense. All I have done is to explain what that sense is and to show that in this sense the right to listen is intelligible as an equal right.

No doubt liberals and others who believe in a perfect right to speak and to listen believe that it is a right in the strong sense of the term. They believe, that is, that if anyone has this right, then everyone else has the duty or obligation not to interfere. The nature of this right varies according to the way in which the connection between the right and the duty is understood. Some theorists speak vaguely, as did Bentham, of a "correlation" of right and duty; this is variously understood by some as an identity, by others as an equivalence, and by still others as only an implication. Since this problem is a general one and not confined to peculiarities of the rights under

[17] W. N. Hohfeld, *Fundamental Legal Conceptions* (New Haven, Conn.: Yale University Press, 1923), pp. 39–40. Cf. R. W. M. Dais, *Jurisprudence* (London: Butterworth's, 1964), pp. 226–227, 230–237.

[18] Hart, "Are There Any Natural Rights?," p. 65.

discussion, I will pass it here.[19] I do not think it matters to our discussion how the "correlation" is understood. Even if the right to listen is a right in this strong sense, it still does not follow that it is always wrong to disrupt listeners and speakers, that it is never right to prevent speakers from exercising their rights and listeners from exercising their rights. Once again, the point is a perfectly general one, applying to every known kind of right, or sense of "right," and I shall explain it in a general way.

Just as every theorist of rights has wanted to say that there is a sense of "right" in which it is "correlated" with duties of others, many theorists of rights have wanted to say that the most important sense of "right" is the sense in which (12) A has the right to do x entails (13) it is wrong for A to be denied, prevented, or interfered with in doing x. Other philosophers, especially during the past half-century, have denied this entailment. They have asserted that (12) entails only (14) there is a presumption of wrongness for A to be denied, prevented, or interfered with in doing x. The crucial difference between those who see the connection between (11) and (12) to be analytic, and those who see the connection between (11) and (13) to be analytic, but the connection between (11) and (12) synthetic, lies in the claim that (14) but not (13) is consistent with (15) it is sometimes right to deny, prevent, or interfere with A doing x.

Sometimes it is said that those who understand (12) so that it entails (13) believe in "absolute" (or what I have called perfect) rights, whereas those who reject this entailment in favor of the entailment of (14) by (12) believe in "prima facie" rights. This nomenclature, like the history of these two different conceptions of what it is to be a right and the connection between *having a right to do x* and *doing the right thing in doing x* need not preoccupy us here.[20] It is enough simply to note that it makes an enormous difference whether the right to listen is thought of on the "absolute" or "prima facie" model. If it is thought of on the former model, then

[19] The issue has been discussed most recently by David Lyons, "The Correlativity of Rights and Duties," *Nous* 4 (1970): 45–55; and David Braybrooke, "The Firm but Untidy Correlativity of Rights and Obligations," *Canadian Journal of Philosophy* 1 (1972): 351–363.

[20] See A. I. Melden, *Rights and Right Conduct* (Oxford: Basil Blackwell, 1959), pp. 16–20.

there is no way in which the case for disruptive interference could be made. One bit of evidence that it is in this sense of "right" that liberals understand the right to listen can be found in the belief that it follows from deliberately disruptive activities that the disrupters deserve to be punished.[21] This conclusion could follow so readily only if the right to listen is a right in the strongest and most absolute sense of that term.

If, however, the right to listen is thought of on the latter, or "prima facie," model, then the advocates of the right to listen are in theory quite vulnerable, given their own presumed commitments to liberal values (apart from free expression itself), such as social justice and exemplary campus initiatives, to reasons why certain speakers on certain topics before certain audiences ought to be disrupted. They have no way of rejecting, in advance and a priori, a hearing to those who plead for the correctness of disruption. Defenders of rights as "prima facie" rights have no way of denouncing the threat of disruption merely by appeal to the right to speak and the right to listen. For these rights only set up presumptions, defeasibilities, and the way is now open in theory to showing a greater harm or unfairness in permitting the speaker to speak than in denying him his audience.

On which model ought we think of the rights to listen and to speak? Clearly, I think, on the latter model. The chief objections to the alternative way of conceiving them are two. First, it cannot be plausibly maintained that the right to listen is a special right of students and faculty and absolute in character, because this is almost certainly going to appear to be a bit of special pleading. To avoid this objection, one will have to defend the model of absolute rights for all rights, or all rights of a certain sort. This tack will lead to even graver objections. For one thing, it will be easy to think up intuitive counterexamples (where by acting on the absolute right, one seems to be doing the wrong thing), with the result that the inference from (12) to (13) will be preserved by the drastic expedient of denying the truth of (12), that is, denying that there is

[21] That having a right justifies others in using force to secure it for the holder was asserted by John Stuart Mill, *Utilitarianism* (1861), chap. 5. Recently, it has been emphasized by Hart, "Are There Any Natural Rights?" pp. 73–75; and "Legal and Moral Obligation," in *Essays in Moral Philosophy*, ed. A. I. Melden (Seattle: University of Washington Press, 1958), pp. 106–107.

the right in question. In order to avoid this result, one will have to dispose of the counterexamples by relying upon moral principles of dubious persuasiveness, for example, passivity in the face of injustice. For reasons like this, as I said, recent philosophers have in general defended rights not on the "absolute" model, but only on the "prima facie" model. Perhaps it should be added that we do not take rights less seriously because we do not take them as absolute and categorical foreclosures of conduct.[22]

The consequence of this for our argument is quite clear. Even if the right to listen is a right in the strong, rather than the weak, sense, it does not follow on the model of "prima facie" rights that from the fact that A has the right to do *x*, it is wrong for A to be denied *x*. Even if it is my duty not to disrupt your speech, a duty that follows (in some purely logical fashion) from your right to give a talk before this audience, it will not follow that it is wrong for me to disrupt. All that follows is that, *ceteris paribus*, or prima facie, it is wrong; there is a presumption against my disruption being right conduct. Thus, the move to unqualified moral condemnation of a disrupter is not made legitimate merely by shifting from thinking of the right to listen as a privilege to thinking of it as a duty-correlated right. To put it another way, "It is always wrong to fail in your duty" or "One ought never to behave contrary to duty" are not implicitly tautologies; they can be significantly denied. The basis for their significant denial will be found in the presence of other morally relevant considerations independent of the duty in question.

My argument so far in this section can be succinctly recapitulated as follows. If there is a right to listen to whomever one pleases, a right to speak on any topic and to say anything about it, these rights are not general but special rights. Moreover, even if they were general rights, they may be rights only in the weak sense of liberties or privileges. There is no obvious reason why they must be rights in the strong sense of entailing counterpart duties of forebearance or noninterference upon other persons. Finally, even if they were rights in this strong sense, that does not entail that it is always wrong to disrupt. The result is that it does not matter what sort of rights the right to listen and the right to speak are; it is

[22] See Ronald W. Dworkin, "Taking Rights Seriously," *The New York Review of Books*, December 17, 1970, pp. 23–30. Reprinted in *Is Law Dead?* ed. Eugene V. Rostow (New York: Simon and Schuster, 1971), pp. 168–194.

not conclusive of anybody's conduct in the face of predictable outrages from a speaker that others have to listen to them and he a
right to utter them, or that it is morally wrong if the audience and
speaker are disrupted. It does not matter how the right to listen
and to speak are obtained; it might be, for example, from a need
essential to the role of persons as students or as faculty engaged in
cognitive development (like the need for electricity and vacuum
pumps in laboratories, chalk and blackboards in classrooms). Having the right and exercising it remain subject to the constraints I
have identified.

Now, it could be argued against me at this point that, even if I
am correct in theory, in theory there is a certain kind of logical
gap between a speaker having the right to speak and a listener
having the right to listen, on the one side, and its being wrong to
disrupt the speaker and his audience, on the other side; still in practice there is no such gap on college and university campuses today,
and thus what I have proved at best is the abstract possibility on
liberal assumptions of justified disruption, and no more. The final
step in my argument constitutes a reply to this objection.

Students, student organizations, faculty, faculty committees, administrators—all these individuals and groups on campus are capable of frivolous, irresponsible, unfair, harmful, dangerous activities in exercise of their official or authorized roles and capacities. In
this respect, they are in no way saved from the sins to which flesh
is normally heir by virtue of their campus status or role. High
scores on the SATs, like an earned Ph.D., guarantee nothing about
the exercise of responsible choice in social relations. I mention this
lest it be thought that students and faculty, in the nature of their
calling or by virtue of their special capacities or the special setting
in which they conduct their daily affairs, are immune from error
and beyond manipulation and being manipulated by others for
interests that have nothing to do with conquering the frontiers of
knowledge. Not even the probability that students, faculty, and administration have superior alertness to unfair, harmful, manipula-
tive activities in the guise of sincere and unprejudiced inquiry can
assure that highly objectionable conduct never occurs on campus in
the course of regular classes, meetings, lectures, and so on. For one
thing, there is no such probability; at least, I doubt whether the history of higher education in this nation gives any basis for supposing

otherwise. We must be wary of being blinded by our own compla-cency, derived from what we believe to be our good intentions and our daily experience, lest we fail to see the ways in which institutions of higher education and all those who are part of these institutions actually use their power for socially harmful ends and are naïve as to the social effects their powerful positions have.

I conclude, therefore, that there is nothing in the nature of uni-versity life or the needs of students and faculty, nothing about the rights of speakers to speak and listeners to listen, nothing about constitutional liberties and local ordinances, nothing about the re-sponsibilities of university authorities, nothing about the duties of persons in audiences that shows in general and without ex-ception that it is wrong to disrupt certain speakers in certain situa-tions. I assert, moreover, that—in virtue of actual abuses of author-ity, actual hypocrisies and inconsistencies by academic institutions and officials, actual structures of power in our society, actual vul-nerabilities and crying needs of many people—it is right to disrupt an advocate of racism, of poor people being taxed to pay what is properly owed by the wealthy, of rich and wealthy nations waging aggressive war against their poorer neighbors, of corporate glut and ecocide, and so forth. It is trivial to say—but it is true—that each case must be judged on its own merits. It is platitudinous to com-plain against student disrupters that in this or that instance they have quite misjudged the facts and therefore disrupt without justi-fication; it may well be true. What is profoundly in error is to think that the disruption of free expression on campus could never be and that it has never been justified.

16. Comments on Bedau's "Free Speech, the Right to Listen, and Disruptive Interference"

BY ALAN PASCH

In choosing to speak on the subject of disruptive interference, Professor Bedau has addressed himself to a topic that puts to the test a number of widely held beliefs about academic freedom and the First Amendment and that has had a special poignance the last few years for many in the academic profession who have witnessed disruptive interference—who have, for example, attended (or, for that matter, disrupted) annual meetings of learned societies. But one can, in this latter connection, wish that in discussing disruption Professor Bedau had cast his net a bit wider. For instance, to anyone seeking a ground for the possible justification of the disruption of the March 1970 meeting of the American Philosophical Association in order to show Vietnam atrocity films and adopt resolutions about political repression on the campus, it is of scant help—when what was disrupted was a symposium entitled "Subcategorization Reconsidered" (an austere and quintessentially academic topic)—to be told by Professor Bedau that, even though the speaker's belief is sincere, his "obscenities deserve to be crushed." Still, it would be helpful to get clear even about the relatively narrow kind of disruption he seems to be talking about, the disruption of speakers whose beliefs all of us here would find morally repugnant. We should be grateful to Bedau for shedding light on this important problem.

The discussion, as we are told, is in two parts, the first dealing with the argument in favor of disruption, the second with the argument against it. Saying that he has not found anywhere in print the argument in favor, which is no doubt "inspired by Marxism," that he does not fully grasp or entirely accept the underlying viewpoint, and that he would rather examine than try to invent the defense of the disrupters, Bedau tries "to set out the general argument . . . in its own quasi-Marxist terms." Quickly overcoming this early diffidence, he speaks thereafter of *his* argument, and he asserts in his final paragraph that "it is right to disrupt an advocate of racism, of poor people being taxed to pay what is properly owed by the wealthy, of rich and wealthy nations waging aggressive war against their poorer neighbors, of corporate glut and ecocide, and so forth." I will refer to this as his strong conclusion, since it would enable whoever accepted it to claim of certain specific speakers in specific situations that persons have a right to disrupt them and that either there is no corresponding right to listen to them, or, if there is, the right to listen is outweighed by the right to disrupt.

Turning to the arguments given by liberals against disruption, Bedau considers the nature of the right to listen and finds that it is a special right, which does not hold for all persons in all circumstances, and that either it is a weak right (in the sense that there is nothing wrong about listening), or, if a strong right (in the sense that it is wrong to interfere with anyone else's listening), it is a weak, or prima facie, strong right and not the strong, or absolute, kind that can never be abrogated in the face of other, overriding, rights. The conclusion he reaches is that there is nothing about the nature of university life or about the needs, rights, liberties, or responsibilities of students, faculty, administration, speakers, or listeners to "show in general and without exception that it is wrong to disrupt certain speakers in certain situations." I will refer to this as his weak conclusion, since it could not be used to sustain the claim, in any specific situation, that the listeners have a right to disrupt the speakers, and since it is compatible with its never being right to disrupt the speakers.

I will confine the remainder of my discussion of Bedau's paper to four comments, apart from those implicit in my account of the paper. Each of the four strikes me as obvious and not very interesting philosophically, but needing to be made; I will make them briefly. One is that Bedau is much less careful about the arguments leading to his strong conclusion than about those leading to his weak conclusion, which is a pity, because what we are thus left with is the shaky and the impotent. But, of course, it would be unrealistic to expect it to be the other way around. Before one could profitably discuss the strong conclusion, at any rate, one would need to know a great deal more than Bedau tells us about the nature of the right to disrupt that he says we have.

The second comment has to do with Bedau's argument that the right to listen is not an absolute but a prima facie one. He says that it cannot be plausibly maintained that it is both absolute and special, "because this is almost certainly going to appear to be a bit of special pleading"—and there are even graver objections to the claim that the right to listen is both absolute and general. In defending academic freedom, however, we are already engaged in a kind of special pleading, and we should therefore count it not a defect—or much of a defect—in an argument defending the right of academics to listen, that it should involve a bit more special pleading. (Bedau occasionally addresses himself to the problem of the right to listen outside the framework of academic freedom, and insofar as he does, of course, this comment is without force.)

The third point hangs on the question, "Who is the university?" According to the second of the arguments defending the strong conclusion, "The vaunted neutrality of the university is in fact false, and plainly so. The government contracts, tax subsidies, classified research, military and police training programs, economic interests of influential trustees and alumni all tell a different story. The university's 'hands off' policy on behalf of allowing anyone duly invited to use its facilities for purposes of speech making masks its tacit but wholehearted support of the existing order." Professor Hughes's metaphor of a minisociety is useful for making my point, though Professor Hughes's point was a normative one about being civilized, whereas I want to call attention to the complexity of a university, to the respect in which it is a microsociety. It is—or normally would be—belaboring the obvious to point out that there are a vast number of things that go on within a university and that it is a crippling and, I think, irrational allocation of moral resources to disable its academic sector because of something unsavory about its nonacademic sector. I do not mean that faculty and students should not concern themselves with the nonacademic sector of the university and agitate to eliminate the unsavory. I mean instead that Bedau is wrong—or that whoever he is speaking for is wrong—in suggesting that the academic vice-president's defense of the right to listen should be ignored because of the "tacit but wholehearted support of the existing social order" by the director of finance.

Finally, there is an unsettling need to call attention to a recurrent feature—perhaps the dominant feature—of the arguments that Bedau has constructed or reconstructed in favor of his strong conclusion, a feature that is to be found also in other papers and responses here. The third argument is that the only interests served by extending toleration, courtesies, liberties, and rights to the spokesmen for oppression are the interests of the oppressors, and one ought not, therefore, extend toleration, courtesies, liberties, and rights to the spokesmen for oppression. One who wishes to use the conclusion as a guide must, of course, know who the spokesmen for oppression are, but whoever pauses to ask the question, "Who are the spokesmen for oppression?" is certain to invite the accusation of being "culpably ignorant or cynically knowledgeable," to borrow a phrase from the first argument. Bedau does, perhaps in anticipation of the question, suggest answers in his fourth argument, but the answers can scarcely be taken seriously by one who takes the question seriously. All but one shift the burden of identifying the speakers who deserve disruption to some concept no more able to do the job than "spokesmen for oppression": dangerous and outrageous doctrines, suave and hypocritical servants of their masters, what the speakers have done or said elsewhere, the purpose of the meeting, and so forth. The single characterization of speakers deserving disruption that might enable us actually to identify someone as such is "pompous and arrogant elitists whose style is *Diktat* and pronunciamento." The trouble with this (apart from its somehow conjuring up an image of a comic-opera college being addressed by Groucho Marx) is that pompous and arrogant elitists whose style is *Diktat* and pronunciamento not only have already infiltrated our faculties but also are to be found on both sides of every question, so that Bedau—assuming he really intends this to be taken seriously—has got it quite wrong. Either we should refuse to listen, and in fact should disrupt, these speakers irrespective of whether they are advocating the extermination of the American Indian or the extermination of prejudice, poverty, and oppression, or else they deserve disruption only when they are speaking in the interest of oppression. In the first case we are disrupting speakers who do not deserve to be disrupted, and in the second we still lack ways of identifying those who do deserve such treatment.

The point of the question about who should be disrupted, and the recurrent feature of many of the arguments Bedau has marshalled for us—and of some of the other arguments we have heard—is that an aprioristic undercurrent is easily discerned which is disturbing and which, insofar as it is to be found in the academic community, is more than disturbing. Packed into the ideas of selective tolerance and "deserving disruption" are a claim to infallibility and a refusal to let the sword cut both ways. Both the claim and the refusal are inimical to the idea of a university. Speaking about democracy, Bertrand Russell remarked during the City College case that "it is necessary that people should learn to endure having their sentiments outraged."[1] To be told now that the university should not provide a forum for "sincere believers in dangerous and outrageous doctrines," or that such speakers, when they do find a forum, deserve to be disrupted, suggests that there is within the academic community today a depressing urgency about Russell's remark.

[1] Nicholas Capaldi, *Clear and Present Danger* (New York: Pegasus, 1969), p. 203.

17. Reply to Alan Pasch

BY HUGO ADAM BEDAU

Except for one or two observations at the end, what
follows is confined to responding to the criticism that Alan Pasch
has written in the first part of his essay, directed to my original
paper. I am grateful to him for his criticisms, although I am un-
persuaded by most of them. I shall take them up roughly in the
order in which he made them.

1. I disagree with Pasch that my explicit discussion of disruption
is of "scant help" in many cases, including the actual case he presents as a counterexample. It may appear that he is right, however,
because my "radical" argument relied heavily on the existence of
what I called "obscenities" that deserve to be "crushed," whereas
in some disruptions we can point, apparently, to no such obscenities.
I do not wish for present purposes to commit myself to the doctrine
that obscenity lies in the eye of the beholder, much less to attribute
any such vulgar doctrine to radicals. Yet what is and what is not
obscene is at the heart, I take it, of Pasch's objection. I suggest that
disruption, like other forms of direct protest, may be justified not
only by the grossest and most violent obscenities in the immediate
vicinity. Consider in particular the harsh and barbaric realities
that some suffer even as others blunt their awareness of these causes
for grievance in the pursuit of trivial exercises in the higher but
decadent learning. Such benign conduct has long ago been con-

demned as "fiddling while Rome burns." Is it not quite possible that
this is how some of the disrupters viewed the immediate situation
in the case Pasch cites?

In such cases, if we think disruption is justified and accept my
radical argument, it will be incumbent on us to believe and to convince others that passivity, indifference, preoccupation with the
finer things in life, and enjoyment of the intrinsic good of philosophical discourse can be obscene when they prevent those involved
from attending to the remedy of extreme injustice suffered by
others. I do not think it is always absurd or impossible or unreasonable to argue in this way. If we think disruption is not
justified, we can still accept my argument; what we cannot do is
accept the judgment that there is obscenity in passivity and indifference, at least, not in the case in question. I have difficulty with
Pasch's use of the example he cites because I believe he starts with
the conviction that the disruption was not justified and that no
obscenities were involved. If this is his view, why should he object
to my analysis, since it can be used to vindicate his position and
condemn the disrupters? The fact that some radicals engaged in a
disruption that they thought to be justified, but which my analysis
shows to be unjustified, is not in itself a very strong objection to
my analysis. After all, radicals can make errors of fact and of judgment in the application of an otherwise sound analysis. It is no use
to Pasch to reply that it is my analysis that is wrong, because the
radicals thought they were justified but not because (as my argument required) obscenities were present and deserving of disruption. For we have seen how radicals might reason to conclude that
obscenities were present after all. I suspect Pasch knows as little
as I do about whether the disrupters in the case he cites would
accept or reject my analysis, in so far as it turns on the issue of
"obscenities deserving to be crushed."

What all this shows is that Pasch's counterexample to my analysis
is inconclusive until and unless we can answer both the question of
whether obscenities were involved in the scene as the disrupters
understood it and the question whether their disruption was justified. I am not convinced that my analysis of the radical argument
is correct, and I would not want it treated as an Archimedean point.
But, surely, the same caution should apply to judgments of the
obscene. I am convinced that my argument can be applied without

ad hoc revisions or gross distortions in order to cover in a plausible way the kind of case Pasch has brought forward against it.

2. Pasch notices a distinction between what he calls the "strong conclusion" and the "weak conclusion" in my paper, and he comments that my arguments for the former are so weak as to leave it "shaky." I do not dispute the distinction he draws between these two "conclusions," but I do object to his assessment of my reasoning behind the "strong" one. I think he believes my reasoning there is worse than it is because he believes my conclusion has an entailment that I do not accept and because he overlooked my denials of this entailment (and therefore did not go on to show my denial to be in error).

Specifically, Pasch correctly asserts that I try to argue to the "strong conclusion" that (*a*) "it is right to disrupt" a racist. But I do not agree, as he insists, that doing so commits me to further conclusion that (*b*) "persons have a right to disrupt" such a speaker in certain situations. He makes it clear that the right to disrupt in (*b*) is to be understood as a strong or absolute right. I think Pasch attacks my reasoning for (*a*) because he erroneously believes that (*a*) entails (*b*), and he believes that I have only very weak arguments for (*b*). What Pasch seems to have overlooked are my remarks at several places where I deny the inference from (*a*) to (*b*). I denied the inference on two different grounds: the quite general ground that there is no direct inference from the truth of "It is right for A to do *x*" to the truth of "A has the right to do *x*"; and the special ground that radicals, as I understand them, no more believe in a perfect or strong right to disrupt (with one exception, to be noted below) than they believe in a perfect right to speak or to listen. Consequently, if I am correct, radicals would assert (*a*) but would go on to deny that doing so commits them to (*b*). It is Pasch, not I, therefore, who must produce some arguments to show that (*a*) does entail (*b*), and that I and anyone else would be inconsistent if we were to accept (*a*) and reject (*b*). Pasch says he does not bother to criticize my argument for (*a*) because he thinks that "before one could profitably . . . do so, one would need to know a great deal more . . .about the nature of the right to disrupt." This may be true for those who believe that (*a*) entails (*b*). But it is not true on my view. Whether, if he were to abandon his belief in this entailment, he would also change his mind about the relative inconclusiveness of my arguments for what he calls my "strong conclusion," I will not try to guess.

The merit of Pasch's doubts about my argument, even if I am correct in diagnosing them to involve the confusion alleged above, is that they point to a considerable omission in my initial essay. He wants to know exactly what I think (a radical ought to think) about "the right to disrupt," and surely that is a plausible desire on his part, one I am sure he shares with others who have heard the paper. Since in my original paper I did not appeal (on behalf of radicals) to any such right or try to establish that there is such a right, it is perhaps understandable that Pasch should have misunderstood my views as I think he did. Let me, therefore, try to say something directly on the matter now, even though I will content myself with drawing out a few strands from the original paper apropos of this issue.

One way to understand a right to disrupt speakers and their listeners in an academic setting is to see it simply as an extension of the right to render negative applause, to boo, hiss, laugh derisively, stomp the floor, and to heckle.[1] A right to do these things is, I take it, understood as part of the tacit structure of the give-and-take between an audience and a speaker, at least in which we might call Hyde Park Corner situations. I am reluctant to see disruption as merely an extension of this right to heckle, because disruption is intended to bring about the end to the exchange between speaker and listener, whereas heckling is meant merely to spice it up, to accelerate the exchange.

Another way to claim the right to disrupt is to do so in the same sense of "right" as it was claimed by blacks and whites in the 1960s that, whatever the law may provide, they had the right to disrupt "separate but equal" facilities by sit-ins, wade-ins, ride-ins, and so forth. This move would turn the right to disrupt an audience in an academic setting into a mode of civil disobedience. But now we encounter a different difficulty. If the right to disrupt and the disruption itself are understood in this way, then the mode of justification has probably been transmuted from radical to liberal premises. The appeal to a right to disrupt in this sense will be a characteristically

---

[1] I am indebted here to a comment made at the Conference by Judith Jarvis Thomson, though I would not want to imply that she would approve of the use I have made of it.

liberal, not radical, maneuver, just as civil disobedience itself is typically a liberal and not a radical mode of political conduct.[2] So I am reluctant to try to understand the idea of a right to disrupt in this fashion. It seems to saddle radicals with a belief in conventional liberal or "bourgeois" rights.

The only way I see to get around this difficulty is to suppose that radicals appeal to a right to disrupt as a special instance of the revolutionary right of the people, or the working class, or the oppressed to take whatever direct action is appropriate to secure their interests. The idea of revolutionary rights, as distinct from the right of revolution itself, is not clear to me, and I will not attempt to say anything more about it here.[3] I must add, however, that any appeal to such revolutionary rights in order to justify disruption of speakers in academic settings (like those cited at the beginning of my original paper) looks semiridiculous to me, and I will not come to its defense. I would even go further and agree with my liberal friends that, in this sense of "right," there has rarely if ever been a right to disrupt speakers on campuses in recent years in this country. If that shows I am no radical, then I can only comment that nowhere in my original paper did I claim or imply that I was one.

3. Is it true, as Pasch argues, that even if I was right when I said that it is a bit of special pleading to maintain that the right to listen is a special and absolute right, this is not "much of a defect," since "in defending academic freedom we are already engaged in a kind of special pleading"? I would point out, as other papers in this Conference show, that there is some uncertainty over the status that academic freedom enjoys as a liberty and as a right. Some defenders of academic freedom, since they see it only as a special case of the general rights of free speech that all men have, would not accept the view that, in claiming academic freedom as a right, they are engaged in a form of special pleading. If, as others think,

---

[2] Radical defenses of civil disobedience are not easy to find; see, e.g., Bruce Pech, "Radical Disobedience and Its Justification," in *Civil Disobedience: Theory and Practice*, ed. H. A. Bedau (New York: Pegasus, 1969), pp. 263–268, and the dilemma posed for Pech's argument, ibid., pp. 216–217.

[3] I have discussed it in an unpublished paper, "Tentative Thoughts on Revolutionary Theory," given in the symposium, "Philosophy and Revolution," at the University of Wisconsin-Milwaukee, April 30, 1971.

the freedoms claimed for and by academics are special in that they
go beyond those properly possessed and enjoyed by others, then
Pasch's riposte may go unchallenged. Even so, however, his suggestion tends to obscure the point I thought I had made (though,
perhaps only obscurely), that the protagonists of an absolute and
special right to listen were engaged in a sort of *philosophical* special pleading. This is not, as I understand it, the kind of special
pleading engaged in (on his view) by the defenders of academic
freedom. They do not (at least, not necessarily) rely on any special
conception of freedom; they declare only that members of an
academic community have a perfectly ordinary freedom. All that is
special about it is that other persons, or even the same persons in
other roles or capacities, lack it. But I was supposing that defenders
of the right to listen must beware of relying on some special *sense*
of "right," especially if, as I believe, they would have to disallow
this sense of the term in elucidating other rights. Tacitly picking
and choosing among senses of "right" is a different sort of special
pleading than is insisting that some but not others have a certain
right. After all, the idea that some people have rights that others
lack is hardly controversial; it is obviously true. But the idea that a
particular right is absolute and is a right in a special sense of
"right" is controversial, or ought to be, since it cries out for philosophical analysis and argument. Since, I take it, Pasch does not
dispute my point that special pleading of a philosophical sort is required for those who would advocate an absolute right to listen,
perhaps it would be best not to obscure this "defect" by coupling it
as he has with a possible further defect of a different kind.

4. Pasch's third comment is a familiar, not implausible, but
nevertheless troubling one. His argument can be recast so that it
looks like this: Since (*a*) we must distinguish between the "academic" and "nonacademic" sectors within a university, and since
(*b*) the "unsavory" antics that provoke and may deserve disruption
do not fall within the academic sector, it follows that (*c*) it is
"wrong" for students and faculty to disrupt within the academic
sector. The argument is not persuasive. Looked at empirically,
premise (*b*) is often false, and conspicuously so in some of the
cases I cited. Professor Richard Herrenstein (to cite him here only
for the sake of argument) is a member of a university faculty, and

when he travels to other campuses he is usually a guest there of other faculty and students. The course curricula on which ROTC relies were voted in on many campuses by the faculties of Arts and Sciences, of which ROTC is usually a department. And so on, in many (even if not all) cases. Presumably, Pasch would not deny that for these cases his argument simply does not apply. Or he might think that it does, once it is slightly revised. The point of his argument seems to be that it is wrong to cause one part of the university to pay for the moral defects of another part. If this is his view, then he would presumably regard it as wrong to interrupt classes in French literature in order to protest ROTC on campus: it is the ROTC classes that should be disrupted (if any should). I mention this possible embellishment in his argument because it brings us to the essence of the matter, which is not in his premise (*b*) but in his premise (*a*). This premise relies upon the principle that the right hand bears no responsibility for what the left hand is doing. But does not reliance upon any such principle make too much out of functional divisions of labor in the typical modern university? Obviously, reformist liberals, not to mention radicals, are not going to accept this principle, as Pasch must know. They are going to remind him that the notion of a "university community" and of a "society of seekers after the truth" (such phrases are often on the lips of university spokesmen) make it artificial to invoke the distinction that he does in (*a*). They will say that to lean on it as Pasch advises is to concede that the university does not belong to the faculty and students first and foremost, but that the non-academic tail (at least, on matters affecting public issues and off-campus politics) may wag the academic dog, that our role as academics rigidly defines the scope of our responsibility and our rights. Here, I want neither to attack nor to defend such views but only to insist that they are held and that those who do hold them will not accept premise (*a*) in the way Pasch wants. Furthermore, I would add, as an objection to the conclusion of Pasch's argument, that disruption in one setting indirectly related to the setting of some grievance may not be merely symbolic, or futile, or irrelevant. It can produce a remedy, as reformers and radicals have learned on other issues long ago. Like the hostility toward indirect civil disobedience in the body politic expressed by former Justice

Abe Fortas and the former Solicitor General Erwin Griswold,[4] Pasch has taken a parallel position regarding campus disruption and thus verges upon their conspicuous errors.[5]

5. I had anticipated Pasch's final comment in the opening section of my paper. Liberals do say, as he does, that "the ideas of selective tolerance and . . . 'deserving disruption'" have packed into them "a claim to infallibility and a refusal to let the sword cut both ways that are inimical to the idea of a university." But is this really true? Radical caucuses and meetings are, in my experience, notorious for the way in which factions disrupt, applying therein to themselves the principle they rely upon in disrupting the university. Where is the inconsistency? Surely, Pasch does not mean to imply that at universities run by radicals, with radical faculty, student body, and administrators in the great majority, the rights of dissenting liberals and conservatives to disrupt are brutally ignored. For there are no such radical universities. Whether, if there were, dissent and disruption would be crushed and, if so, on what grounds (e.g., to prevent ideological counterrevolution), we can only guess. Accusing radical disrupters of implied claims to infallibility is, I think, mostly a hangover that liberals suffer from after having read or dimly remembered) Mill's *On Liberty*. It is not an inference I would be tempted to make from the disrupter's actual conduct.

Finally, I am pleased to be reminded of Russell's sage advice, because it is to liberals, not to radicals, that his words apply most aptly at present. It has been the inability of most faculties to accept the outrage of their liberal sentiments provoked by the conduct of radicals, hippies, crazies, and ordinary dissenters, that has been a destructive factor in universities during the past few years whenever major disruptions have occurred. Liberals on campuses from Berkeley to Columbia seemed to have incredible difficulty in appreciating the fact that, in most cases, the grievances that provoked disruption were large scale, chronic, and legitimate, and the disruptions were not mere self-indulgent antics of irresponsible adolescents. Business as usual—which for academics meant talk, read, lis-

---

[4] See Abe Fortas, *Concerning Dissent and Civil Disobedience* (New York: Signet, 1968); and Erwin N. Griswold, "Dissent—1968," *Tulane Law Review* 42 (1968): 726–739.

[5] See my paper, "Civil Disobedience and Personal Responsibility for Injustice," *The Monist* 54 (1970): 517–535.

ten, write, meet, telephone as usual—in the face of social crisis is what these faculty could not cheerfully interrupt. They could not bear to see their liberal freedom and rights, and the civilized sentiments behind them, abused and outraged. Well, I agree with Russell. It is necessary that they should learn to endure having these sentiments outraged.

6. After reviewing Pasch's comments and my own notes on the discussion at the Conference, I am inclined to conclude that the major claims of my original paper stand essentially unscathed by the criticism. My original purpose was twofold: The first was to show what a radical argument for disruption of speech on campus looks like, on the assumption that liberals need more familiarity with such arguments if they are to cope with them reasonably. My other purpose was to show how complex and inconclusive was the standard liberal doctrine about the nature of rights, including the right to listen, on the assumption that liberals tend to underestimate these features. Professor Pasch, like other critics at the Conference, did not attempt to show how I had misunderstood the radical argument or how it might be made stronger. Instead, like the others, he showed that he thought it was weak and that he was content to leave it in that condition. Nor did he and other critics at the Conference attempt to show how I had misunderstood the standard liberal theory of rights, or how it is much stronger than I suppose it to be if only it is correctly stated. It is tempting to infer from this that the radical argument for disruption is as strong and the liberal theory of rights no stronger than I portrayed them as being. Whether further criticism, directed at these major claims of the paper, could cause me to alter substantially what I wrote I do not know.

18. Comments on Bedau's Reply

BY ALAN PASCH

1. I appear to have been mistaken in supposing that when Professor Bedau was talking about the justification of disruption, a disruption of a kind he could not have had in mind is that of a metaphysical symposium entitled "Subcategorization Reconsidered" at a meeting of a learned society. The reason I thought he was discussing something quite different is that he spoke of disrupting speakers whose "obscenities deserve to be crushed." Alas, when I thought I was casually remarking the occurrence of what he and I would agree is another kind of disruption, Bedau not only took me to be challenging him with a counterexample, but also he denied that it is a counterexample : ". . . enjoyment of the intrinsic good of philosophical discourse can be obscene."

Bedau's strategy is to portray a point of view from which the event in question—the philosophical symposium—might appear to be obscene. The portrayal, like a number of others he gives us, exhibits a genuine flair for the subtle and penetrating appreciation of a viewpoint he professes not to be his own. "Consider in particular the harsh and barbaric realities that some suffer even as others blunt their awareness of these causes for grievance in the

NOTE: The numbering of these comments corresponds to that of Bedau's replies.

pursuit of trivial exercises in the higher but decadent learning. Such benign conduct has long ago been condemned as 'fiddling while Rome burns.' Is it not quite possible that this is how some of the disrupters viewed the immediate situation in the case Pasch cites?"

I think it is not only quite possible but also almost certain that Bedau has succeeded in capturing the viewpoint, or at least a part of the viewpoint, of the disrupters. I also think the viewpoint is wrong. It was, after all, Nero who fiddled while Rome burned, and what was remarkable about his fiddling is not that fiddling was going on but that he was supposed to be putting out the fires instead. This is not to say that if he had been putting out the fires he would not have been entitled to a little relaxation, nor that metaphysicians ought never to engage in political action, nor even that circumstances justifying the disruption of the symposium— circumstances in which its continuance would have been "obscene" —are inconceivable. It is only to say that performance of one's duties, and "preoccupation with the finer things in life," even though pursued amid harsh and barbaric realities and at the cost of "attending to the remedy of extreme injustice suffered by others," are not obscene and do not deserve to be crushed.

I am very unsure, however, about whether and where I have joined issue with Bedau. It seems clear that he is not presenting the argument for disruption as his own; at times he appears instead merely to be polishing and perfecting the argument—transforming it into a cameo to be held up for our aesthetic contemplation. From this standpoint he would doubtless maintain, in discussing the point of view he has so carefully presented, that it is false that I have betrayed my utter failure to understand what he is doing. Still, he displays the position as something more than an *objet d'art*: "I do not think it is always absurd or impossible or unreasonable to argue in this way." Perhaps, then, Bedau and I are in agreement, since I too can conceive of circumstances that would justify disruption of the symposium. But, no, the kind of circumstance I have in mind is a bomb about to go off in the back of the hall (clear and present danger), where Bedau has to be alluding to poverty and unjust war. He must, in other words, be claiming, on his own behalf and not merely in an effort to portray the radicalist position, that it is sometimes reasonable to argue that a metaphysical sym-

posium should be disrupted on the ground that the injustice, the
oppression, the exploitation rampant in the world render the symposium obscene. (A further obstacle to understanding Bedau's intentions and to responding to his paper is that although he calls his
paper "Free Speech, the Right to Listen, and Disruptive Interference," he appears to be as interested, or more interested, in what
a specifically *radical* argument for the right to disrupt would be
like. Thus, he is unwilling to construe disruption as civil disobedience and to argue for it in ways that have become familiar in recent years, because it "seems to saddle radicals with a belief in
conventional liberal or 'bourgeois' rights.")

Whether "Subcategorization Reconsidered" is or could be obscene is not the only problem raised by Bedau's reply in connection
with that happening in 1970. Bedau asks why I should object to his
analysis if I believe that the symposium was not obscene and that
the disruption of it was not justified, "since it can be used to vindicate [Pasch's] position and condemn the disrupters." If my
reading of Bedau's paper is correct (and I can find no other interpretation), the radical argument as he reconstructs it is that (1)
obscenities deserve to be crushed, and (2) the symposium is an
obscenity, and therefore (3) the symposium deserves to be crushed.
What Bedau means in saying the analysis can be used to vindicate
my position seems to be that if I agree that obscenities deserve to
be crushed, then, by denying that the symposium is an obscenity, I
can still deny that the symposium deserves to be crushed and thus
find the ground I need for condemning the disrupters. Given the
argument whose premises are (1) and (2) and whose conclusion
is (3), in other words, and given my conviction that (3) is false,
I ought not to object to (1), because I also happen to think that
(2) is false and this saves me from having to infer (3). Thus, Bedau says, I can use his analysis to vindicate my position (the position that (3) is false). The logic is a miracle of versatility. It should
convince me also that obliquities deserve to be crushed, since I
don't think that the symposium is an obliquity (actually I am
rather less sure of this than I am that it isn't an obscenity), and I
can thus once more vindicate my position by escaping the conclusion that the symposium deserves to be crushed.

Radical logic aside, my reply to Bedau's question about why I
should object to his analysis is that, even though acceptance of (1)

does not commit me to acceptance of (3), I happen not to accept (1). I do not think obscenities deserve to be crushed.

2. Bedau has quite rightly taken me to task for moving so easily from (*a*) "it is right to disrupt" to (*b*) "persons have a right to disrupt." My doing so is to be attributed, however, not to a belief that (*a*) implies (*b*), but to sheer carelessness. I used both (*a*) and (*b*) to refer to Bedau's conclusion that "it is right to disrupt an advocate of racism," and I then compounded the confusion by calling this his strong conclusion, by which I meant not that it is a strong right (for, as Bedau points out, it is not a right at all), but merely that it is strong in comparison with what I called his weak conclusion: that nothing shows "in general and without exception that it is wrong to disrupt certain speakers in certain situations." Nor, in calling the first conclusion strong and the second weak, did I mean that the first but not the second is absolute; again, it is not rights that we are talking about. What I meant is merely that the first conclusion could be used in certain specific situations to defend disruption and is in this sense stronger than the second conclusion, which could never be used in a specific situation to defend disruption. I still think that Bedau's arguments for his "strong" conclusion are weak and that we need to know more about the circumstances in which it is right to disrupt. I am sorry these points got obfuscated by my illicit move from (*a*) to (*b*).

3. Bedau thinks I have failed to distinguish between two kinds of special pleading and that, in failing to distinguish, I have obscured a point of his. I have to confess that I have not succeeded in separating the two kinds of special pleading he wants to keep distinct, and I am thus inclined to believe that there is only one kind. But, of course, my ability to make distinctions does not depend on my seeing the need for them, and I will try to make the distinction I believe Bedau is talking about in order to discuss his complaint.

Of the two kinds of special pleading he talks about, one may be called *ordinary* and the other *philosophical*. But, in order to explain this difference, another distinction is helpful, this one between two kinds of special rights and liberties. There are those rights and liberties that are special in the ordinary sense and those that are special in the philosophical sense; I will refer to these as "O-special" and "P-special" rights and liberties, respectively. Bedau speaks of

O-special rights as special in the sense that some persons have them
and others do not, or that some or all persons have them in some
circumstances but not in others. Special pleading insofar as it may
be involved in the defense of O-special rights or liberties, is ordinary special pleading. To the extent that academic freedom is
special, it is O-special: ". . . members of an academic community
have a perfectly ordinary freedom. All that is special about it is that
other persons, or even the same persons in other roles or capacities, lack it." If, as I suggested, the defenders of academic freedom
are engaged in special pleading, it is ordinary special pleading they
are engaged in.

The example of a P-special right that occurred in Bedau's paper
is the right to listen, considered (but only as a hypothetical case)
as an absolute and special right. Anyone who attempted to defend
it as absolute and special would have to engage in a kind of special
pleading that is philosophical, not ordinary. It might be supposed
that what is P-special about this right (or would be P-special about
it if it existed) is not a matter of there being a special class of persons who have it—not a matter, in other words, of those character-
istics that make academic freedom O-special. However, this is not as
clear as one might wish, since what Bedau was considering in his
paper is the right to listen as "a special right of students and faculty,"
which would appear to make the right to listen O-special instead
of P-special and thus to involve in its defense the same kind of
special pleading involved in the defense of academic freedom as
special. Perhaps what Bedau has in mind is that it is the existence
of a special class of persons who have academic freedom that
makes academic freedom O-special, whereas it is not the existence of
a special class of persons who have the right to listen that makes the
right to listen P-special. A right or liberty, he might want to say, is
O-special if its being special depends solely on there being persons
who have it and persons who do not, and it is P-special if, even
though belonging only to some persons and not to others, it is not
just this consideration on which its being special depends.

On the basis of what other considerations, then, may a P-special
right or liberty be said to be special? Bedau's answer seems to be
that what makes it P-special is not some *characteristic* of the right
or the liberty but the right or the liberty itself. One gets the impression that an O-special right is not really special, because, al-

though some characteristic of the right is special, the right itself is "perfectly ordinary." A P-special right, on the other hand, really is special, because the right itself, and not simply some characteristic of it, is special. It hardly needs to be pointed out that this is an extremely metaphysical notion of a special right or liberty. One can understand why Bedau thinks that those who defend it are "engaged in a sort of *philosophical* special pleading," unlike those who defend academic freedom, which, even if special, is only O-special and thus calls only for ordinary special pleading. One can understand why Bedau wants to disallow the philosophical special pleading he thinks is required for a defense of the right to listen as a special and absolute right, and why he is annoyed by my coupling it with the relatively innocuous kind of special pleading associated with the defense of academic freedom as a special freedom.

One can understand, but one is not repentant. For I do not believe that Bedau is entitled to speak of more than one sense in which rights and liberties are special, and therefore I do not believe the basis exists for the distinction he has drawn between two kinds of special pleading. To say that academic freedom, if special, is a perfectly ordinary freedom that some people have and other people do not have is, in the context in which Bedau says it, to suggest that what *makes* academic freedom special is that some people have it and others do not. But surely it is not just that some people happen to have it and others happen to lack it; the people who have it have it for a reason, the people who lack it lack it for a reason, and to specify the reasons is to say what is special about academic freedom.

But in this, academic freedom is no different than the right to listen—considered as absolute and special. Describing what it is about the right to listen that would be considered special, if it were special, is tantamount to specifying the reasons some persons would have that right and others would not. The specification could, of course, be very difficult, especially if the claim (or hypothesis) were that the right is absolute as well as special. It is clear, moreover, that Bedau finds this difficulty significant; part of the reason, if not the entire reason, for his claim that a defense of the right to listen as special and absolute would have to be in terms of a special sense of "right" is that the idea "cries out for philosophical analysis and argument," and he pointedly contrasts this with its being "obviously true" that some people have rights that others lack. But he exaggerates the contrast; I do not think he finds it obviously true—or obviously false—that academic freedom is special, and, indeed, it is presumably the need for philosophical analysis and argument that underlies the present conference on the concept of academic freedom.

In any case, there is not a great deal of promise in the analytical techniques of inventing a new sense of "special" or a new sense of "right" whenever we find ourselves confronted with a special right that is badly in need of analysis, or of supposing that there must be something peculiarly "philosophical" about ill-understood rights. It is better to proceed on the assumption that the liberty or the right is—as special rights and liberties go—perfectly ordinary, and only if we are otherwise unable to get clear about it should we declare it to be new or deviant. What is true in this respect about special rights and liberties is also true about special pleading. In his reply, Bedau may have left out some reasons for drawing the distinction he did, but, on the basis of what he has told us, the distinction is not justified.

4. Bedau is correct in saying that the essence of my comment about the complexity of the university is in the premise about the academic and nonacademic sectors of the university. It is not enough just to draw the distinction, however. The premise was perhaps summed up best in my statement that "it is a crippling and, I think, irrational allocation of moral resources to disable [the university's] academic sector because of something unsavory about its nonacademic sector." The reason I made this point in terms of the academic and nonacademic sectors is that I was responding to a passage in which Bedau seems primarily to be talking about the university's involvement with other institutions—government, industry, the military, and so forth. But, although I find the distinction between the university's academic sector and its nonacademic sector useful, the premise could, as Bedau recognizes, be reformulated to cover the disruption of French classes by students and faculty protesting the presence on campus of ROTC and the disruption of visiting speakers by students and faculty objecting to the visitors' published views. That the primary commitment of faculty and students in a university is to *education* would be either spelled out in

the reformulation or would be a presupposition of it, and I think this is the point at which I would be attacked by radicals and "reformist liberals" (who Bedau now throws into the discussion, perhaps to indicate the enormity of my error). Although some reformers and radicals may deny that the primary commitment of faculty and students is to education, what is more likely is that the conflict between us will show up in my believing and their not believing that the commitment is violated when French classes and visiting speakers are disrupted. This, at any rate, is the point on which I think debate should focus, and on this point the question of the efficacy of disruption (which Bedau introduces as an objection to my conclusion that disruption is wrong) has no bearing.

5. It seems to me disingenuous of Bedau to cite the disruption of radical meetings by radical factions as evidence of the willingness of radicals to let the sword cut both ways. If by "radical meetings" he means meetings of radicals for, say, organizational purposes, what goes on at radical meetings is clearly irrelevant to the question of whether an aprioristic claim to infallibility underlies disruptive interference. If, on the other hand, he is talking about public lectures on campus by radical speakers, then, if the disrupters are members of a faction significantly *different* than that of the speakers, this is no more an instance of "applying . . . to themselves the principle they rely upon in disrupting the university" than would be the disruption by Americans for Democratic Action of a lecture by a longtime Democratic senator from the Deep South. If the disrupters are members of the *same* faction as that of the speakers but suddenly find themselves in sharp *disagreement* with what is being said, then their being members of the same faction becomes less significant than the disagreement which leads them to disrupt, and that disagreement prevents this too from being an instance of applying their disruptive principle to themselves. If Bedau has in mind the disruption of the speakers by members of the *same* faction who *agree* with what is being said, then he would have to cite an actual instance in order to escape the charge of frivolity. (In each instance, Bedau's helpful distinction between disrupting and heckling must be borne in mind.) Finally, my claim that disruption is inimical to the idea of a university was directed not toward radicals but toward those who disrupt; disruption of radical speakers by liberals or conservatives is as much to be deplored as the kind Bedau talks about.

However, disruption on principle is more profoundly inimical than what might be called disruptive acts of passion, and to the extent that it is, as suggested by Bedau, radicals who disrupt on principle, I believe there is a profound conflict between the radical position and the idea of a university, a conflict that is not diminished by whatever discrepancy there may be between the multiversity of the present day and the idea of a university.

Bedau's *tu quoque* about Russell's remark is scarcely to the point. Beyond any doubt, many liberals need to take Russell's maxim to heart. What is at issue, however, is "selective tolerance" and the right to disrupt in a university, and my point was, quite obviously, that those who would disrupt, or deny a forum to "sincere believers in dangerous and outrageous doctrines"—not to mention those who merely wish to continue their "pursuit of trivial exercises in the higher but decadent learning"—should learn to endure having their sentiments outraged. To be told that this advice applies most aptly to those who react against the disrupters is altogether unhelpful. Surely Bedau cannot mean that those who disrupted were justified because of the reprisals subsequently taken against them.

However, I do not mean to be replying to Bedau merely that both parties—"faculties" and "radicals, hippies, crazies, and ordinary dissenters," to borrow his improbable scenario—are guilty, but the radicals *et al.* did it first. I mean instead to be saying that what the disrupters are guilty of is more serious than the sins of the liberals who were blind to the legitimate grievances of the former. It is more serious because disruption strikes at the nerve of the university, and this in turn is due to the claim to infallibility and the refusal to let the sword cut both ways, which are implicit in the act of disruption and which are inimical to the idea of a university, and about which Professor Bedau has said nothing to alter my belief.

Part Five

◇◇

T. M. Scanlon here follows some other writers in this volume in searching for nonconsequentialist grounds for a defense of academic freedom. His focus is on research, and his argument turns on the inconsistency of hiring a man to find and publish the truth and then restricting his freedom to do so. That this defense will carry us only a certain distance he is quick to acknowledge. It applies only to universities that, like most, claim to be dedicated to finding and publishing the truth and that leave the decision of what directions to follow in research to professionally qualified faculty experts. It also leaves open the question of how universities may regulate their research activities without violating academic freedom. Can good reasons be offered for restricting the right of academics to engage in certain kinds of research? On what grounds should the choice be made to support one line of research but not another? Are there moral restraints on the individual faculty member in choosing a line of research? Far-ranging questions are raised by Scanlon's paper. Judith Thomson recognizes the force of the argument from inconsistency but emphasizes that it applies only to interference of the university with research or publication. Most of the hard problems are left, including the problem of what criteria should govern the decision to support or not to support a line of research.

T. M. Scanlon is associate professor of philosophy at Princeton University. Judith Jarvis Thomson is professor of philosophy at the Massachusetts Institute of Technology.

19. Academic Freedom and the Control of Research

BY T. M. SCANLON

"Academic freedom" appears to refer to a special privilege of teachers and scholars to be free from some kinds of regulation by the institutions that employ them or by others, a privilege that goes beyond the rights that all citizens enjoy to freedom of thought and expression, freedom of association, and freedom from persecution or economic discrimination on political or religious grounds. Many of the cases that have been discussed under the heading of academic freedom can be adequately explained as violations of these more general rights or of specific rights arising from contractual relations between the parties concerned. But there seems to be a notion of academic freedom that goes beyond these rights in placing limitations on the ways in which those who hire scholars or teachers can specify what is to be done by those whom they have hired. In this paper I will give one account, perhaps only a partial account, of this notion of academic freedom. I will then discuss the ways in which universities may, consistent with this notion of academic freedom, place restrictions on the kinds of research projects that they will support.[1]

[1] Discussions of an earlier draft of this paper at the Conference in Austin and subsequently at a meeting of the Society for Ethical and Legal Philosophy have helped me to see, though not always to avoid, a number of difficulties and pitfalls. I am grateful to the participants in those discussions and also to Clark Glymour for much helpful criticism.

In my defense of academic freedom I will avoid as far as possible consequentialist arguments to the effect that institutions in which academic freedom is recognized are likely to yield better results than other institutions or that the benefits of having such institutions outweigh the costs involved. I avoid such arguments, first, because the long-range consequences of the policies in question depend upon so many considerations that they seem to me almost impossible to estimate, and, second, because any argument that appeals to these consequences must rely heavily on an assignment of values to various intellectual activities and objectives relative to other goals, and this seems to me an unsatisfactorily sensitive point on which to rest an argument for what may already strike many as a special kind of class privilege for intellectuals. Quite possibly any complete account of academic freedom will have to face these difficulties and deal with them directly, but I will attempt to describe a narrow doctrine of academic freedom that handles at least certain central questions without invoking consequentialist calculations.

My argument proceeds by elaboration and analogy from the following imaginary situation. Suppose that one person, call him the monarch, who is longer on money than on the time or inclination to do research, decides that the best way for him to be well informed on certain subjects is to hire another person, call him the counselor, to spend full time investigating these subjects and reporting his findings. Once the monarch has made this decision and as long as he does not revoke it—as long, that is, as he continues to justify his support of the counselor in the way just described—it is irrational for him to attempt to influence the counselor to report anything other than his own considered opinions on the matters he is hired to investigate. Not just any attempt to affect what the counselor says constitutes an attempt to influence him in the sense I have in mind. There would be no objection on the grounds I am considering to the monarch's insisting that the counselor consider certain evidence that the monarch believed relevant to his investigations. Nor would there be any objection on these grounds to the monarch's undertaking to motivate his counselor by decreeing that he will be shot if his findings turn out to be false according to some objective standard. What would be irrational in the sense I have in mind would be, for example, for the monarch to forbid his counselor to consider certain evidence even if he thought it relevant, or for him to decree that the counselor will be fired if his findings run contrary to the opinions of the monarch's senile father. The irrationality of these actions is independent of the question whether the strategy of hiring the counselor is a good one to start with or whether the results it produces are worth the costs involved. All that is involved here is the truism that, if you are paying to hear someone's opinion because you think his opinions likely to be correct, it is irrational to try to get him to give you something else in place of his true opinion. This truism holds no matter what the monarch's reasons for interfering with his counselor may be. It would be just as irrational to try to get your counselor to report a certain thing (whether he believes it or not) because you believe that thing to be true as to try to get him to report something because you think it puts you in a particularly good light or is apt to please a neighboring potentate from whom you are expecting a favor. It may be objected here that, if you value the favor more than the counselor's testimony (by which *you* won't be misled anyway), it may be perfectly rational for you to induce him to testify in the desired way. But to act on this reasoning would be just to suspend his duties as counselor temporarily and make him instead an instrument of propaganda. The irrationality I have in mind arises only if the monarch attempts to influence the content of the reports that the counselor submits to him qua counselor, reports that he continues to regard and to urge others to regard as particularly worthy of belief because they represent the counselor's opinions.

The narrow doctrine of academic freedom that I wish to defend is just the extension to universities of the principle that a monarch should avoid the kind of irrationality I have just described. In addition to the constraint that this principle places on him, our monarch may also have good reason to undertake positive measures to protect his counselor from factors that might tend to influence his reports. He might, for example, try to prevent the counselor from becoming dependent, economically or otherwise, on persons (including the monarch himself) who might try to influence his reports (or even do so without trying by inadvertently revealing what it would please them to hear). There will be various methods for isolating and protecting the counselor to achieve this end, one of which would obviously be to make him financially independent for life.

Since, however, these methods may cost money or involve the sacrifice of other ends, it will not generally be a requirement of reason that the monarch employ any one of them. Which ones it is worthwhile for him to use can only be determined by balancing these competing ends against the value he places on the counselor's testimony. We may think of these methods as ranked along a continuum according to their cost. Where this cost is negligible, the monarch's refusal to employ them may constitute a kind of irrationality: he is knowingly failing to employ the most effective available means to his ends. But the irrationality I have described above goes beyond this. It involves not merely failure to make one's chosen means more efficient but also active subversion of those means.

If our monarch is particularly rich, unusually curious, or particularly paranoid or insecure, he may want to have more than one counselor in his service. All the remarks made so far would then apply to his behavior with respect to each of these counselors. The problem of guarding counselors against influence is likely to be particularly important, since, if he is to get the benefit of having more than one counselor, the monarch must ensure that no one of them controls what the others report to him. This aim might be secured by keeping them totally independent, perhaps even ignorant of each other's existence, but this need not be done: presumably, it would be more efficient to have them aware of each other's findings and able to respond and criticize each other but unable to influence each other in any way that would be vicious in the sense described above.

There will be a wide range of ways in which a stable of advisers of this sort could be organized. One extreme would be represented by a group of independent and autonomous individuals, each of whom gives his own views to the monarch who then chooses among them. At the other extreme would be a tightly organized and disciplined group of investigators, who work as a team with centralized procedures for subdividing a given problem and assigning parts to individuals, for making partial decisions, and for shifting manpower from one subquestion to another to maximize marginal productivity. The result produced by such a team would be a single, unified view of the subject in question.

As long as the autonomy of each individual's input into the system is maintained, neither of these systems of organization is inconsistent with the narrow concept of academic freedom as I have described it. In both cases, the principle of academic freedom is the basis for claims that members of the group may advance against each other or against their common employer to be free from attempts to influence them in ways that defeat the purpose of their participation in the system.

Groups of counselors may differ widely in their degree of independence from their respective monarchs. A modern university can be seen as a group of counselors that has virtual autonomy. It has become self-perpetuating in that it chooses its own members and self-governing in that it, or its members, choose the questions to be investigated rather than being handed these questions by the monarch. But it is essential to the idea of a university as it is generally understood that this choice of questions is to be made (and the answers pursued) within the framework provided by the common and publicly recognized conception of certain academic fields of inquiry and the methods appropriate to them. These features distinguish a university not only from a research firm that answers particular questions on contract but also from a sectarian institution, such as a church or a religious order, and they are features that are characteristic of universities (and most other schools) considered as educational institutions as well as centers for research.

A minister who loses the faith and says so openly can be dismissed from his church with no violation of academic freedom (or an analogous "clerical freedom"), nor would any violation of academic freedom be involved in the dismissal of a teacher who taught Darwin's *Origin of Species* in a school that was specifically organized to offer an education without evolution for the children of a certain sect. But teachers in what I am tempted to call "genuine" schools and universities are hired not to maintain specific doctrines but to teach the truth about certain subjects according to the generally accepted standards of those subjects. They therefore have a basis for complaint when attempts are made to influence their work in ways contrary to these standards.

In the analytical model I employed earlier, the monarch fulfilled a number of separable functions. He was simultaneously the person who employed the counselors, the person who set the questions they were to pursue, the person who, at least in the first instance, was supposed to benefit from their answers, and, finally, as the person who created the office of counselor for a certain purpose, he was also the person to whom claims to academic freedom were most appropriately addressed. In the description of a university just given, the person of the monarch has disappeared, and these functions are widely scattered. In a university as I have described it, hiring decisions are taken over by the institution itself, and decisions regarding what questions are to be investigated are made by the institution and its individual members within the canons of the relevant subjects. The justification for a university appeals to the benefits that it brings not to any one individual but to the society or world as a whole. Finally, claims to academic freedom in the sense I have described are appropriately addressed to anyone who accepts it as the function of the university to investigate and teach the truth as determined by the accepted canons of certain recognized subjects.

Thus, claims based on this notion of academic freedom may be pressed by members of a university against each other, against those who represent the university as an institution, or against persons outside the university who accept its purpose as I have described it. Alternatively, the university itself may appeal to the principle of academic freedom to support its claims to be free from certain pressures that may be directed against it, for example, by its financial supporters, private and public, who may try to place conditions on their continued support.

The clearest violations of academic freedom in the narrow sense have occurred when teachers have been threatened with dismissal or reprisals for maintaining that certain unpopular views might actually be the truth in their subjects (revisionist historians, early teachers of natural selection, atheistic or amoral philosophers). The principle of academic freedom as I have described it provides us with an argument against such actions only to the extent that those who undertake them are simultaneously committed to a certain conception of a university. For a person who takes the view that the proper function of a university is to propagate and defend the Christian faith, no irrationality is involved in attempting to ensure that no teacher is retained who does not remain true to this function.

This dependence on appeals to the internal inconsistency of

certain views may seem to make the notion of academic freedom I have described hopelessly weak, particularly in view of the fact that the thesis about universities and Christianity mentioned in the preceding sentence is probably held by a number of university presidents today and certainly was twenty years ago. To this kind of criticism I have three responses. First, a person's views on the proper function of universities are revealed not only in his direct statements on this question but also in the claims he is prepared to make as to why universities should be supported, what those who attend universities may expect to gain, and why the teaching and other output of universities is particularly deserving of intellectual attention. While it may be easy to modify one's direct remarks about the function of universities in order to avoid the kind of direct irrationality to which I have been appealing, it is considerably more difficult to bring all of one's claims about universities into line with a revised account of their function. Second, unlike the imaginary institution of counselor that I described earlier, universities are not defined, created, or changed merely by the decisions of one man. While there may be no such thing as a fixed and immutable account of *"the* function of a university," in order for such institutions to operate there must be, at any given time, some general understanding, rough perhaps, of what is expected of those who work and teach in a university, and this understanding cannot be too widely at variance with the claims the university makes to those who support it and to prospective students. The existence of such a partial consensus does not, of course, mean that anyone with a different view of what universities should be doing is wrong, but only that his idea represents a possible change. If, as I would claim, the features of universities to which I have appealed are central to the notion as we now know it, then any proposed change that would affect the basis of academic freedom as I have described it would represent a fundamental departure. When such a revision is put forward self-consciously and consistently, however, the appeal to academic freedom does not, by itself, constitute an objection that those who propose the revision need accept. In such a case the appeal to academic freedom is perhaps best understood as one addressed not to a threatening opponent but to fellow supporters of the existing view of the function of universities, calling their attention to the nature of the threat and perhaps also suggesting that they have reasons to provide universities and their members with protection against it.

Finally, while appeals to "the function" of an institution seem to me inherently fuzzy and philosophically unsatisfying, examples such as that of the antievolutionist school mentioned above convince me that an appeal of this kind is required in order to defend a notion of academic freedom that goes beyond normal civil rights and existing contractual obligations.

As I have described it, academic freedom does not involve a right to do anything one wants, even within the limits of one's field, or a right to be free from even very demanding and specific restrictions on which questions in one's field one is to pursue. The degree of individual autonomy allowed to individual researchers can vary widely from institution to institution, even among institutions that lay equal claims to serve the function that I have held to be typical of universities. In this section I want to investigate the degree to which universities may, consistent with academic freedom, regulate the research activities of their members with a view not only to the academic value of particular research projects but also to their probable consequences.

What constraints apply to an individual scholar in his choice of which lines of research to pursue?[2] To begin with, there are the canons of his subject, which indicate what kinds of investigation could possibly lead to new and interesting results and what kinds could not. There are also moral constraints. Whether or not we suppose a person to be under a positive requirement to choose those lines of research he believes likely to be most beneficial to mankind as a whole, he is at least under a requirement not to pursue work that is simply trivial or wasteful. Moreover, there surely are cases in which the foreseeable applications of certain kinds of research are such as to make it morally impermissible for that research to be undertaken. It is perhaps easiest to think of examples based in military applications of research in the physical sciences, but these are surely not the only cases. Of course, it is difficult to predict with any degree of certainty what applications a given piece of research

2 The following discussion draws on my "Individual Responsibility and Political Obligation," Proceedings of the Working Group in Philosophy, Science, and Technology, mimeographed (MIT, The Hunsaker Fund, 1973).

is likely to have. Even when the exact range of possible applications is not clear, however, if one knows who controls the resources essential to making whatever applications there are to be, one may have good grounds for predicting what kinds of applications will be pursued and for what ends they will be applied. There clearly are cases where this kind of information alone can make it immoral to pursue certain lines of research or at least to make the results of one's research known.[3]

These moral restrictions apply to individual scientists and to individuals who may underwrite or commission research by others. Do they also apply to universities? If so, they would require universities to decide what research to support not only with regard to its theoretical importance but also with regard to its possible beneficial or harmful applications, and in at least some cases they would require universities to refuse support to those engaged in certain kinds of research.

How would one argue that universities should not exercise this kind of control over the research activities of their members? For them to exercise this control is not obviously inconsistent with academic freedom as I have defined it. It may seem, however, that the injection of considerations other than purely theoretical ones into the research decisions of universities is somehow inconsistent with their proper function. One might support this intuition by appealing to the model I have used above: It is rational for the monarch to shield his counselors from any influence or pressure that might motivate them to report anything other than their best judgment on the matters they are asked to investigate. Thus, it might be concluded, to get the most from such institutions as universities, one should organize them with the understanding that the sole responsibility of those involved is to ascertain and report the truth about their respective subjects. But from the fact that it is rational for the monarch who wants to get the most out of his counselors to have them *believe* that their sole responsibility and obligation is to him, it by no means follows that this is *true*. This is obvious in the case in which the monarch is a Hitler, but the theo-

---

[3] I will concentrate on the question of university controls on research rather than controls on publication, since a decision regarding what research to support is one that cannot in any case be avoided while the institution of controls on publication raises complicating questions of freedom of expression.

retical point remains the same if he is a benevolent despot, the democratically constituted sovereign of a progressive state, or, as is generally the case when the "counselor" is a university, no one in particular, or, more accurately, those persons, whomever they may be, who are in a position to make use of the information that the university and its members provide.

From the fact that my weak notion of academic freedom does not bar the exercise of controls of the kind I have suggested, one might conclude just that this notion is too weak. Its most obvious extension would be through a consequentialist argument to the conclusion that there is no system of controls of this kind that could prevent enough harmful consequences to offset the loss in scholarship and beneficial applications that would result from its misuse or mistaken use. I do not think that this conclusion can be established, but I will not offer a direct argument against it. In what follows, however, I will try to suggest how those cases that may seem to be the most obvious abuses of such a policy of controls can be distinguished from the cases in which I have claimed that controls are required.

In the discussion so far I have been thinking in terms of examples drawn from the natural sciences, such as research in physics, chemistry, or biology, that would have obvious application in the development of new and more destructive weapons. There are obviously similar examples in the social sciences; new results about the psychology of individuals or about the stability or instability of social institutions could have enormous and devastating consequences when placed in certain hands. But as far as consequences alone are concerned, research in philosophy, history, economics, or political theory can have consequences serious enough to raise problems of the kind I have been considering. Research in these areas could undermine the legitimacy of institutions, provoke factionalism and violent conflict, and, in general, bring about a crumbling of the consensus necessary to hold social institutions together. Results of this kind are likely to occur in just those cases where the propositions under investigation are matters of wide concern and are thought to be of extreme importance by at least a large number of people. I take it that on most people's understanding of academic freedom it would be entirely unacceptable to empower universities to refuse to underwrite research into questions of this kind whenever serious consequences seemed likely to ensue. On the contrary, one has a tendency to say that intellectuals have a positive responsibility *to* investigate such questions, especially when important decisions must be taken and the stakes are high for everyone.

But if we wish to maintain that in some cases a university should support and even encourage research on certain questions despite the consequences that the publication of the findings of this research may have, while in other cases the likelihood of certain harmful consequences makes it morally impermissible to support some research, then we must support this contention with some account of the difference between these cases. We must therefore take a closer look at what I have called the moral constraints that apply to a university's research decisions.

I have so far spoken as if the principal constraint of this kind consisted in a prohibition against bringing about certain kinds of bad consequences or against supporting pieces of research whose bad consequences greatly outweighed the good. But this manner of speaking is obviously much too loose. To begin with, in considering the consequences of research, one must take into account not only the consequences narrowly construed, for example, in terms of lives saved or lost, but also the character of the actions through which these consequences are produced. It makes a difference, for example, whether a piece of research contributes to a country's defense against an unprovoked attack or to the prosecution of a cruel war of economic expansion, and this difference persists even if the contribution is in neither case decisive and its net effect in terms of lives lost or saved is the same. But the moral constraint we are concerned with cannot be understood simply in terms of "bringing about" consequences, even when these are construed in this broader fashion. For there are a great many different ways in which it may be true that certain consequences would not have occurred but for the publication of a certain piece of research, and the differences between these are in many cases morally significant. For example, a piece of research might bring about certain violent actions by providing the necessary means, by providing a rationale, or by provoking them as a response. More to the present point, there are many situations in which one of the likeliest ways to bring about morally impermissible actions is to lead people to believe that these acts are in fact morally blameless. To many who hold the conserva-

tive position on abortion it may seem that this is what has in fact
happened with respect to that issue, and there surely are cases in
which something similar has happened with respect to military
policy when the erosion of popular moral scruples has made politically possible the development and use of weaponry previously un-
used or unbuilt. Thus, if the moral constraints on the support of
research are ones that forbid supporting research that would lead
to certain kinds of immoral action, then there will be cases in which
research supporting the conclusion that certain acts are morally
blameless will itself be permissible only if these actions are *in fact*
morally blameless. This might mean, for example (assuming that if
abortion is wrong then widespread abortions would be a very
serious matter), that research in moral philosophy that is likely to
convince many of the permissibility of abortion should not be
supported if abortion is wrong. I take it that this is an unacceptable
conclusion, since it seems clear to me that the permissibility of research into the moral status of abortion does not depend on the
permissibility of abortion itself.

If, then, not all the foreseeable consequences that will be brought
about (in the broadest sense) by the publication of a piece of research are relevant to determining the moral permissibility of supporting that research, which consequences are so relevant and
which are not? I do not have a general answer to this question, but
cases of the kind just considered lead me to the conclusion that,
where we are concerned with the consequences that research may
have through its influence on the actions of third parties, the relevant moral constraint should be understood not as a prohibition
against bringing about certain consequences but, more narrowly,
as a prohibition against aiding certain immoral courses of action.
Construing the constraint in this way avoids the problem we have
just considered, since convincing someone that a certain course of
action is morally permissible (or even, perhaps, that it is desirable)
is not *aiding* him in that course of action in the relevant sense. It
would be aiding him in this sense, however, to provide him with
the means he requires or to contribute to his deliberations as to
which means are most appropriate to his immoral ends. It seems to
me that those cases in which it seems clearest to us that it is immoral
to support a certain line of research are cases in which we believe

that that research will give aid of this kind to courses of action that we regard as gravely immoral.

This way of understanding the constraint also fits with our intuitions in cases of the kind alluded to at the outset of this discussion where research findings may be expected to promote civil disorder, revolution, or civil war. Our judgment in such cases seems to be heavily dependent on the aims and motives we ascribe to those who are moved by the information the research provides. If we suppose that this information moves them because of what they take to be its implications concerning the justice or legitimacy of their institutions, then even if we think their subsequent actions entirely wrong and immoral, we are inclined to believe that the research should not be stopped on this account. On the other hand, if we suppose that they are committed to a program of racial or religious persecution and that the research in question makes known to them the means or the opportunity for final drastic action against the persecuted group, then we are much less inclined to say that the research should be allowed to proceed "despite the consequences."

I am not claiming that the communication of information leading others to adopt heinous courses of action is always itself morally blameless provided only that one does not aid these courses of action once they are conceived. But it does seem to me that there are conditions under which this is so and that these conditions apply in many of the cases in which we tend to think that a course of research should be allowed to proceed despite its bad consequences (and even if these consequences are not counterbalanced by compensatory good effects).

One class of cases in which we blame a person who, without evil intent, conveys information that sets off a chain of actions is represented by the case of the busybody who brings about a murder by telling a jealous and volatile person of his spouse's infidelity. Our judgment in such cases depends, however, on attributing extreme irrationality or a pathological tendency to violence to the person to whom the information is given, conditions which, when known, impose special standards of care. We would also blame a person who, knowing that others would make important choices based on the information he conveys, nonetheless presents groundless speculation as fact or conveys his information in a misleading or distorted fashion. Similarly, we may blame a person whose word has some special authority and who issues a judgment, knowing that those who will rely upon his authority will systematically misunderstand the information he conveys or will receive only a distorted version of it.

We can conceive of cases analogous to these in which the information in question is just the findings of university-supported research work. In such cases the positive grounds *for* the support of that research are undermined, since, due either to the character of the findings themselves, the incapacity of the audience, or the failure of effective communication, the contribution that the research would make to intelligent understanding and rational deliberation is, at least temporarily, severely reduced. In addition, when the issues involved are important and the actions to be taken have serious consequences, there may be independent moral grounds for abstaining from research (on the questions at issue) while these conditions last.

But such cases are extremely rare, and the cases we are primarily concerned with are those in which such conditions are absent, that is, in which (*a*) the research in question is not trivial and its conclusions are reached in ways that accord with the standards of the relevant disciplines; (*b*) the results of the research are accurately and nontendentiously reported, and a fair representation of these results (rather than just a garbled or systematically distorted version) is made generally available; and (*c*) the agents who can be expected to act on these results are capable of understanding them and meet everyday standards of rationality. It is under some reasonable approximation to these conditions that, I wish to maintain, the thesis set forth above holds, namely, that a university is not under a general moral constraint to avoid supporting research that will lead, through the actions of others, to certain kinds of consequences, but only under the narrower constraint to avoid aiding certain immoral courses of action.

This conclusion, even if it is true, is extremely vague and does not take us very far. There are obviously more and less direct ways to aid a course of action; some courses of action are more immoral than others; and most programs of research that in some way aid immoral courses of action also have more positive effects that may or may not tip the moral scales in their favor. A great deal more would have to be said about all these matters of degree and of balancing before we would have a principle that would help us to decide whether a given piece of research can or cannot morally be supported. I have not attempted to develop such a principle here. My aim has been the more limited one of explaining how it could be true that, in some cases, the consequences that research may be foreseen to have made it immoral to support that research, while, in other cases, research should be allowed to proceed despite what appear to be equally serious consequences.

The explanation I have given has relied on a distinction between aiding an immoral course of action and leading a person to adopt such a course of action by, for example, leading him to believe it to be morally blameless. While I am convinced that this distinction, or one closely related to it,[4] is required to deal with the problems we have been considering, I cannot deny that the distinction and its application are beset by numerous difficulties. There is one apparent difficulty that I would like to forestall, however, and this arises from the fact that there are numerous cases in which the most obvious way in which one might aid an immoral course of action is to persuade others to join in it, for example, by leading them to believe that it is morally innocent. Suppose that a piece of research, otherwise quite respectable, could be foreseen to have this effect. Would this consequence be one that could be regarded as raising a moral barrier to supporting that research? In my view it would not. The initial effect of the research, the one through which the other effects involved in this example are achieved, lies in its contribution to people's deliberation on the moral status of the acts in question. If, as I claimed in discussing the case of abortion, those acts of individuals (that a piece of research brings about through its effect on their moral deliberations) do not count against the support of that research, then this must remain true when those acts are pursued in concert with others. Thus, the course of action that is aided must be one adopted by those whose behavior is initially affected by the information that the research provides.

Even when only a single person is involved, however, there are cases in which the same piece of information may be said to both aid a course of action and to lead to the adoption of one. For there

[4] A related distinction is discussed in my "A Theory of Freedom of Expression," *Philosophy and Public Affairs* 1 (1972): 204–226.

is certainly a sense in which a person is said to adopt a course of action only when he sees and chooses some particular means to his end, and in this sense a piece of information that contributed to a person's choice of appropriate means to his ends would be said to lead to the adoption of a course of action as well as to aid one in the sense I have described above. In such cases, if the course of action that is *aided* is immoral, then the information in question falls within the scope of the moral constraint I have been discussing. For example, suppose that a man is inclined to murder his rich uncle in order to aid a charity that will benefit from the old man's will. One day he comes into possession of information indicating a foolproof way to get rid of the uncle without being caught, so he acts at once. This information aids an immoral course of action in the sense I have been considering and does so even if the man had not decided to murder his uncle (and perhaps had not even thought about doing so) until the foolproof means occurred to him.

Nothing in the moral argument with which I have just been concerned distinguished the case of universities from the more general case of individuals who bring about unfortunate consequences by imparting information to others. But this distinction may seem quite important. Even some who agree with my claims about university research decisions may feel that there is (to say the least) something suspect about an individual who undertakes on his own initiative to provide others with information that, he has reason to believe, may lead them to decisions whose consequences are ultimately disastrous. We want to say, I think, that such an individual, if he does not exercise his option to remain silent, should at least set forth his reasons for believing one course to be a disastrous one. But if he is then asked directly for information that he believes will influence the person toward this course, what should he do? (Note that the case in question cannot be Kant's[5] example in which a would-be murderer asks where his intended victim is hiding; for, in that case, giving the information sought would constitute aiding an

[5] Immanuel Kant, "On a Supposed Right to Tell Lies from Benevolent Motives," in *Kant's Critique of Practical Reason and other Works on the Theory of Ethics*, trans. T. K. Abbott (New York: Longmans, Green and Co., 1909), pp. 361–365. See also Kant's lectures "Duties towards Others: Truthfulness" and "Responsibility for Consequences" in *Lectures on Ethics*, ed. L. W. Beck (New York: Harper Torchbooks, 1963), pp. 224–234, 59–60.

immoral course of action in the sense previously discussed. Instead, the interlocutor should be thought of as an as yet quite innocent person agonizing over some difficult choice.) I do not think that an individual in such a situation is morally required to remain silent, although he may be *entitled* to do so unless his position places him under some special obligation to speak.

What is special about the case of a university is just that its position does place it under such an obligation. In most of the cases I have mentioned in which we think that research should be supported despite possible serious consequences, we think not merely that it *may* be allowed to proceed but also that a refusal to allow it to do so because of the threatening consequences would constitute a failure on the part of the university to discharge its responsibility. This is true for two related reasons.

First, the cases in question are, by hypothesis, ones in which the outcome of the research will have an influence on important choices facing members of the society, and this is prima facie a reason to expect that the issues to be investigated are themselves important (although it is of course conceivable that people might be greatly exercised by matters that are in themselves wholly trivial). The second reason appeals to the notion of the function of a university discussed in the first part of this paper. It is the function of a university in the sense discussed there to contribute to intelligent understanding and rational deliberation on the part of the populace (its "monarch"). Its function is not to produce that selection of information which it believes will lead members of the populace to form (what it regards as) true beliefs and to make (what it regards as) correct decisions. Thus, a university that quite generally made its research decisions with an eye to the consequences would have departed from the function that (currently, at least) people have good reason to expect it to perform. Merely to have observed, however, that the proper function of a university requires that its decisions be based on considerations other than producing the best consequences would not have solved the problem with which the second part of this paper has been concerned. We have also had to explain how there would be cases in which it is morally permissible to discharge this function despite the consequences of doing so.

To conclude, I should indicate where the moral constraint that I have been discussing falls within a more general outline of the questions a university administration may legitimately consider in deciding whether or not to support a given piece of research. First, the administration must consider whether it is conceived and can be expected to be carried out and reported in ways that meet the relevant intellectual standards. Second, if the resources required by the research are scarce ones, the administration must consider the theoretical and practical significance of this research relative to other uses of the same resources. Third, it must consider whether there may be moral considerations that make it immoral to support this research *at all*, quite apart from considerations of resource allocation. Moral problems might be raised by the methods used in a piece of research or by the effects of its publication. In this paper I have been concerned with one class of problems of this latter sort, namely, moral problems raised by the actions that the results of the research might lead or enable others to perform. But the effects of publication are not limited to such actions. To mention one other kind of effect, the publication of certain findings may result in some individuals being held up to public scorn and ridicule or may damage their reputation in a way that, in serious cases, may undermine the basis of their self-respect and prevent others from regarding them as full members of the community. Historical research must frequently raise problems of this kind, and they certainly are a factor in the recent controversy over research on I.Q. and race. In many cases the beneficial consequences of research may make it worth paying a certain price of this kind, but this is something that must be determined in each case, and it seems clearly to be a part of legitimate decisions by universities to weigh these considerations.

20. Academic Freedom and Research

BY JUDITH JARVIS THOMSON

Teachers and scholars have constitutionally guaranteed civil rights, just as all other citizens do. They also have such special rights as their contracts with their employer-institutions provide for—such as the right to be paid this or that amount, for work of this or that kind, for this or that period of time. Do teachers and scholars have any further rights and privileges, rights possessed by no other citizen and possessed by teachers and scholars merely because they are teachers and scholars? I am half inclined to think they do not. Professor Van Alstyne's contribution to this symposium argues, very convincingly, I think, that those rights, the violation of which we commonly think of as violations of something very special, *academic freedom*, are merely civil rights, guaranteed under the Constitution. Those rights and liberties that we think of as constituting academic freedom are, in his view, merely some among the many rights and liberties guaranteed to every citizen. As Professor Scanlon says, claiming that teachers and scholars must be granted academic freedom strikes many people as claiming that teachers and scholars must be granted a "special kind of class privilege," an immunity that other people who work for a living have not managed to talk fast enough, or cleverly enough, to be able to provide themselves with; if Van Alstyne is right, this is a mistake—everyone who works for a living has those immunities that teachers and scholars have.

Van Alstyne's main point, I take it, is this: what we centrally and crucially claim for ourselves is that neither our employer-institutions, nor anyone else, may impose sanctions on us for extramural utterances—we may not be fired, suspended, or fined for what we say outside our classrooms, however much what we say may conflict with the moral or political sentiments of the community at large, or the administrations of our employer-institutions in particular. But then, as Van Alstyne says, *no* public servant may have sanctions imposed on him for extramural utterances—policemen, firemen, and civil servants generally are *all* immune from firing, suspension, or fines for what they say off the job, however much the community, or their superiors, may dislike what was said.

Public servant. It is precisely this that leaves me only half convinced. Some teachers and scholars are, of course, employed by institutions that are entirely supported out of the public purse; academic freedom in their case, then, appears to be explained by Van Alstyne's account. Others are employed by institutions that are not entirely supported by the public purse, but only granted certain public benefits, such as tax exemptions; and perhaps it is plausible to suppose that Van Alstyne's account covers them, too. But what if I open a small university in my basement and accept no public aid in the running of it? A purely private institution, run to provide instruction for those who wish to pay for it, and to provide information for me. (I rather fancy hearing the latest news about the universe.) To construct a metaphor from Scanlon's model: I am monarch in my basement. Will the Constitution protect any member of my staff whose contract I choose not to renew because of his extramural utterances? I should have thought not. It goes without saying that I am no expert in constitutional matters, but I should have thought that it is entirely within your rights to dismiss someone whom you have privately hired (your cleaning woman, for example) if you happen not to like his (or her) politics. Yet couldn't a member of my university staff whom I refuse to renew on such a ground claim that my act constituted a violation of academic freedom? We presumably do not think that academic freedom is possessed only by those who are employed by institutions that are in some measure publicly supported. So perhaps there is more to academic freedom than Van Alstyne's account allows for.

Scanlon plainly thinks so. He says there "seems to be a notion of academic freedom that goes beyond . . . normal civil rights and existing contractual obligations"; and in the first part of his paper he explains its nature and justification. Suppose a monarch, rich and curious, but lazy, hires some "counselors" to do research for him; he would be acting irrationally if he attempted to influence his counselors in ways contrary to the standards of the disciplines in which he wants them to work—if you have hired a man to do something for you, it is irrational to make it difficult or impossible for him to do it. The analogy is ingenious. Our situation is illuminated by it; it *is* irrational for a community to support an institution of higher learning, an institution whose purposes are the increase and dissemination of knowledge, and at the same time to make it difficult or impossible for those employed by that institution to increase and disseminate knowledge.

But there seem to me to be difficulties. In the first place, I suspect that what Scanlon's account provides us with—beyond ordinary civil rights and contractual guarantees—will be felt by many to be fairly meager stuff. Consider the case of a young assistant professor at a university that is in no measure publicly supported (e.g., my Basement University); and suppose his contract is not renewed, because of an antiwar speech he makes on Boston Common. What comfort does Scanlon give him? I am not absolutely certain Scanlon has any comfort at all to give. Would the monarch be acting irrationally in dropping a counselor on such a ground as this? After all, the market nowadays is full of clever counselors in search of jobs. And it is not as if the monarch here makes it difficult or impossible for the job he wants done to be done; he merely replaces the current doer of the job with another, who is more to his liking.

Or suppose it could be made out that the monarch does act irrationally. Then Scanlon would have comfort to give: "Ah, yes, a dreadful thing; your institution has acted irrationally in refusing to renew your contract!" But it is cold comfort, and the exclamation point is rather a joke. Irrationality, after all, is fairly well at home on university campuses, and the complaint "They've acted irrationally" is hardly likely to raise any eyebrows. If this is what a violation of academic freedom—which is not a violation of a civil right or a contractual obligation—comes to, then it does not come to very much.

On the other hand, in fairness to Scanlon, it ought to be said that he did not have this kind of case in mind. What he had in mind, I think, is not the possibility that a university administration will fire, suspend, or fine a teacher for extramural utterances, but rather the possibility that a university administration will interfere in his research by attempting to influence its content and results. Scanlon's "analytical model" in fact seems to be constructed precisely in order to shed light on such cases as these—that is, to be intended precisely to explain what is wrong with interfering in this way in the work of a teacher and scholar. So if Scanlon does not tell us, or does not tell us in a satisfying way, what has gone wrong in the case of the man who is fired, Scanlon can say: I never meant to, I meant only to tell you what has gone wrong in the kind of case *I* have in mind. It is, obviously, open to Scanlon to say that we have more than one right over and above our civil and contractual rights and that he is at the moment attending to only one of them.

Scanlon's further aim, of course, is to explain how it is that, although he has given an explanation of why universities may not interfere in the research activities of their employees (it is irrational to do so), they may nevertheless prevent research of certain kinds from being undertaken at the university—his job, then, is to characterize and justify the limits (i.e., to explain which and why). But before turning to this matter, I think we ought to stop for a moment to ask just what rights teachers and scholars do have in this area. There is no need to justify a university's stopping research unless scholars have at least a prima facie right to immunity from such regulation, so we should ask about that first.

A university teacher's salary is paid to him primarily for the teaching he does; but it is paid to him also to do research, partly in the belief that his teaching will be the better for it, partly in order simply to increase knowledge. As things stand, the choice of research topic is normally left entirely to the discretion of the teacher himself, subject only to financial constraints (e.g., if expensive equipment is needed, he may be expected to get financial support for it from outside the university). Now, we should ask: Is it a teacher's *right* that he choose his own research project? Does my university violate a right of mine, does it, in particular, violate my academic freedom, if it tells me that I may not work at research project *P* during that part of my time that I am paid to do research in? It seems to me quite unclear that it does.

Of course it might be asked how, in any case, the university could enforce its demand that I not work at project *P*. In the hard sciences, I suppose it would be easy: the university need merely refuse to allow me to use its space and facilities. In the softer sciences, such as sociology, it would perhaps be less easy; but the university could, anyway, refuse access to its computers. But what does it do with Professor Jones, whose work requires only pencil and paper and who is willing to buy his own? Here something fairly drastic would be required, I suppose: the university could, for example, increase his teaching load to a point where carrying it requires a full forty-hour week, thus in effect refusing to pay Jones to do any research at all. If Jones still wants to go on with project *P*, he will have to do it nights, week ends, and holidays—on his own time, that is.

As things stand, we expect, and past practice justifies us in expecting, that we will be allowed to work at any research projects we choose during that part of our time in which we are paid to do research. Anyone who is suddenly told, "We don't approve your research project; so this year you teach forty hours a week," has —to say the least—ground for complaint. But what if universities had always operated under different rules? What if it had been standard practice for everyone to have to submit his research plans for approval (e.g., to an elected faculty body, charged with making decisions in light of its best opinion of what is in the best long-range interest of the community)? I see consequentialist reasons to think this would be a bad system; it seems to me there is every reason to think that the community is best served in the long run if its scholars are allowed to choose their own research topics, and, in any case, the system would be open to appalling abuses. But I see no reason to think that those who teach and work under such a system would be suffering from institutionalized violation of rights. For most universities, it is, after all, the community that pays the bills; and surely A has not the right to dispose of what B pays for, unless B, or B's representative, wishes to give him that right.

Indeed, I should have thought that to the extent to which

Scanlon's "analytical model" *is* a model of the university, the suggestion I make here really is a plausible one. The monarch might think it would be in his own best long-range interest to let his counselors decide what they wish to work at. But he might not. And for some cases it might be entirely rational for him to think not —and then entirely rational for him to say, "No, not on my time do you work at that!"

In fact, I suspect that Scanlon does not himself think of the existing freedom possessed by academics to choose their own research topics as a *right*. If he had thought it a right, he would (I suspect) have defended it on stronger grounds. For it can hardly be the case that a man has a right to do *x*, but that the only complaint we can make against one who prevents him is, "You're being irrational."

If this is correct, then what Scanlon is dealing with in the second part of his paper is not academic freedom, not any right that teachers and scholars have that goes beyond their civil and contractual rights, but rather something quite different. I think the point comes out particularly clearly if we contrast the central problem of the second part of Scanlon's present paper with the central problem of his exceedingly interesting earlier paper on freedom of expression.[1] In that paper, Scanlon's problem may, I think, be put as follows: Suppose you were the person, or group of persons, charged by the community with deciding what acts of expression (speech, writing, publication) shall or shall not be permitted; and suppose you have excellent reason to think that a number of acts of expression would, if undertaken, have consequences in which the bad outweighs the good (e.g., by virtue of causing second parties to do harms to third parties). Which, if any, should you permit the undertaking of, and why? An exact analogue of that problem would be the following: Suppose you were the person, or group of persons, charged by the community with deciding what research projects people shall or shall not be permitted to undertake; and suppose you have excellent reason to think that a number of research projects would, if undertaken, have consequences in which the bad outweighs the good (e.g., by virtue of causing second parties to do harms to third

[1] T. M. Scanlon, "A Theory of Freedom of Expression," *Philosophy and Public Affairs* 1, no. 2 (Winter 1972): 204–226.

parties). Which, if any, should you permit the undertaking of, and why? Now, Scanlon is *not* dealing with this problem in the second half of his present paper. Scanlon is not here asking under what conditions the community, or its representatives, can enter a man's house and prevent him from undertaking research in his own kitchen, on his own time.[2] A man has a prima facie right to do what he likes in his own kitchen, on his own time, just as he has a prima facie right to say, write, or publish what he likes; and so the mere fact that, in the consequences, bad will outweigh good does not by itself show that the community can intervene and prevent the act. Something more is needed than a mere weighing of consequences; and as Scanlon suggests in his earlier paper, we must certainly pay heed to the question of how those consequences will get brought about.

But as far as I can see, the question Scanlon deals with here is quite different, and, I think, may be put as follows: Suppose you were the person, or group of persons, charged by the community with deciding what research projects the community shall or shall not support the undertaking of; and suppose you have excellent reason to think that a number of research projects would, if undertaken, have consequences in which the bad outweighs the good (e.g., by virtue of causing second parties to do harms to third parties). Which, if any, should you commit the community to the supporting of, and why? As I see it, no one has a prima facie right that the community shall *support* his research projects,[3] so solving this problem does not require a balancing of consequences against his *rights*. Scanlon may well be right in thinking that it is an important consideration in making the decision in any given case, that

[2] Scanlon had asked us to "suppose some misanthropic inventor were to discover a simple method whereby anyone could make nerve gas in his kitchen out of gasoline, table salt, and urine" (ibid., p. 211); and he had said that it seemed to him clearly permissible to make it illegal for the inventor to print his recipe on handbills and give them out at street corners. But now suppose he hasn't yet discovered the method and merely tells us he plans to do research on it nights in his kitchen. Would it be permissible to make it illegal for him even to begin? Supposing that, however misanthropic, he's a first-rate chemist, who usually does find what he sets about to find?

[3] In particular, the misanthropic chemist of the preceding footnote has no prima facie right that the community, or its universities, shall *support* his work in his kitchen.

it be asked just how the bad consequences are brought about. But since, if I am correct, the researcher's rights are not in question, the difficulty is not that of balancing radically different kinds of moral consideration (consequences against rights), but rather that of assessing in just precisely what the community's long-range interest lies—no less a difficulty, but a different difficulty all the same.

APPENDIX

In these pages it becomes clear that quite different conceptions of academic freedom may be distinguished and that the backing offered for claims to academic freedom will depend upon the conception that is presupposed. It therefore seemed to Judith Thomson worth setting out a statement on academic freedom that specifically adopts one conception of academic freedom, draws out the appropriate consequences concerning the rights and duties of academics, and offers a justification of claims to academic freedom. The editor has obtained permission from Judith Thomson to publish her statement in the hope that it may usefully be contrasted with statements already available.

A PROPOSED STATEMENT ON ACADEMIC FREEDOM

BY JUDITH JARVIS THOMSON

1. Teachers in institutions of higher education are citizens, and therefore possess all the rights of citizens. These rights include, among others, the right to speak out freely on matters of public concern and to participate in lawful political activity.

If a person has a right to do a thing, then no one may prevent him from exercising that right, either by force or by the threat of sanctions, and no one may impose sanctions after the fact for an exercise of that right.

Therefore no institution of higher education may threaten a faculty member with sanctions, or impose sanctions after the fact, for an exercise of his right to speak and to participate in lawful political activity.

2. Teachers in institutions of higher education are scholars and teachers as well as citizens: they are employed by their institutions to discover, and to transmit to their students and to the public at large, the truth as they see it in their respective disciplines.

It is both irrational and unjust to employ a person to do a thing and then to prevent him from doing it, either by force or by the threat of sanctions; it is both irrational and unjust for an employer to impose sanctions after the fact for a person's performing an activity that he was employed to perform.

Therefore no institution of higher education may threaten a faculty member with sanctions, or impose sanctions on him after the fact, for teaching, conducting research, or making public the result of that research, in accordance with the truth as he sees it.

3. Like all other citizens, the teacher in an institution of higher education has certain obligations and duties, deriving from the fact that he is a citizen. For example, a citizen ought not abuse his right to speak out freely on matters of public concern: he ought to speak the truth as he sees it, to exercise restraint in the expression of his views, and to show respect for the opinions of others. He ought to act reliably and honorably in his dealings with others; and he ought to abide by the law, except, perhaps, in such circumstances as make civil disobedience the only way in which an injustice may be eliminated. Democratic government is possible only when a sizeable proportion of citizens are willing to accept such constraints on their behavior.

Any employee has certain obligations and duties beyond those that derive from the fact that he is a citizen; he has those obligations and duties that attach to the job he is employed to do. In particular, the teacher in an institution of higher education ought, among other things, to teach, and to publish in his discipline, only what is in accordance with the truth as he sees it; he ought in the classroom and in his scholarly writings to give and take credit only where it is due; and he ought to allow open expression and discussion in the classroom of scholarly views that conflict with his own.

4. If a person fails to carry out the obligations attached to his job, then his employer has ground for imposing sanctions on him, up to and including dismissal in case of a gross dereliction of duty. By contrast, a man who fails to carry out some obligation of a citizen has not thereby given his employer ground for imposing sanctions, unless it is demonstrable that his failure bears directly on his fitness to do his job. For example, a teacher in an institution of higher education may be sanctioned for presenting to his classes research results that he knows to be false, or for plagiarizing; he may *not* be sanctioned for intemperate utterances in a public forum on a matter of public concern, or for acts of civil disobedience, or for any other falling short of the ideal of good citizenship, unless it is demonstrable that the failure in question bears directly on his fitness to serve on a faculty, that is, on his fitness to join with others in the enterprise of discovering and transmitting the truth.

BIBLIOGRAPHY

SOME SUGGESTIONS FOR FURTHER READING

Thanks are due to Professor Fritz Machlup, of Princeton University, who
supplied us with many of the items on this list. For bibliographical references before 1925, see Julia E. Johnsen, comp., "Academic Freedom,"
The Reference Shelf, vol. 3, no. 6 (New York: H. W. Wilson, 1925). Additional bibliographical references will be found in Robert M. McIver,
Academic Freedom in Our Time (New York: Columbia University Press,
1955); and Samuel Gorovitz, ed., *Freedom and Order in the University*
(Cleveland: The Press of Western Reserve University, 1967).

American Association of University Professors. *AAUP Bulletin*. 60 vols.,
  1915 to present.
————. "AAUP 1956 Statement on Academic Freedom and Tenure in
  the Quest for National Security." *AAUP Bulletin* 42 (Spring 1956):
  54–61. Reprinted in *Policy Documents and Reports, 1973 Edition*, pp.
  24–27. Washington, D.C.: American Association of University Profes-
  sors, 1973.
————. *The 1915 Declaration of Principles*. In *Academic Freedom and
  Tenure*, edited by Louis Joughin, pp. 155–176. Madison: University of
  Wisconsin Press, 1969.
American Association of University Professors and Association of American
  Colleges. *1940 Statement of Principles on Academic Freedom and
  Tenure*. In *Policy Documents and Reports, 1973 Edition*, pp. 1–3.
  Washington, D.C.: American Association of University Professors, 1973.
American Civil Liberties Union. *Academic Freedom and Civil Liberties
  of Students in Colleges and Universities*. New York: 1956, 1959, 1961.
Baade, Hans W., ed. *Academic Freedom*. Dobbs Ferry, New York:
  Oceana Publications, 1964.

Buckley, William F., Jr. *God and Man at Yale: The Superstitions of "Academic Freedom,"* Chicago: Henry Regnery Co., 1951.

Capen, Samuel P. "Privileges and Immunities." *AAUP Bulletin* 23 (1937): 190–201.

Carlson, Anton J., and Arthur O. Lovejoy. "Teachers' Oath Laws: Statement of Committee B." *AAUP Bulletin* 23 (1937): 27–29.

Carnegie Foundation for the Advancement of Teaching. *Neutrality or Partisanship: A Dilemma of Academic Institutions.* Bulletin no. 34. New York: Carnegie Foundation for the Advancement of Teaching, 1971. (Essays by Fritz Machlup, Walter Metzger, and Richard Sullivan.)

Conant, James B. *Education and Liberty.* Cambridge, Mass.: Harvard University Press, 1953.

Cushman, Robert E. *Academic Freedom and Responsibility.* Ithaca, New York: Cornell University Press, 1952.

de Raeymaeker, L. *Truth and Freedom.* Pittsburgh: Duquesne University Press, 1955.

Eliot, Charles W. *Academic Freedom.* Ithaca, New York: Andrus & Church, 1907.

Goodman, Paul. *Growing Up Absurd.* London: V. Gollancz, 1961. (See especially Appendix D, "The Freedom to be Academic.")

Gorovitz, Samuel, ed. *Freedom and Order in the University.* Cleveland: The Press of Western Reserve University, 1967. (Essays by Paul Goodman, Walter Metzger, Sanford Kadish, John Searle, and Mortimer Kadish. Cf. Bibliography, pp. 207–215.)

Hofstadter, Richard. *Anti-Intellectualism in American Life.* New York: Alfred A. Knopf, 1963.

————, and Walter P. Metzger. *The Development of Academic Freedom in the United States.* New York: Columbia University Press, 1955.

Hook, Sidney. *Heresy, Yes—Conspiracy, No.* New York: John Day Co., 1953.

————, ed. *In Defense of Academic Freedom.* New York: Pegasus, 1971.

Joughin, Louis, ed. *Academic Freedom and Tenure. A Handbook of the American Association of University Professors.* Madison: University of Wisconsin Press, 1969.

Kantorowicz, Ernst H. *The Fundamental Issue: Documents and Notes on the University of California Loyalty Oath.* Berkeley: Privately printed, 1950.

Kirk, Russell. *Academic Freedom: An Essay in Definition.* Chicago: Henry Regnery Co., 1955.

Lazarsfeld, Paul F., and Wagner Thielens, Jr. *The Academic Mind: Social Scientists in a Time of Crisis.* Glencoe, Ill.: Free Press, 1958.

Lippmann, Walter. *American Inquisitors.* New York: Macmillan Co., 1928.

Lovejoy, Arthur O. "Academic Freedom," In *Encyclopaedia of the Social Sciences* I, 384–388. New York: Macmillan Co., 1937.

McCallister, W. J. *The Growth of Freedom in Education.* London: Constable, 1931.

Machlup, Fritz. "On Some Misconceptions Concerning Academic Freedom." *AAUP Bulletin* 41 (Winter 1955): 753–784.

MacIver, Robert M. *Academic Freedom in Our Time.* New York: Columbia University Press, 1955.

Meiklejohn, Alexander. *Freedom and the College.* New York: Century Co., 1923.

Metzger, W. P.; S. H. Kadish; A. De Bardeleben; and E. J. Bloustein. *Dimensions of Academic Freedom.* Urbana: University of Illinois Press, 1969.

Morrow, Glenn R. "Academic Freedom," In *International Encyclopaedia of the Social Sciences* I, 4–10. New York: Macmillan Co. and Free Press, 1968.

Murphy, Arthur E. "Concerning Academic Freedom." In *Reason and the Common Good,* edited by Marcus Singer, William Hay, and Arthur E. Murphy, chap. 26. Englewood Cliffs, New Jersey: Prentice-Hall, 1963.

Rose, Arnold M. *Libel and Academic Freedom.* Toronto: Copy Clark, 1968.

Royce, Josiah. "The Freedom of Teaching," *The Overland Monthly,* n.s., 2 (September 1883).

Searle, John. *The Campus War.* New York and Cleveland: World Publishing Co., 1971.

Shryock, Richard H. "The Academic Profession in the United States," *AAUP Bulletin* 38 (Spring 1952): 32–70.

————, ed. *The Status of University Teachers.* Ghent, Belgium: International Association of University Professors and Lecturers, 1961.

Silber, John. "Academic Freedom." *Alcalde* 52 (November 1963): 10–14.

Sutton, Robert B. "European and American Concepts of Academic Freedom, 1500–1914." Ph.D. dissertation, University of Missouri, 1950.

Sweezy v. New Hampshire, 354 U.S. 234 (1956).

Van Alstyne, William W. "Student Academic Freedom and the Rule-Making Powers of Public Universities: Some Constitutional Considerations." *Law in Transition Quarterly* 2 (Winter 1965): 1–34.

Veblen, Thorstein. *The Higher Learning in America.* New York: Huebsch, 1918.

Yakovlev, Boris A., ed. *Academic Freedom under the Soviet Regime.* Munich, Germany: Institute for the Study of the History and Culture of the USSR, 1954.

INDEX

Academic community. *See also* University
  as a just and humane society, 173
  nature of, 131, 173
  as a religious community, xxiii
Academic freedom
  arguments for
    argument from inconsistency, 235, 238–241, 245, 257, 264
    consequentialist, vii, xiii–xvi, 45, 46, 98, 99, 101–103, 105, 238, 246
    deontological, 101–102, 105
    "expectations principle," 46–49, 52–53, 77
    moral, 44–51
    nonconsequentialist, vii, xiii–xvi, 50, 98, 101, 103, 105, 238
  as a branch of civil liberty, viii, xvi, 57, 64–70, 77–81, 152, 221
  classical theory of, 87–89, 92, 94–95
  common conception of, x–xi, xxii, 52–54, (right to pursue the truth) 102–103, 106
  as freedom *from*, in addition to freedom *to*, 173–174
  as "freedom" rather than "right," 71
  as an instrumental value, 45
  as intrinsically valuable, xvi
  mechanisms for the protection of, 73–77. *See also* Tenure
  as a method of internally policing professional activity, 16, 23–24, 26
  one vs. many model of, 10–11, 32
  as a right, collective, xxi
  as a right, distributive, xxi
  as a right, general, xvi
  as a right, moral, xiv, xv, 44–51
  as a right, prudentially justifiable, xiv–xv
  as a right, special, xvi, 57, 69, 71, 77, 87, 128, 222, 229–232, 237
  as a right, subordinate to class interests, 7–9, 19
  as serving the interests of the ruling class, 27, 37, 41
  as a social value, 172
  as a specific vocational necessity, 68
  of students, 92–96, 168
Academic Freedom and Tenure: A Handbook of the AAUP (Joughin), 145
Academic neutrality, 35, 113, 114, 123
  concept of, 35
  right of, 24–25, 31, 34–35
Academic profession, purpose of, 78
Academics
  as citizens, xviii, xx, 94, 263–264
  as "functionaries," viii–x, 8–12, 16, 21, 25–26, 36–37, 39, 42, 108
  as having special status, 88
  as members of an interest group, viii, 108
  professional evaluation of, xi, 74–77, 103, 105–106, 115–116, 129, 154–155
  as professionals, 112–113, 115, 118–120, 123
  professional standards of, 15–19, 31, 33, 43
  as serving social interests, 105
AAUP, 3, 44, 57, 62, 70, 75, 77, 82–84, 112, 114, 123, 129, 138, 149,